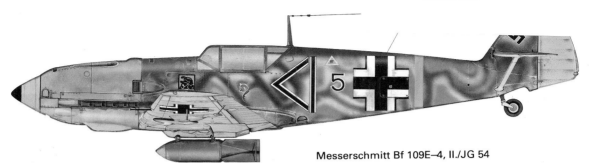

Messerschmitt Bf 109E–4, II./JG 54

JG 54

Jagdgeschwader 54 Grünherz

JG 54

Jagdgeschwader 54 Grünherz
ACES OF THE EASTERN FRONT

Jerry Scutts

Airlife
England

Copyright © Jerry Scutts, 1992

First published in 1992 by Airlife Publishing Ltd.

British Library Cataloguing in Publication Data

A catalogue record for this book is available
from the British Library

Printed by Livesey Ltd. Shrewsbury.

Airlife Publishing Ltd.

101 Longden Road, Shrewsbury SY3 9EB, England.

Contents

Introduction

Flying into action with the flanks of its Messerschmitt 109s and Focke-Wulf 190s emblazoned with a huge, unmistakable green heart, *Jagdgeschwader* 54 was one of the most distinguished of the German Luftwaffe's wartime fighter units. Enjoying a reputation for tenacity and skill in battle second to none, JG 54 numbered among its ranks such outstanding pilots as Hannes Trautloft, Hans Philipp and the legendary Walter Nowotny. Like other first line Luftwaffe fighter formations the *Grünherz* fought the Allies for nearly six years over the vast European battlefronts, from Warsaw to London, Belgrade to Moscow and back to its very roots in the German homeland.

During its existence JG 54's pilots shot down over 9,000 enemy aircraft and flew from some 200 different airfields. Rarely did these men shy away from reflecting their *esprit de corps* in colourful unit badges, rows of victory bars and highly individualistic aircraft paint schemes. Within the story of JG 54 there are to be found incidents that are typical of other *Jagdgeschwaderen*, all of which had their share of heady victory and humiliating defeat. But in some respects, JG 54 was unique.

It was the last — apart from those units raised during the war — of the Jagdgeschwaderen to be officially brought together as a three-Gruppen unit. This union did not take place until the summer of 1940 and it was towards the end of that year before the unofficial title 'Grünherz' was brought into widespread use.

JG 54's experience as a fighter unit was indivisibly interwoven with the waxing and waning fortunes of the Luftwaffe and the entire Third Reich. Very ably led, it managed to hold together surprisingly well under the rigours of that toughest of all fighting fronts, Russia, where its victory tally was unsurpassed. It also served well in Europe immediately after the invasion, where the fields of north-western France became the last resting place of an appallingly high number of German fighter pilots.

When the over-reached *Wehrmacht* began its long retreat on all fronts, the *Jagdflieger* maintained what protection it could. Like most other Jagdgeschwaderen, JG 54 had its component Gruppen split for most of the war to fight on two fronts. Embroiled in the Herculean, hopeless task of preventing Germany being laid waste by Allied bombing, its increasingly youthful and inexperienced pilots smashed themselves against an aerial juggernaut which rapidly eclipsed anything the Germans themselves had fielded. In defending their homeland, the Luftwaffe fighter force fought as desperately as the men of Poland, Yugoslavia, Russia and other nations had done when their own countries were mercilessly attacked by Hitler's legions.

Any story of the wartime Luftwaffe is also inextricably interwoven with the stranger-than-fiction saga of the men who led it first to victory and then to utter defeat. If any one fighting force can be said to have been more misused after the initial euphoria of victory, the German air force must be a prime contender for that dubious distinction.

But the defeat of the Luftwaffe in 1945 had its roots not in the aircraft factories of Britian or the US, the training schools in Canada or the sheer tenacity of the Russian people to resist the invader of their country at almost any cost. All these factors contributed in great measure — but it was the German high command that brought about the demise so quickly.

There will always be an irony in the story of a force which had at operational level the ablest band of men ever to take the controls of military aircraft — and at high command level a group of self-seeking, jealous and fearful individuals, hamstrung by political ambition in the claustrophobic atmosphere of Hitler's Third Reich. Continually deploying the Luftwaffe in ill-defined and highly optimistic operational ventures for which there was no precedent, these men found that the promise of airpower's ability to win a long war, when a conflict of far shorter duration had been planned, could not be fulfilled.

That the first-line Luftwaffe formations, particularly those equipped with fighters, continued to fly and fight so well in defence of a cause that was clearly lost as early as the winter of 1940 was at the very least, remarkable. Even when the ring of Allied steel was crushing the life out of the remains of the Third Reich, the *Jagdwaffe* continued to operate, some units receiving examples of the most technically advanced military aircraft in the world. But even these turbojet machines, flown by some of the ablest and most experienced pilots anywhere, could not reverse the situation when their own military infrastructure had been destroyed.

The following narrative is the story of the 'Green Hearts' from formation to defeat. The author makes no claim that the result is in any way definitive and at some future date an expanded history of this and other Luftwaffe fighter units would be welcomed by him.

The narrative for this Airlife book stems primarily from translations of a number of German language publications and in particulary *Die Grünherzjager* compiled by Werner Held, Hannes Trautloft and Ekkehard Bob, published by Podzun-Pallas-Verlag in 1985.

To this framework the author has added more than double the amount of information to be found in this invaluable starting point, adding material from a large number of German, US and British sources. It is to be hoped that the result adds something to the aerial history of World War Two by bringing the information contained herein to a wider audience, for English-language narratives of Luftwaffe units are still very few in number, even fifty years or so on from the conflict which saw their rise to eminence.

Although the bulk of the interpretations and conclusions made here are the author's alone — as are any errors or omissions, for which apologies are duly made — invaluable assistance was given by Ron Mackay, who translated the original German publication upon which the narrative is broadly based. My thanks to him for his efforts, without which the task could have been much harder. Also, my thanks to J. Richard Smith, the doyen of Luftwaffe operational matters, and to Fritz Ungar, Jim Crow, Peter Petrick, Jeff Ethell, Michael Payne, Chris Shores, Paul D'Orley, Brian Marsh, Richard L. Ward, Bruce Robertson, Eddie Creek, Dave Howley, and the staffs of the Bundesarchiv, Koblenz and the Finnish Air Force archives — photos from which were kindly loaned by Kari Stenman.

Typifying the highly successful fighter pilots who were the cornerstone of the Luftwaffe throughout the war, Hubert 'Hubs' Mütherich wears the Knight's Cross immediately after presentation, on 6 August 1941. Then Staffelkapitan of 5./JG 54, Mütherich had eight British, two Yugoslavian and twenty-seven Russian aircraft to his credit, all duly recorded on the rudder of his Bf 109F, 'Black 10'. When he was killed in action on 9 September that year, 'Hubs' had a score of forty-three. He was then JG 54's most successful Staffelkapitan and had previously served with I./JG 77.

Chapter 1

BUILD-UP TO BLITZKRIEG

During the 1930s, the creators of Nazi Germany's new military might placed due emphasis on the importance of airpower, rarely doubting the propaganda value of a Luftwaffe strong in all branches. This was at a time when other European powers, particularly France and Britain, were relatively weak in terms of modern warplanes. Although much emphasis was to be placed on the use of dive bombers and lightly armed and armoured medium bombers to spearhead a new form of short range, army support warfare known as *Blitzkrieg* or 'Lightning war', the important part that would be played by fighter aircraft in any future conflict was also studied and given practical application. Even before Adolf Hitler signed the decree that officially established the *Reichsluftwaffe* as a separate branch of the armed forces, on 26 February 1936, a fighter unit existed. This was *Jagdgeschwader* 132, which had been created on 1 April 1934.

As the Luftwaffe gradually expanded under the energetic command of Hermann Goering, new fighter units were created under the three-digit numbering system which served as a code to identify the type, strength and location of each one within ten different areas of the Reich known as *Luftgau* or air districts. In their turn,

these Geschwaderen were groupings of individual *Staffeln*, most of which were composed of men from the same area of Germany and Austria, and which commonly bore names with strong local associations, similar to militia forces raised for military duty in bygone times. It was from these units, largely renumbered prior to the outbreak of World War Two, that the twelve full Jagdgeschwaderen that would undertake the vast majority of wartime sorties came into being.

The designation changes were in certain cases slow to be implemented and were to continue in use into the early part of the war; there is considerable evidence that some of the outdated ones were used in reports even after they had become obsolete. This was probably not accidental as it did serve to indicate that the Luftwaffe had more operational *Gruppen* than was actually the case. Anything that bolstered the illusion that Germany was already stronger in the air than some of her European neighbours, and rapidly gaining on the major powers in terms of active units and the number of modern aircraft that were in service, was grist to the propaganda ministry's mill and Hitler's plans for a 'new order' in Europe.

After the Anschluss of 1938, the Austrian Air Force was absorbed by the Luftwaffe and among the assets the Germans acquired were a number of Fiat CR 30s, shown here in the 'Lion of Aspern' markings that would become synonymous with JG 54. In 1939, the parent unit was identified as I./JG 138, which became I./JG 76 and finally II./JG 54. *(J. Ethell)*.

Among the new aircraft types developed and test-flown during this period was the one that would assume the most importance when the Luftwaffe's greatest test came, the Messerschmitt Bf 109. A light, agile monoplane, the Bf 109 in early Junkers Jumo-engined form, began to replace obsolescent *Jagdwaffe* biplane fighters in 1937, the year in which it received its baptism of fire in the Spanish Civil War. However, re-equipment at home was slow and by the time of the Austrian *Anschluss* of March 1938, there were but six Gruppen of Bf 109Bs based in Germany, either equipped or in the process of converting. A further six were still flying the Arado Ar 68 and in the case of I./JG 136, the Heinkel He 51C-2 biplane.

Production of the Bf 109 at the main Augsburg plant proceeded at a steady pace throughout the turbulent months prior to the outbreak of world war, and although the Messerschmitt concern did not establish any production records, Hitler's successful brinkmanship did not, perhaps fortunately for Germany, plunge the country into a premature conflict. Tacit agreement, through inaction, by the rest of Europe allowed the German Chancellor's increasingly threatening territorial de-

mands and blatant military expansionism to continue without armed conflict.

Iberian origins

While the Führer sought to modify the national boundaries of Europe in an atmosphere of increasingly uneasy peace, the Condor Legion was honing its combat doctrine under real war conditions in Spain. Ably supporting Franco's nationalist cause, the Legion's fighter element found a fortuitous and convenient training ground. The largest possible number of pilots and ground personnel spent an average of ten months with *Jagdgruppe* 88 before returning home to share their experience of modern warfare.

Among the young pilots who made their mark in Spain was Hannes Trautloft. A native of Grossobringen in Thuringia, Trautloft arrived in the country on 7 August 1936 aboard the freighter *Usaramo*, along with five other pilots, eight mechanics and six He 51 fighters. The group was led by *Oberleutnant* Eberhard.

The original intention had been merely to transfer the Heinkels to the Nationalists and for the German group to return home. But there was some doubt as to the ability of the new owners to use the Heinkels effectively. With one aircraft already written off by a Spanish pilot, the German group flew the remaining five machines to Escalona via Salamanca. The handover duly took place, but the Germans were appalled to witness two more He 51 crash landings the very first time the Spaniards began operations.

Eberhard, realising that unfamiliarity with the German aircraft made the Spanish pilots marginally more dangerous to themselves than to their Republican opponents, obtained authorisation from Berlin for his small group to stay in Spain and fly the Heinkels themselves. *Jagdstaffel Eberhard* consequently became the initial fighter unit of the Condor Legion.

On 13 August Trautloft had the dubious distinction of becoming the first German pilot to be shot down over Spain. Having attacked and damaged a Republican Potez which burned but refused to go down, Trautloft was concentrating on another pass when the enemy aircraft suddenly burst into flames and the crew promptly bailed out. Then without warning, bullets began hitting his own aircraft. The He 51 quickly became uncontrollable and Trautloft himself took to his parachute.

As he floated down, the chagrined German pilot noted a couple of things. One was that he was hardly dressed in regulation uniform — shorts, an open-necked shirt and tennis shoes — the other was the Dewoitine fighter that had shot him down coming in, seemingly for another attempt to kill him. Luckily the Republican pilot either missed or held his fire and Trautloft found himself staggering against the wall of a farmhouse.

Again his luck held in that nobody came to investigate the disturbance and after dark he crawled into an olive grove — where he was discovered by about eighty well-armed men. Realising that his 'uniform' would take some explaining — whichever side these people supported — Trautloft stood up slowly. A sergeant stuck a pistol in his stomach and punched him in the mouth. Very worried by this time, Hannes Trautloft reached for his passport. Another punch connected. There was nothing for it but to say something relevant. The only problem was that Trautloft's command of Spanish was practically nil. Then, noticing that his antagonist was wearing a red and yellow badge, Trautloft used nearly his entire Spanish vocabulary. 'Viva Franco', he said weakly. On hearing this, the sergeant

Mainstay of the Luftwaffe fighter formations during the late 1930s, the Heinkel He 51 was generally a docile type – although mishaps did occur. This example is believed to have served with I./JG 70. *(Peter Petrick)*.

flung his arms around the German pilot and kissed him.

In a very short time, the German Heinkel unit became heavily engaged in the fighting over the Madrid Front, flying up to five sorties a day. Another of Trautloft's victories, a Breguet Bre 19 two-seater, fell in late August. One of three that were intercepted while they were intent on attacking Nationalist positions, the Breguet observers were dropping small bombs by hand from the second cockpit. Shooting down one of their number gave Trautloft little trouble; it was described by him as 'a copy book attack.'

A further sixteen Heinkels arrived from Germany in September, enough to equip the first Staffel of Jagdgruppe 88. Through a desire to perpetuate the 'green heart' of his homeland and express a little individuality, Trautloft also gave an early indication of his future Luftwaffe command. A green heart was duly painted on the fuselage of his He 51.

On 9 December 1936 Ltn Trautloft was ordered to Tablada airfield, Seville to test-fly a prototype of the exciting new monoplane fighter developed by Messerschmitt AG; as yet only a number of prototypes existed but examples of these had been shipped to Spain for evaluation under actual combat conditions. Trautloft duly set out from his base at Vitoria in an old car, fog having eliminated the chance of flying to Seville. He arrived on the 10th only to find that the aircraft he was due to test fly, the Bf 109 V3, (civil registered D-IOOY) had crashed on take off within hours of his being summoned to Seville. Trautloft was obliged to wait until the Bf 109 V4 (D-IALY) was made ready.

Trautloft finally got to fly the Bf 109 V4 on 14 December and despite the lack of a proper ground check out, he quickly realised the enormous potential of the machine. He demonstrated this by rapidly overhauling an Italian Fiat CR 32, then reckoned to be the fastest aircraft in Spanish skies.

The succeeding weeks were to be a little frustrating for Trautloft, who had to await the outcome of continual attention by the mechanics to cure a catalogue of teething troubles with the Bf 109 prototype. But none of these changed his opinion that here was an outstand-ing aircraft, one that the Legion could use to advantage. He went on to evaluate the V4 for a brief period on the Madrid front during January 1937.

Trautloft scored four confirmed victories in Spain before returning home. Among other pilots who would help provide a fund of experience to form the cadres of the new fighter Jagdgeschwaderen then being raised in Germany and who cut their combat teeth in Iberian skies, was Hubertus von Bonin. His subsequent career in JG 54 was built on the confidence generated by a score of four kills in Spain.

When he got back to Germany in late February 1937, Trautloft was summoned to Berlin to meet Hitler. Waiting in an ante-room in the Reich Chancellery, an aide noted a strange smell. It was Trautloft's hair oil, which he had bought in Spain. The aide was horrified. He told Trautloft he could not possibly meet the Führer smelling like that and to wash it off immediately. Although his audience with Hitler was only supposed to last ten minutes, Trautloft stayed an hour. Trautloft was amazed at how much the German leader already knew about the situation in Spain, but he was able to stress the urgent need to have Jagdgruppe 88 fully re-equipped with the Bf 109. Hitler promised to see to it and by April 1937, 2./JG 88 had received enough Bf 109Bs to fully replace its He 51s. Almost at once the new German fighter demonstrated its marked superiority over virtually all other aircraft in Spain and numerous pilots who would later build on this early combat experience flew the potent fighter on the Nationalist side to materially assist Franco's ultimate victory.

Origins

In the meantime, the Luftwaffe continued to expand, enough Gruppen being created to enable the formation of a sizeable fighter force, each Geschwader being composed of three Gruppen, each in turn with a nominal strength of three Staffeln. The three-digit designations continued in use by the majority of new Jagdgeschwaderen raised at that time.

As far as the formation of Jagdgeschwader 54 was concerned, the origins of the unit were

These Bf 109D-Is represented the new generation of fighter aircraft that the Germans were soon to deploy with devastating effect. *(Ethell)*.

quite diverse, which was not in itself unusual. What did mark the unit out from other first line Jagdgeschwaderen was the length of time it took to bring all its component Gruppen together, and indeed for the designation to be officially promulgated in Luftwaffe records as a fighter formation of standard size.

The units that made up JG 54 for most of World War Two were as follows: I Gruppe drew its original personnel cadre from I./JG 70 which was raised at Herzogenaurach near Nuremberg in July 1939 and commanded by Major von Cramon. I./JG 70 provided most of the original personnel of the Gruppe, including the bulk of the groundcrew who were local to the Nuremberg region. It was therefore appropriate that the Gruppe should adopt the Nuremberg city coat of arms as its emblem, this consisting of a vertically-divided shield with a black heraldic bird on the left and red and white diagonal stripes on the right.

Equipped with the Arado Ar 69 pending the delivery of the Bf 109, I Gruppe also briefly operated the Avia B-534, air and groundcrews conducting a full operational evaluation of the Czech biplane fighter during the summer of 1939. I./JG 70 became I./JG 54 on 15 September 1939.

II Gruppe was actually JG 54's oldest. Stemming from the former *Jagdgruppe Wein-Aspern* it became I./JG 138 on 1 July 1938, following the Austrian Anschluss of February-March that year. Commanded by Hptm Muller-Reinsburg, the unit continued to be manned largely by Austrian nationals, many of whom had served in the *Luftstreitkrafte*, the Austrian Air Force.

Absorbed into the Luftwaffe and flying the He 51 and Fiat CR 30 pending delivery of the Bf 109D, I./JG 138 became I./JG 76 before being designated II./JG 54 on 6 April 1940. The Aspern coat of arms, a black lion's head surmounting a white cross on a red field, became the II Gruppe emblem.

On 15 July 1939 Major Martin Mettig's I./JG 21 became III./JG 54 while it was based at Jesau and Gutenfeld in East Prussia. A large proportion of the groundcrew had been born in Prussia and again an emblem with local connections was chosen, in this case the Jesau cross with three diving aircraft superimposed. It differed from the similar emblem of III./JG 27 in that the background to the black cross was red rather than white and the shield outline was white, that of JG 27 being yellow. III Gruppe's new designation was seemingly slow to be officially changed in Luftwaffe records, for it was to be known as JG 21 for almost another year, certainly through to the end of the battle of France.

Late in July 1938 the man who would lead JG 54 in a little over two years' time was in Zurich for the fourth International Flying Meeting which lasted from 23 July to 1 August. Trautloft led a *Kette* of three Bf 109s to win the speed race event and, in general, Germany impressed all the visitors with the undeniable quality of her new aircraft and the skill of their pilots. For many observers, it was a sobering experience to witness the strides the Germans had made in the last few years.

Trautloft subsequently became an instructor at the fighter flying school at Berlin-Werneuchen, commanded by Major Theo Osterkamp.

Equipped with the Bf 109, He 51 and Ar 68, this school provided the nucleus of personnel for a fourth Gruppe of JG 132; the first Jagdgeschwader to be formed for service in the Reichsluftwaffe. IV Gruppe was established on 1 July 1938 and Trautloft became Staffelkapitan of 10./JG 132 at the time of Hitler's invasion of Czechoslovakia in March 1939; it was an extremely tense time for many Germans, including men of the Luftwaffe, who felt this latest coup, albeit a bloodless one, would surely lead to war with France or Britain, probably both. Knowing that Germany's strength in the air was not as great as the propagandists boasted, few wanted military action at that time.

But again war was averted and the build-up of the Luftwaffe continued unhindered during the last months of uneasy peace. Throughout

Modestly powered and armed, the Bf 109D was relatively short lived in Luftwaffe service, although the small number of similar 'C' models sent to Spain gave a good account of themselves under combat conditions. This Bf 109D-1, with a striking spiral spinner design and radio mast pennant, was part of I./JG 21 in 1939. *(Bundesarchiv).*

the summer of 1939, fighter, dive bomber and medium bomber Gruppen were established and re-equipped and by late August Hitler's war plan for the attack on Poland, while still something of a gamble, had a better chance of success. On 1 September, German troops violated the border and invaded Polish territory.

Ostmarkflug

By 2 September 1939 there were 811 Bf 109s on Luftwaffe charge, 771 of which were on the strength of operational units. Of this total, 676 were serviceable on that date. Equipped mainly with the Bf 109C and D, with a few of the new E-1 models on strength, JG 54 prepared for combat over Poland. In the event, only II and III Gruppen (then identified as I./JG 76 and I./JG 21 respectively) participated briefly in the campaign that sparked off World War Two , I Gruppe (I./JG 70) remaining on alert at Herzogenaurach. In total, the Luftwaffe committed five Gruppen of Bf 109s, totalling 202 machines in four different models, to Operation Ostmark.

For the Polish campaign, I./JG 21 and I./JG 76 were grouped under two of the four Luftflotten formed for war operations. The former unit operated with Luftflotte 1 and had twenty-nine Bf 109Cs and Es on strength, with one machine unserviceable on the eve of war. I./JG 76 came under the operational command of Luftflotte 4 and fielded forty-five Bf 109Es from its total strength of forty-nine aircraft.

To oppose the Germans, the Polish Air Force had about 1,900 aircraft of all types, including reserves and those under repair, the strength of training units and auxiliaries. By far the most dangerous to the Luftwaffe was the PAF fighter force, consisting of 132 P.11 and thirty P.7 gull-winged monoplanes armed with a quartet of machine guns. Although obsolete, these single-seaters enjoyed a high degree of manoeuvrability and were quite capable of inflicting serious damage on Luftwaffe aircraft, particularly bombers which were, in 1939, poorly armed with minimal armour protection for the crew and vital airframe areas.

Pre-positioned on airfields in East Prussia, Silesia and Czechoslovakia for their initial period of combat flying, from 1 September 1939 JG 54's pilots flew a variety of operations, including close escort to Ju 87 dive bombers,

Frei Jagd or 'free hunt' patrols — independent fighter sweeps not tied to escort or other support work — and ground strafing attacks. While the Jagdwaffe had long trained for war, the actual event proved traumatic for some pilots, among them Dietrich Hrabak. He suffered the forgettable distinction of being one of the first German pilots to be shot down in World War Two when he was forced to belly-land after his first sortie on 1 September.

Supporting the advancing Panzers and infantry, JG 54's fighters soon occupied the abandoned Polish airfields at Bialystok and Camicy near Radom. The Polish Air Force had implemented a programme of dispersal of the bulk of its combat aircraft to second line airfields, leaving most of the twelve major bases, the location of which was well known to the Germans, with only second-line aircraft and trainers. About seventy-five emergency airfields were then in use.

As a result of the wide — perhaps too wide — dispersion achieved by the Polish Air Force, it was never able to marshal enough fighters to make concerted and damaging attacks on German bomber and Stuka formations. And with extremely poor communications to start with, the defenders quickly lost all hope of rallying to mount any appreciable resistance of this kind once the attack had started. Early German air attacks on the road and rail network, plus the destruction of the radio stations at Babic and Lacy, all but prevented rapid movement to areas in danger of being overrun. Early warning of German penetrations could therefore not be relayed in time for counter-attacks to be mounted, and no cohesive defence was possible. Inclement weather also played its part, with poor visibility hampering both sides to some degree, but the Poles marginally more, and particularly so their vital fighter interceptor units.

Only over Warsaw, starting in the morning of 1 September, was the Polish fighter force able to deliver some degree of disruption to waves of Luftwaffe aircraft, primarily He 111s, flown largely by men who were getting their first taste of war. That afternoon, in better visibility, about thirty PZL fighters so unnerved the bomber crews that some broke formation and jettisoned their bombs away from the city.

Pictured during the Polish campaign, where a number of German pilots who would later be the stars of JG 54 opened their victory tallies, Bf 109D-1 'Yellow 2' probably from 9./JG 76, formates on a sister aircraft. In total the embryo Grünherztrager scored twelve victories in Poland. *(Petrick)*.

Those bombs that were dropped began the battering that the unfortunate Polish capital was to suffer in nearly six years of war.

Otherwise, the resistance put up by the PAF was rarely anything but sporadic, although dogfights showed that the defenders did not lack determination and high courage in their endeavours to stop the invaders. German pilots, among them Hans Philipp (then flying with I./JG 76), and Gustav Rodel of I./JG 21, recorded their first aerial victories of the war over Poland. Essentially however, the campaign was not marked by intense fighter versus fighter activity by the Bf 109 units. It was spearheaded by Ju 87 and He 123 dive bombers and medium bombers, with the Bf 110's heavy cannon armament appearing to vindicate the almost unique German concept of the heavy 'destroyer' fighter. Polish airmen regarded the *Zerstorers* as their most dangerous opponents.

Rather than risk further destruction to Warsaw after five day's bombing, the military commander sued for unconditional surrender on 27 September. Having weathered numerous operational deficiencies and a few tactical errors, the Germans had nevertheless achieved victory in the remarkably short space of one

month. In total the entire Polish campaign, tinged as it was with the considerable risk that France and Britain would offer tangible aid to a beleaguered ally following their declaration of war on Germany, was completed in thirty-six days without any interference from outside.

Luftwaffe losses from enemy air attacks and ground fire, plus operational accidents, often as a result of unfamiliarity with equipment, misreading of signals and general teething troubles under the pressure of war, were relatively high. The Polish fighter force claimed a total of 126 victories but German figures place the Luftwaffe's total losses much higher at 285. It included sixty-seven Bf 109s, twelve Bf 110s, thirty-one Ju 87s and no less than seventy-eight twin-engined bombers of all types. Added to the losses of reconnaissance and transport aircraft and non-operational accidents the total reached 564 aircraft, or about twenty-five percent of operational strength.

Among the units that had been operational over Poland was 2./JG 77, led by Hannes Trautloft. Promoted to the rank of Hauptmann, Trautloft subsequently became Kommodore of III./JG 51 on 19 September. JG 54's participation in Ostmark ended on 9 October, three days after all armed resistance in Poland had ceased, and its component Gruppen took up station in southern and western Germany on home defense duties. I Gruppe was based at Boblingen, Fredrichshafen and Eutigen bie Horb, II Gruppe's Staffeln used Gelnhausen, Rhein-Main, Walldorf and Ober-Ulm, while III Gruppe dispersed to Pantlunne, Hopsten, Krefeld, Munster and Munchen-Gladbach.

When a movement order was received, ground crews would arrive at the satellite base in advance, having travelled by air or road, and set up the essential services that the flying unit would need for the duration of its stay. Such training was to prove invaluable when the Luftwaffe began its highly mobile war, base changes throughout the conflict in some cases running into hundreds. During World War Two a similar policy was followed whenever poss-

A JG 76 pilot studies a map of his operational area before flying a sortie in 'White 2' in the background. Possibly taken after war in Europe had been declared, the photo reflects the great care taken by pilots of both sides not to overfly sensitive areas and thereby cause an 'international incident'.

This allocation of a number of different airfields to each Jagdgeschwader had become standard practice in the Luftwaffe and enabled units to move rapidly from place to place for training duties and participation in exercises. The majority of airfields, all of which were grass strips, had only minimal installations and support facilities and were manned by very small units of personnel.

ible; it enabled operational and training sorties to be flown from the less forward airfields and had the additional advantage of dispersing each Gruppe in the event of enemy air attack.

While based in Germany after the Polish campaign, the six Staffeln of I. and III./JG 54, as well as JG 76, completed re-equipment with the Bf 109E and embarked on an intensive period of conversion training. These potent new machines, although very unforgiving of inattentiveness — as were all models of the Bf 109 — were soon found to be significantly superior to the earlier models. I./JG 76 had been among the recipients of some of the first Bf 109E-3s powered by the DB 601Aa engine, and in most cases, armed with two 20mm MG FF wing cannon in place of MG 17 machine guns. This and all other Emils had the chunky nose shape with numerous bulges and bumps necessitated by a more powerful engine surmounted by a pair of 7.9mm machine guns in troughs above the block. Those unmistakable contours would soon be very familiar indeed. . .

'Sitzkrieg'

During the so-called *Sitzkrieg* or Phoney War, JG 54 honed its battle tactics with the Bf 109. Sorties were flown as far as the French border, in the vicinity of which German pilots occasionally encountered small numbers of Allied aircraft, among them *Armée de l'Air* Morane 406s and Curtiss Hawks, and Hurricanes and Blenheims of the RAF. Although they had initially been forbidden to cross the border into

French airspace and thereby possibly provoke an 'international incident', despite the fact that a state of war existed, the Jagdflieger did indulge in some small-scale skirmishing when enemy aircraft penetrated German airspace. These clashes quickly turned into a series of vicious combats as both sides increased overflights, particularly by reconnaissance aircraft. They demonstrated the relative quality of the types flown by each side — and for the Allies the realisation of how good a fighter the Luftwaffe had in the Bf 109 was far from welcome news.

The component Gruppen of JG 54 underwent some personnel changes before combat operations were launched in Western Europe, Hubertus von Bonin taking command of I Gruppe on 28 December 1939. Major Albert Blumensaat became the Kommandeur of II Gruppe on 10 January 1940 and on 2 February Martin Mettig was named as the first Kommodore of Jagdgeschwader 54. His place at the head of III Gruppe was taken by Hauptmann Fritz Ultsch.

The phoney war continued, but before long both sides were obliged to be more concerned

An unusual paint scheme applied to a Bf 109E-1 of Stab I./JG 54 at Friedrichshafen in 1939. It appears to have consisted of a light washable distemper over the standard dark green finish, possibly for a tactical exercise.

with combatting the increasingly harsh winter conditions that prevailed over the Western Front; as the first full year of the war dawned, temperatures plunged and heavy snowfalls blanketed aerodromes for days on end. Flying was severely curtailed.

With the onset of better weather, sorties on both sides gradually increased in size and frequency. Aircraft losses were relatively few in number and the period did not highlight any marked superiority on either side, these early Western Front sorties being tempered with a good deal of caution, particularly on the part of the Germans. The Jagdflieger were often aloft to escort reconnaissance Dorniers which were very active at this time and the pilots were obliged to see that the bombers carried out their duties and returned home safely. Unfortunately, reconnaissance was just what the French were trying to prevent and a number of dogfights ensued as enemy fighters, often successfully, strove to intercept.

In their turn, German fighter pilots did their best to stop film being taken of Luftwaffe activity, their own preparations being much more sensitive than anything that went on over the other side of the border. Occasionally the aerial engagements went badly wrong for the Jagdflieger, as on 3 January, when four Bf 109s were shot down, although one of the French aircraft involved in two separate combats was destroyed by a pilot of I./JG 54. Five aircraft from I Gruppe succeeded in despatching a Potez 63 of GR II/55, which had itself been responsible for downing one of the Bf 109s.

On 10 January, Reinhard Seiler, then in command of 1. Staffel, shot down another Potez 63. Seiler had only joined I Gruppe in December 1939 and the new Staffelkapitän's first victory was duly celebrated. Two days later the temperature plunged again and ground fog brought another period of much reduced activity on both sides of the line.

Despite the fact that they were often outnumbered by the Messerschmitts, French fighter pilots generally gave a good account of themselves; their three most modern indigenous types, the Dewoitine D.520, Morane-Saulnier MS 406 and Bloch 152 (which was not available in any numbers until later), plus the US-built Curtiss Hawk 75, were well armed and man-

oeuvrable and could be dangerous opponents, particularly if they engaged with a tactical advantage. The Bf 109E had however a top speed some 50mph faster than all the French fighters, and German pilots could often use this edge to break off combat. In armament, the French fighters were even more closely matched against the Bf 109s, as unlike the Hawk 75, and every British aircraft that operated over France, all of them had been designed to take cannon armament.

During the Sitzkrieg the range of German fighter sweeps over enemy territory was gradually extended, the Jagdflieger now frequently meeting French and British pilots who were well able to offer a dangerous challenge if combat was joined. Small numbers of Luftwaffe aircraft had been destroyed on frequent occasions by Allied fighters and this attrition rate continued to climb. Up to 1 May 1940, the Germans admitted the loss of 937 aircraft since the start of operations over Poland. In contrast, the Armée de l'Air's early war sorties had cost sixty-three aircraft downed in combat out of a grand total of 914 lost, the majority of these being attributable to accidents.

Some time before the German invasion was launched, the French had had ample chance to evaluate the fighter type that, used en masse, would prove an almost invincible adversary. On 22 November a young Leutnant of I./JG 76 (believed to have been named Schultz) experienced a problem with his aircraft and was obliged to make a wheels-up landing near Puttelange in Luxembourg, 15km southeast of the capital. The much-vaunted Maginot Line ran through that area and the German pilot was duly captured and turned over to a French infantry regiment guarding the sector.

Badly damaged in the crash landing, and therefore useful only insofar as it was examined closely, the Bf 109E (Wr Nr 1251 marked Yellow 11) was dismantled and transported to Paris, there to be reassembled and placed on public display in the window of a department store on the Avenue des Champs Elysées.

Parisians who paid to view the wrecked fighter doubtless little realised that they were inspecting the one type of aircraft that was, more than any other, to cause the downfall of their country. There was some unwitting irony

Although the 'Sitzkrieg' generally kept both sides' nerves needlessly on edge, there *were* incidents and casualties, among them members of JG 76 who came down on the wrong side of the lines. One Bf 109E, WrNr 1251, fell at Puttelange south of Luxembourg in December 1939 and after examination by the Armée de l'Air it was displayed in a store on the Avenue des Champs d'Elysées to raise funds for an air force charity. *(via M. Payne).*

in the fact that proceeds from the exhibit went to a French Air Force charity. . .

Three Bf 109s had actually fallen into French hands on 22 November, and the other two intact examples were flight-evaluated. One, previously the property of II./JG 51, was soon destroyed in an accident, but the other provided the French, British and later the Americans with their first details of the Bf 109. This Fieseler-built machine also fell into Allied hands courtesy of I./JG 76, when Feldwebel Karl Hier, who had seen service in Spain, experienced fog and was obliged to force-land. His aircraft came to rest in an orchard at Woerth, in the Bas-Rhine region, 40km north of Strasbourg.

Transported to Orleans-Bricy on 6 December, Wr Nr 1304 (White 1) made seven flights before the end of the month and, somewhat

soberingly, more than confirmed performance figures put out by the Germans. It was to avail the French little that five hours' initial test flying, curtailed by prevailing bad weather, also revealed some shortcomings of the Bf 109. A further series of flights against contemporary French fighters was conducted until late April 1940, when the aircraft was shipped to Britain for further examination as AE479. It was subsequently sent to the USA.

Karl Hier, briefly incarcerated by the French, was, along with a number of other pilots who had come down on the wrong side of the lines, duly released by the conquering Germans. He rejoined his unit in June 1940 and flew throughout the Battle of Britain before being lost over the North Sea on 15 November. Then a member of 4.Staffel, Hier went down following combat with British fighters.

The Battle for France

Numerically, the Armée de l'Air was the strongest air force the Germans had yet faced in Europe. But numbers were deceiving. While there was a nucleus of modern fighters, reconnaissance aircraft and bombers, the larger part of the force was composed of types which were obsolete — and in some cases, decidedly antique! On the eve of the attack in the West, the entire French air force was distributed among four separate Zones of Operation and subordinated to army commands in each area; in addition the *Aeronavale* had aircraft, primarily for maritime reconnaissance, with a handful of bombers, fighters and torpedo attack types distributed on land bases throughout Metropolitan France. Others were embarked on naval vessels or based in French North Africa.

The French striking forces that would bear the responsibility of resisting the German attack were boosted by a sizeable part of the RAF's light bomber and fighter force, much of which was then based on French soil as part of the Air Component (with twelve first-line squadrons) and Advanced Air Striking Force, with another twelve. A total of 416 British machines were therefore available to operate alongside 515 operational French fighters, 210 modern bombers and roughly the same number of miscellaneous types used for a variety of tasks, including reconnaissance and observation.

But the relative strengths available to each side about to engage in the spring of 1940 pale into insignificance when the outmoded thinking of the French high command is taken into account. No nationwide defence plan, based on close air-ground cooperation and enjoying the flexibility required for modern warfare, had been implemented. The vast land mass of Metropolitan France demanded the most mobile and rapid front line forces, backed by in-depth reserves that could be moved to trouble spots quickly; instead much reliance was placed on the fixed fortifications of the Maginot Line and poorly-equipped forces totally unprepared for anything approaching the German Blitzkrieg. Fully expecting that this conflict would be much like the static trench warfare of World War One, the French failed to grasp the advantages inherent in intelligent deployment of highly mobile armoured spearheads acting as a shield for advancing infantry.

When the Germans launched their sudden attack on Holland and Belgium in the early hours of 10 May 1940, JG 54 was not directly involved but was held in readiness for the main thrust on France. As part of Wolfram von Richtofen's VIII *Fliegerkorps*, otherwise composed of JG 27, LG 2 with HS 123 dive bombers and three *Stukageschwaderen* with Ju 87Bs, JG 54's three Gruppen continued to be led by Major Martin Mettig.

By quickly occupying four key airfields in Norway and executing the rapid neutralisation of Denmark, Hitler secured his northern flank for the main assault on Western Europe — codenamed *Weserubung*. Equally rapid completion of the first phase of this operation saw the vital bridges over the Albert Canal in German hands within hours. After five days of fighting, the Dutch surrendered, by which time the sweeping Wehrmacht drive towards the Channel coast was well underway. To subdue France the Germans committed two Luftflotten, representing a force of 3,530 aircraft, plus transports and gliders. It was the most powerful air striking force the world had yet seen.

Two German army groups thrusting north through the Ardennes, skirting entirely the fixed fortifications of the Maginot Line, and southwards towards Sedan, forced a fifty mile breach in French defences in thirty-six hours. Bomber escort, strafing attacks and free hunt sorties occupied JG 54 and other fighter units of VIII Fliegerkorps and Jagdfliegerfuhrer 2 and 3, a total of seventeen Bf 109 Gruppen — an increasing number of French and British aircrews began finding out the hard way just how effective a fighter umbrella the Luftwaffe had established for this huge operation.

As the German Panzers raced through France the Jagdflieger hacked the Armée de l'Air out of the sky, destroyed its aircraft on the ground and punched irreparable holes in a disorganised defence network that was generally tied too closely to Army units, many of which were quickly decimated or had ceased to exist. Hard put to stem the columns of tanks and infantry, the British Air Component and Advanced Air Striking Force similarly suffered an appalling casualty rate — particularly among Battle and Blenheim crews — as they flung themselves into storms of flak and ran the gauntlet of the ever-present shield of Bf 109s. The situation grew more critical as the days of May passed without a sign that the enemy advance was even being forced to pause in its headlong rush.

The pace of operations was exhausting: to prevent the recapture of the vital bridges over the River Meuse and the Abert Canal, the Jagdflieger flew 340 sorties in two days, shooting down twenty-eight Allied aircraft for the loss of four of their own. Under the operational command of JG 27, II./JG 54, I./JG 1 and I./JG 27 coordinated their sorties to provide the necessary protection. III Gruppe JG 54 continued to operate as I./JG 21 and in turn this unit had I./JG 26 under its control.

The first days of fighting brought heavy aircraft casualties on both sides. On 11 May I./JG 21 suffered its first loss of the campaign when a Bf 109E fell victim to a Hurricane over Rotterdam. JG 54 and other fighter units occasionally found their most dangerous adversaries to be not Allied fighters — but French flak. If not a major hazard for the Germans throughout the battle, enemy AA fire did nevertheless exact a toll of the Jagdflieger. On 12 May I./JG 54 lost two aircraft to this cause, one over Luxeuil, the other over Hebevilliers.

After striking Allied columns in the vicinity of Liége, the Luftwaffe spearheaded a sudden switch in the direction of battle on 13 May, when the Panzers of XIX and XXI Army

Capitano Furio Niclot of the Regia Aeronautica pictured with one of II./JG 54's Bf 109Es, probably in France following Italy's declaration of war on the Allied powers. *(E. J. Creek).*

Korps raced for Sedan. Pinning down the defences now became the main task, spearheaded, as was much of the French operation, by the scream of Stukas.

The French fighter force had, however, reacted quickly to Luftwaffe raids and continued to inflict casualties — when they could avoid or penetrate the Messerschmitt screen. Sedan was the focus on 14 May, the German 'Day of the Fighters'. No less than 814 sorties were flown by the Jagdflieger, individual pilots flying up to seven sorties from dawn to dusk. Losses were high on both sides, but the Germans claimed no less than eighty-nine victories.

Attempting to destroy the pontoon bridges across the Meuse and the Panzer columns queueing up to cross, the Allied air forces were slaughtered by flak and fighters. First, the French threw in all available aircraft, including antiquated night bombers. When they achieved nothing, the RAF mustered every serviceable bomber it had in France, launching seventy-one sorties between 15.00 and 16.00. Although they had the protection of about 250 Allied fighters, the Jagdwaffe could put up three times that number in the critical sector. The result was all but inevitable. Falling on the all but useless Battles and outclassed Blenheims, the Bf 109s were a major factor in the RAF's losses for the day, which totalled sixty-nine aircraft to all causes. The German fighter casualties amounted to thirteen Bf 109s, twelve of which were shot down in aerial combat.

The British light bomber squadrons had suffered grievously, to the tune of thirty-one Battles and fifteen Blenheims; more serious was the decimation of the fighter squadrons, which lost twenty Hurricanes. Clearly, such an attrition rate could not be borne for long and, for France, the end was near. The French Prime Minister's telephone call to Winston Churchill early on 15 May admitted as much.

While the fate of France hung in the balance and the British War Cabinet discussed the merits of sending more fighter squadrons across the Channel, the war went on. May 1940 continued to be synonymous with disaster for the Allied air forces.

RAF losses were significantly less on the 16th but they began to rise again on subsequent days. For the Jagdflieger, the pace hardly slackened: the defences of Luxeuil shot down another Bf 109E on 16 May when I./JG 54 carried out a strafing attack on the airfield. The pilot was made a prisoner. JG 21 also lost an aircraft, this time the cause being the fire of an RAF Hurricane. Other branches of the Luftwaffe, particularly the bomber and reconnaissance elements, suffered heavy casualties.

As well as exhausting air defence operations, Luftwaffe fighters were required to undertake escort to Hs 126 observation aircraft, which were a vital link in the chain of command directing the German advance. Flying immediately ahead of the tanks, the spotter crews provided up-to-the-minute situation reports which enabled French strongpoints to be knocked out as they were located, by air attack or artillery fire.

As the French were forced to abandon airfield after airfield, the Luftwaffe occupied many of them to keep in range of their own advance. JG 54, in common with other Jagdgeschwaderen, frequently moved base during those momentous weeks. Supporting the army divisions thrusting towards the Channel coast, the Jagdgeschwader's area of operations was primarily northeast of Paris, its forward bases, including Vitry en Artois, Guise, Baulie and Cambrai, being located in a rough arc around the capital.

By 22 May, III Gruppe had reached Cambrai, an airfield it shared with the Hs 123 biplane dive bombers of II./LG 2. Gruppenkommandeur Werner Ultsch had a heavy responsibility in planning his Messerschmitt sorties to provide maximum protection, keeping enemy fighters away from the slow, vulnerable Henschels, which were nevertheless highly effective if aerial opposition was light.

On the 22nd, orders were received to escort a Henschel attack on a potentially dangerous column of French tanks, accompanied by infantry in soft-skinned vehicles, which had been observed less than four miles from Cambrai. Four Hs 123s of Stab.II./LG 2 opened the assault, followed by the whole Gruppe attacking in waves, well protected by III./JG 54's Bf 109s. The small 100-pound bombs carried by the dive bombers were enough to halt the column, whereupon the Bf 109s raked it with cannon and machine gun fire. After causing extensive damage, the fighters and dive bombers broke off, as German flak units, using their guns as artillery, ranged in on the column to complete its destruction.

Elsewhere on 22 May, I./JG 21 had a Bf 109 posted as missing; five days later this unit had another aircraft go missing, plus one Bf 109E badly damaged during combat. A further E-1 was almost totally destroyed in a disastrous take-off crash.

Very few people, least of all the Germans themselves, had believed that the French campaign would be over so quickly. The suddenness of the collapse, compounded by a disorganised defence, and the unexpected direction of the main armoured thrust through the Ardennes, plus the lightning thrust at Sedan, caught the defenders off balance. Seemingly incapable of reaction with the necessary speed to unexpected situations, the French high command allowed the enemy to gain too much of a foothold before retaliating. By the time it did so, it was too late.

The lack of a mobile defence in any great strength, able to move from a quieter sector to offer significant resistance in areas under imminent threat of capture or encirclement, highlighted fatal flaws in planning and the French Army never recovered from its early setbacks.

In the air, the principles of Blitzkrieg were once more fully employed by the Germans, with dive bombers wreaking both military and pyschological damage ahead of the Panzers. But it was the Jagdflieger and flak batteries which quickly ensured that any gains on the ground were exploited without crippling casualties. If German fighters did not defeat the numerous courageous attempts by Allied airpower to destroy their tanks and infantry on the roads and fields of France, those bombers which did get through were decimated by the flak guns. In addition, strafing attacks on French and British columns, themselves often hampered by large groups of panic-stricken refugees, only added to the nightmare.

Such was the degree of German ascendency over the Allied air forces that Britain quickly faced a terrible choice — to throw in even more Hurricane squadrons to take on the Bf

109s and probably see them utterly destroyed — or to pull back and consolidate the defence of the British Isles. When the French themselves perceived the situation as hopeless, there was little alternative. The remaining British fighter squadrons, many of them woefully under strength and depleted by the sheer scale of the air operations, not to mention German ground attacks which had destroyed considerable amounts of equipment, bid adieu to France, to await whatever came next.

Hitler's incredible order to halt the Panzer columns short of Dunkirk on 24 May meant that the Jagdflieger were obliged to support other Luftwaffe elements tasked with cutting off the seaborne lifeline of the British Expeditionary Force and preventing hundreds of thousands of Allied troops escaping to England. It was an extremely difficult job. Many units had been in action with little respite for six weeks and men were on the point of exhaustion. Goering nevertheless assured his Fuhrer that the Luftwaffe could accomplish the annihilation of the BEF on the French beaches. Hitler concurred and the Panzers marked time.

Although the Luftwaffe Commander-in-Chief badly misjudged the task at hand, he had no precedent exactly like the situation at Dunkirk, with its yawning seaborne escape route; he assumed — if he gave it a great deal of thought at all — that his dive bombers would repeat what they had already accomplished against any type of land target across half of Europe. There is little evidence to suggest that he appreciated the different conditions prevailing at Dunkirk.

When the evacuation began on 30 May, JG 54 and other units met RAF fighters (including Spitfires for the first time) over the beaches and the Channel, doing their best to keep the Luftwaffe away from the rescue fleet. In great part, they succeeded. And by deploying a vast fleet of small boats to support ships of the Royal Navy and French Navy, the British managed to spirit away more than 338,000 men.

It was all but impossible for bombers to destroy more than a small proportion of this large makeshift rescue fleet or indeed to decimate large groups of troops waiting on the soft, sandy beaches. Bad weather significantly hampered air operations and when they did get

When the Bf 109E entered service, the Luftwaffe had a world-class fighter, more than capable of beating any opposition when war came. But it was often also planning and tactics that gave the Germans the upper hand. These Bf 109E-1s in the widely-used pre-war dark green camouflate, are in service with I./JG 76 during pre-war manoeuvres on a forward airfield. *(J. V. Crow).*

through, many German crews saw their bombs detonate with reduced blast effect in the sand; palls of smoke from sabotaged oil storage tanks reduced visibility. And above the clouds lurked the fighters of the Royal Air Force. These machines were not manned by pilots fatigued after long weeks of operations over France, but by eager individuals flying from airfields in England. Almost to a man, they were spoiling for a fight.

Largely unseen by the troops awaiting rescue, these fighter squadrons from England maintained patrols over Dunkirk and harried the Luftwaffe bombers saddled with the chore of preventing the largest military evacuation in history. The German fighter units took on their British opposite numbers, and both sides suffered casualties, but tasked as they were primarily with bomber escort, the Bf 109s could do little to prevent men being taken off the beaches in thousands. And giving chase across the Channel in order to reduce RAF fighter attacks was hardly recommended for the health of the Jagdflieger!

In the euphoria of defeating France, the Allied success at Dunkirk was dismissed by the Germans as a temporary setback, doubtless one to be rectified once those troops who had escaped were either killed or captured when the Wehrmacht invaded England. But militarily it was a defeat — virtually defenceless and squeezed into a confined area, those troops should have been captured with relative ease. In military terms, it was a job for infantry and tanks, not aircraft. Operation Dynamo was the first of a series of setbacks stemming from a wasteful misuse of the Luftwaffe that would eventually prove fatal for Germany.

Both I./JG 21 and I./JG 54 suffered casualties on 29 May. The former unit recorded a Bf 109 as totally destroyed in a crash-landing at Moncy-Breton, the latter having a Bf 109 suffer sixty percent damage in a forced landing following combat.

The Luftwaffe's French campaign culminated in Operation Paula, an ambitious series of large-scale bomber and fighter strikes on the airfields surrounding Paris on 3 June. German fighters engaged Armée de l'Air squadrons equipped with a variety of aircraft types including the new Bloch 152, tasked with defending the capital, and destroyed seventeen French aircraft. Overall however, Paula failed to knock out the Paris airfields, a fact that would soon benefit their new occupiers who did not have to undertake extensive repairs.

A much reduced level of combat marked the month of June, although Luftwaffe units continued to suffer losses from both operational and non-operational causes. The ever-present risk of accidents happening under the pressure of combat flying claimed numerous victims and no unit was immune.

A combat over Evreux on 14 June involved Bf 109s of JG 54's 3.Staffel. One Messerschmitt was shot down and the pilot, Ltn Angski, killed. According to the Luftwaffe Quartermaster General's daily returns of aircraft losses, this was the last casualty suffered by JG 54 in the battle of France, the outcome of which was now hardly in doubt. The daily loss totals for the Luftwaffe from 10 May to 24 June put JG

54's casualties at six aircraft destroyed or damaged, and those for JG 21 at nine.

With the armistice of 22 June, there came a welcome lull for the German forces; the Luftwaffe enjoyed a breathing space in which to replace aircraft lost in the air battles of the previous weeks and make good personnel casualties suffered by absorbing new pilots. In general, it was a time to savour a very sweet victory and for units to get used to new operational surroundings on what had become the most forward airfields in Reich territory.

Fighter and other units welcomed back men who had briefly been the unwelcome guests of the French, among them Uffz Hager of I Gruppe. He had taken off to carry out an air test on 30 May and had failed to return. It was assumed that the pilot had been killed and his aircraft lost — but in fact Hager had made a safe landing on a French rather than German-occupied airfield at Orconte, near St Dizier.

Being surrounded by French and Czech airmen was not a happy moment for Hager who nevertheless survived his misadventure.

The very speed of the German advance through France occasionally proved hazardous to lost fighter pilots. This Bf 109 of I./JG 54 landed in fading light at the airfield at Orconte, west of St Dizier on 30 May 1940, the pilot finding to his dismay that it was still occupied by the French. The aircraft was repainted in French national insignia for air tests. *(M. Payne).*

His aircraft was subsequently painted in French markings.

While there was now a little time to take stock, the German fighter units prepared to move up and occupy airfields in the Pas de Calais. It was almost certain that there would be future operations against the RAF; airfields nearest to England would therefore be necessary for fighter sorties, but few pilots then had any idea what the British would do. It was certainly possible that the nearest French airfields would be attacked by the RAF and however near-suicidal such action might be, the Germans took precautions. Sandbagged dispersals, each capable of accommodating a single Bf 109, were built on many aerodromes and to make the aircraft less conspicuous from the air, camouflage netting was slung between the protective revetment walls.

Numerous French airstrips in this forward area lacked all but the barest facilities and, on the majority of bases, these had to be constructed from whatever materials were at hand. Packing cases were saved to double as engine and equipment work stands, heavy-duty hoists were fabricated and vehicles of all kinds, many of them of French origin, were pressed into service. Care had to be taken to keep the German aero engines in good order, as dust was a considerable problem during the spring of 1940, necessitating the fitting of supercharger air intake filters at some bases, where dry weather could create minor dust storms whenever one or more aircraft took off.

Fortunately for the Luftwaffe ground crews, and a significant number of coerced French personnel, the fine weather enabled a good deal of servicing to be carried out in the open on airfields where covered facilities were often at a premium. At that time the early Bf 109E-1 was in widespread service, along with the less numerous E-3. Both Messerschmitt sub-types initially lacked sufficient armour protection for the pilot, although 'bolt-on' plates had been developed and were now being supplied to front line units. Retrofitting these plates, by securing them to the seat and canopy framing, was a relatively simple task; they added fifty-three pounds of 8mm protection to the seat and 28.6 pounds to shield the pilot's head in the form of a backplate. It appears though that individual pilots foreswore any additional weight being added to their aircraft, despite the increased safety aspect, as by no means all Bf 109s were so fitted. This attitude was not unique to the Germans; before, during and since World War Two anything that adds weight to a fighter — and inevitably carries a performance penalty — has been anathema to fighter pilots!

The workload of the ground crews was considerable and included, when time permitted, repainting fighters in specified tactical camouflage, and applying revised national markings, following directives which changed the presentation of the *Balkenkreuz* and *Hakenkreuz* on the Bf 109 in both location and size. Any Bf 109 serving in a front-line unit and which still bore the older, predominantly dark green airframe upper surfaces, now emerged from the paint shops with two-thirds of the fuselage light blue, and a straight-edged splinter camouflage in two shades of green applied to those surfaces likely to be visible from directly above.

Orders to change the camouflage and markings of all first-line Bf 109s had been issued following close scrutiny of the effectiveness of camouflage paint during operations over Poland, and by the start of the French campaign this change had been widely implemented. However, individual machines retained their old markings, as the respraying of every aircraft, even in a single Staffel, took time. Operational considerations naturally took precedence, but by the start of the period of intensive flying over the Channel, where a much lighter paint scheme would help to merge the now higher-flying Messerschmitts with the backdrop of the sky, standardisation had all but been achieved. Apart from the application of localised tactical markings, often in water-soluble paints, Bf 109s, like their RAF opposite numbers, looked remarkably uniform as far as their overall colour scheme was concerned.

Unlike other Jagdgeschwaderen, JG 54 did not remain long on French soil after the armistice but was dispersed to airfields in Holland and Norway. The Luftwaffe now had an immense area of Europe to police and while some second-line units were employed on the occupation task, the combat-ready fighter units

Unencumbered by the need for cockpit armour and heavier canopy framing, the Bf 109D offered excellent vision for the pilot. Mechanics probe the innards of the Junkers Jumo engine, while armourers attend to the ammunition in this view. The spiral treatment on the spinner was in the Staffel colour, yellow in this case. *(Bundesarchiv)*.

were rotated through newly-conquered territory until any positive new Allied move was identified. No immediate orders to attack across the Channel were received.

All Gruppen of JG 54 withdrew from France on 21 June to occupy Eindhoven and Schipol (I Gruppe), Wallhaven and Vlissingen (II Gruppe) and Soesterburg and Bergen (III Gruppe). From these bases the Geschwader mounted patrols, ever on the lookout for RAF reconnaissance aircraft, a small number of which were intercepted. If the British crews were in a position to fight back, the interceptors did not always have things their own way.

Action of this kind came early for Oblt Hans Schmoller-Haldy, Staffelkapitan of III./JG 54. With other members of his Schwarm, he attacked a Blenheim flying near Rotterdam on 26 June — and what should have been a relatively easy kill turned into a painful, albeit short, break from operations.

The Blenheim rear gunner fired back as the Bf 109s swept in, one burst of about twenty rounds hitting Schmoller-Haldy's aircraft and wounding him in the left foot. The German pilot broke off the attack and made quickly for base, blood spurting from his foot. Managing to carry out a landing that was none too easy in the circumstances, the Staffelkapitan's machine promptly nosed-over. Schmoller-Haldy was rushed to hospital at Tilburg. A month's enforced rest followed until he was discharged at the end of July.

Such forays over enemy occupied areas of the continent were vital but extremely hazardous for the RAF bombers. Decimated as they had been in France, Blenheim crews continued to be sent out unescorted in small numbers to obtain what photographs they could of German activities and to drop a small weight of bombs on a variety of targets. Little more than nuisance raids most of the time, the light, relatively slow and poorly-armed bombers were very vulnerable to Bf 109s if they were caught in clear weather conditions. The foregoing incident was typical of many during the period, the RAF despatching a total of thirteen Blenheims on 26 June to various points in Germany. One aircraft was tasked with reconnaissance, the rest carrying bombs. Only three aircraft in fact bombed and one was lost — possibly that attacked by Schmoller-Haldy.

For JG 54 and other fighter units, this interlude was to be short lived; when, somewhat to Hitler's surprise, the British refused to sue for peace or even to enter into negotiations, the Luftwaffe was faced with an assault on England. Its task would be to gain air superiority over the RAF as a prerequisite to invasion, once that particular option appeared as the only way that Germany could remove a dangerous adversary at the limit of its conquest in Western Europe. Unless the war now took a dramatic turn the British would fight, and the bulk of the front line German fighter units were to be committed to the battle ahead.

When direct military confrontation with England became inevitable, a great many Germans viewed the prospect with considerable alarm, not the least of whom were the Luftwaffe aircrews, and particularly the fighter pilots: keyed up and eager as the Jagdflieger were, there were few amongst them who did not, despite outward confidence and exuberance, harbour some reservations about the magnitude of the task ahead.

Those who had flown against the RAF at Dunkirk had realised that the British had, in their Spitfire, a fighter that appeared to be as good as their own Emils, while the Hurricane, although not to be afforded the same degree of respect, was also more numerous and more than capable of shooting down the Bf 109, as the fighting over France had shown. At that time, not many Spitfires had been met in action, but the first-hand accounts by pilots who had done so, and the reports that had been circulated about its performance, were not encouraging.

Previously, German air and ground forces

Ground crewmen pose with the Gruppen-Adjutant's aircraft of Stab II./JG 54 on a French airfield in May 1940. The photo shows that external rear-view mirrors were favoured by individual German pilots. *(Crow)*.

had worked together to demoralise the opposition and cause widespread chaos which they quickly turned to advantage. Over the Channel and south Eastern England the Luftwaffe would be on its own. Initially at least, there would be no ground forces to support and no identifiable front line. it was also known that the British had radar and were therefore in a position to obtain some form of advance warning of incoming raids. Fairly obviously, the Jagdflieger would have as a primary task the one not welcomed by fighter forces anywhere — bomber escort. As the build-up of units on the French coast continued, they awaited orders. Speculation was rife, particularly as to the timescale of the Führer's next move.

Pilots also realised that a standard Bf 109E with a full fuel load — no external tanks yet having been delivered to operational units — would be near the limits of its 412-mile maximum range if it needed to penetrate as far inland as the outskirts of London. Flying that distance, even from the most forward French airfields, would leave a scant eight to ten minutes for combat. And in between their home bases and the Luftwaffe's primary targets in south-east England lay the English Channel, a waterway which was still twenty miles wide at its narrowest point. That fact alone introduced a cautionary note for the German fighter pilots, as the need to traverse such an expanse of water in order to join combat had not yet been a factor in operational plans. This phase of the war, a lot of them knew, would be different. . .

Chapter 2

CHANNEL FRONT

It was 30 June before Goering circulated orders to his field commanders to commence operations in the first phase of what the British were to call the Battle of Britain. No such campaign title was ever recognised or used by the Luftwaffe at the time, the mid-1940 phase of the struggle for Europe being merely an extension of Operation Weserubung, the attack on France and the Low Countries. With the offensive extending further and further from the forward French bases, *Kanal Kampf* or 'Channel Front' was the generic term most commonly used for the opening rounds of the war against the RAF in that area.

Sub-division of the battle into various phases — at least prior to August when the main period of operations was deemed to begin — was also not recognised as such by the Germans. These phases are however, convenient and are used here when necessary because there was a series of discernable changes in tactics on the part of the Luftwaffe — generally forced upon it by the degree of opposition encountered — and no little impatience on the part of the German high command.

Combat over the Channel and south eastern England rapidly began to extend Hitler's time-scale for the invasion, but changes in tactics were often little more than operational experiments designed to tempt the defenders up to battle superior forces and be destroyed. For its part, the RAF largely refused to become bait in the German trap.

Although the Luftwaffe began air attacks on the British Isles and shipping in the Straits of Dover during July with a significant superiority in aircraft, they were used in relatively small numbers, at no time approaching the scale of the mass formation attacks that came later. Plans for achieving a series of goals that would have enabled a sea and airborne invasion to succeed lacked sound intelligence data on the location of the main Fighter Command airfields, British centres of aircraft production and repair and in particular, the vital function of the Radio Direction Finding stations.

It was not that the Gemans lacked good photographic coverage of most of the important targets in south-east England; the reverse was the case. Reconnaissance flights had begun some time before the start of the hostilities and by the time of the Battle of Britain, the target folders were full. What was missing was the ability to determine an order of target priority.

Also, it was German policy to use the Luftwaffe to create panic among the British civil population — as indeed it had on the continent and might well have done in England if the Wehrmacht and Panzers had landed and were known to be a few miles behind the bomb craters. Although a land dimension was completely missing, it was the 'mixture as before'.

Forged as a tactical, ground support force, the Luftwaffe was now saddled with the immense responsibility of a strategic role. While the task of subjugating England by airpower looked the same as before, the Germans were actually embarking upon an entirely different type of operation. While it was true that the Luftwaffe had previously been instrumental in forcing Hitler's enemies to capitulate quickly, no other country had had anything like the defences available to the British — or the advantages of an island location.

A significant factor was that the Luftwaffe also totally lacked the element of surprise which had helped to carry it so decisively through Poland, France and the Low Countries. It now faced a fully-alerted foe, well organised and better equipped in terms of fighters than any nation Germany had previously faced. The failure to build up the necessary comprehensive picture of where the main targets were and their relative importance to the integrated air defence of the British Isles was to cost Germany dear. Throughout the Battle of Britain, the Germans never fully understood how Fighter

Command's defence of south-east England functioned.

As the early stages of the assault unfolded, the Luftwaffe commanders therefore suffered increasingly from a lack of reliable intelligence, particularly in realising exactly what damage their bombers had inflicted on the vital sector stations and the Chain Home RDF network, and the strength of the defences on any given day. Without such information, it is small wonder that they failed to exploit the advantages actually gained — and these were fairly substantial at different periods.

On 6 July, there was further rationalisation of the Jagdwaffe. The remaining pre-war designations, some of which had survived until that time, were finally dropped. Thus I./JG 21 officially became III./JG 54 and other units took on the designations under which they would generally operate until the end of the war. Hubertus von Bonin and Fritz Ultsch remained in command of I and III Gruppen respectively, as did Major Kraut, leading II Gruppe for another five days. On 11 July, Hptm Winterer took over.

A tripod-mounted range-finder framing a Bf 109E of 2.Staffel JG 21 (later 8./JG 54) in France. The forward position of the numeral on the Bf 109 was one of a number of non-standard marking practices favoured by JG 54 throughout its existence.

Shipping and Britain's port facilities were given priority in the assault phase that began on 8 July and although other targets were attacked, both sides were then probing, testing out relative strengths. What the Luftwaffe met, in the shape of Hurricanes and Spitfires, was not at all encouraging.

While the British fighters were by no means an unknown factor, it gradually began to be realised that RDF was serving the enemy even better than had been suspected, enabling him to place fighters to effectively counter Luftwaffe raids without the need to mount fuel-consuming and pilot-fatiguing standing patrols to cover all the approaches from France. Modest though the Luftwaffe effort often was in terms of the number of aircraft involved in these early engagements, for its part the RAF knew it was up against a formidable foe. In particular, the Jagdflieger were treated with great respect, the generally well-flown Bf 109s being more than worthy adversaries for the British pilots.

Shortly before its combat debut over the Channel, JG 54 had been issued with the Bf 109E-4. Externally similar to the preceding E-3, it dispensed with the engine-mounted MG FF/M cannon and had a tip plate to blank-off the hole in the spinner. Having a cannon set to fire directly along the fighter's centreline was a sound enough proposition, but the weapon had proved so troublesome in service on earlier versions that its usefulness was doubtful. The Bf 109E-4 reverted to the 'standard' armament of two cowling-mounted MG 17 7.9mm machine guns and a single MG FF 20mm cannon in each wing.

Thus equipped the E-4 had a ceiling of 34,500 feet and a top speed of 348 mph at 15,000 feet. In terms of altitude, a competently handled 109 could fight on even terms with the Spitfire Mk I, while it had around 1,000 feet maximum height advantage over the MkI Hurricane. But overall, there was not much difference in the qualities of all three fighter types, success in action depending on the pilot's experience, speed of reaction and relative position when combat was joined. The maxim 'He who has height controls the battle' held true most of the time.

The battle was the first in which the ability of fighters to turn inside their opponents really came to the fore, and in this respect, the Spitfire had an edge over the Bf 109. Fitted with automatic wing leading edge slats, the Messerschmitt could be a handful at high speeds as the controls became progressively heavier. In extreme situations the lack of in-flight trimming of the rudder or ailerons made itself felt as the pilot needed more and more pressure to change direction or to sideslip for a good firing position. Having to keep his foot down on the portside rudder pedal quickly induced fatigue and led to the curious condition of the pilot being able to make a faster turn to the left than the right.

In sum, the Bf 109 was a far better dogfighting aircraft at low speeds, below 250 mph, when it could roll rapidly. But as the speed built up, the stiff controls could induce difficult, even fatal characteristics. More than once a Bf 109 pilot was lost when trying to follow a Hurricane or Spitfire which had executed a high speed half roll and 'split-S' below 5,000 feet. In trying to follow with the throttle wide open, it did happen that the German aircraft simply could not pull out of the dive in time.

On the evening of 19 July Hitler made 'a last appeal to reason' to the British people. In an awesome Reichstag ceremony almost dripping with war fever, the German Chancellor promoted his Luftwaffe and Wehrmacht generals, the air force recipients of the rank of Field Marshal including Erhard Milch, Albert Kesselring and Hugo Sperrle. On Hermann Goering Hitler bestowed the ultimate and unique accolade of *Reichsmarschall*. The reaction from Britain was predictable.

JG 54's area defence duty in Holland did not end until late July when it was ordered to move to northern France. Elements of I Gruppe arrived on the first day of the month, 3. Staffel occupying Campagne-les-Guines (usually shortened to simply Campagne to avoid confusion with the airfields closer to the town of Guines) on that date. It had an establishment of 150 airmen, nine pilots and eleven Bf 109s plus, initially, two extra pilots who returned to Schipol after delivering their aircraft. When all of I Gruppe was ensconced, Campagne housed around thirty-five Bf 109Es, enough for the pilots of three Staffeln plus the Geschwader-Stab, led by Otto Hohne. Typically, the Stab

Bf 109E 'Red 7' belonging to II Gruppe after a crash-landing in France in 1940. *(M. Payne).*

flight was composed of four aircraft flown by the Kommodore, adjutant and two NCOs.

As part of Albert Kesselring's Luftflotte 2, JG 54 came under the tactical command of Jagdfliegerfuhrer 2, headquartered at Wissant on the coast of the Pas-de-Calais region. The Geschwader occupied bases about ten miles inland, with Hptm Winterer's II Gruppe going to Hardinghen and III Gruppe primarily using Guines-Sud and Guines-West, the town of Guines lying seven miles south of Calais. There was some switching around of airfields, as II Gruppe subsequently moved to Campagne to co-locate with I Gruppe. All JG 54's airfields were close to each other and it was common for individual Staffeln to operate from alternate bases throughout the Kanalkampf period. It was the first time that the Geschwader had been able to fly from nearly adjacent airfields, which saved considerable time in forming up for combat sorties.

Luftflotte 2's fighter complement was otherwise composed of JG 3, 26, 51 and 52, plus LG 2, ZG 26 and ZG 76, the latter three units flying the Bf 110 and the remainder the Bf 109E, altogether a formidable force. The group-ings of Jagdgeschwaderen for Channel Front operations brought all three Gruppen of JG 54 together to operate as a cohesive unit for the first time since the war began, although there continued to be rotations back to Holland.

Being able to station its component Staffeln on adjacent French airfields — indeed the entire fighter element was close, grouped on airfields on a twenty to twenty-five mile radius around Calais — was not only to cement the esprit de corps of the unit, but to forge a bond between the pilots and ground crews — the ubiquitous 'black men' without whom no Luftwaffe unit could have functioned. The aircraftsmen and mechanics laboured long and hard to provide the maximum number of aircraft for each day's operations.

By the time JG 54 arrived on the Channel coast, the operations of July had brought mixed success for the Germans; the British fighters, although very aggressive when they could be tempted to do battle, were now more quantifiable. A number of fine pilots had however already paid the price of trying to destroy the RAF over its own territory and it was fairly obvious that wearing the enemy down was going to take time.

Fighter availability for JG 54 at the start of its period of Channel Front operations peaked at between sixty and eighty machines. Three or four sorties per aircraft per day were not uncommon as the pilots not only mounted offensive patrols over the Channel, but carried out sweeps to protect air-sea rescue vessels against RAF attack, mounted escort to damaged bombers straggling back to base, and flew sorties over the Franco-Belgian coastline, away from the focus of the main assault on England. These latter were undertaken to counter British bombing and reconnaissance flights aimed primarily at destroying barges being assembled for the planned invasion.

Irrespective of whether or not cross-Channel operations were flown, each fighter Gruppe was obliged to maintain aircraft at a state of immediate readiness in case of air attack, often throughout the hours of daylight. Such alert flights would typically be composed of two or three Rotten, depending on the number of aircraft that could be spared. Stand-down would come as soon as was deemed safe, but it was rarely before dusk. The time would be whiled away by reading, sleep or endless games of skat, the three-handed card game with universal appeal in Germany.

Routine fighter patrols were flown at altitudes ranging from 12,000 to 30,000 feet, under Jafu 2 control and co-ordination within the Geschwader. Such sorties, although tedious, were useful to replacement pilots who might have arrived at their designated forward airfield with relatively few hours in their logbooks — although at this stage of the war the majority had operational experience — and were unfamiliar with the surrounding terrain, diversionary airfields and so forth. In this arena, familiarity with the prevailing conditions was fundamental to survival.

Bad weather began to be welcomed as the pressure of combat mounted, and while the weeks of that momentous summer left precious little time for leave, pilots were glad to get away on rest days or when, for various reasons, flying operations were cancelled. When a break was possible, most JG 54 pilots headed for the comforts of Lille.

Fighter combat in Spain during the civil war and the earlier campaigns in Europe had enabled the Germans to test a range of battle tactics 'in the ring'; one of the most important of these was to radically change they way single-seat fighters were deployed in combat, leading to a considerable advantage for the Jagdflieger over the largely outmoded tactics of the RAF. The British fighters, generally using time-honoured 'V' formations which had inherent visual and manoeuvrability disadvantages, were often surprised by the speed at which the Germans were able to change formation using their highly flexible basic 'finger four' formation.

The Jagdflieger also made it standard practice to fly in mutual support, the basic *Schwarm* or flight of four fighters being sub-divided into two *Rotten* (cell or pair). This basic fighting unit was composed of the *Rottenfuhrer* and his wingman or *Katchmarek*. It was the latter's job to guard his leader's tail and not to go chasing his own targets. It was a highly flexible system which time and again proved much sounder than any other fighter formation.

This slight edge was enhanced by the fuel injection engines fitted to the Bf 109s. No German pilot had to contend with a windmilling propeller resulting from a fuel-starved engine as did Spitfire and Hurricane pilots on occasions when their aircraft were thrown into negative-G manoeuvres. The carburettor fuel system of the Rolls-Royce Merlin could give pilots an anxious moment or two until the engine picked up again.

On the other hand, sorties over the Channel forced Luftwaffe pilots to constantly watch their aircraft's fuel consumption and, by careful throttle control, try to stretch out the average eighty minutes' flight time to keep something in reserve for combat. Watching the fuel gauge became something of an obsession over the uninviting waters of the Channel, and more than one pilot sat in his cockpit willing the low fuel warning red light not to come on before the coast of France passed under his wings.

Should the worst happen and the Bf 109 pilot be forced to bail out over the Channel, he had quickly to divest himself of his Mae West and parachute harness and clamber into a one-man dinghy inflated by compressed air. The dinghy was stowed under the parachute pack in the 109's seat pan and the pilot sat on both, a not too comfortable arrangement, particularly for a tall man. There was also the slight risk of the dinghy inadvertently inflating. It did happen to at least one pilot, who was actually forced out of his cockpit by the steadily expanding rubber boat!

Once in the water, the downed Jagdflieger would be kept afloat by an inflatable Mae West or the older style kapok-filled lifejacket. To mark his position he used fluoscene, a chemical dye which stained the sea bright green or yellow. This was designed to attract the attention of aircraft of the *Seenotflugkommando* air sea rescue service or one of the converted assault boats manned by Wehrmacht crews staioned at several points along the French coast to rescue aircrew.

Provided that he managed to get clear of the aircraft — the Bf 109 generally sank inside five minutes — the pilot stood an even chance of rescue, hopefully by his own side. Enemy surface craft, usually RAF rescue launches, naturally considered German fighter pilots fair game and there were occasions when both sides raced each other to be first to reach a

dinghy. But in general, the Germans were far better placed to rescue downed pilots, the RAF being extremely short of surface rescue craft at that time.

At first, being picked up by the other side was considered only a temporary inconvenience by German airmen, who assumed they would soon be freed by their invading armies. Sometimes, even a successful pick-up by one of the rescue service's He 59 seaplanes was not a guarantee of safe journey home. These slow biplanes could easily fall victim to prowling RAF fighters and later in the battle, suspecting that ambulance aircraft were carrying out reconnaissance sorties, the British deliberately shot them down. A Bf 109 escort therefore became highly necessary to protect them.

The first major clash in the battle came for JG 54 on 5 August, when 1. and 3. Staffeln bounced six Spitfires of No. 64 Squadron over the Kent coast at 08.30 and shot down two. Not emerging entirely unscathed from the brief combat, the German force had one Bf 109 damaged by return fire, with the result that the pilot had to force-land at Beauvais.

Down in the dunes on the Dutch coast (believed to be Beveland) Bf 109E 'Black 4' of II./JG 54 awaits the crash crews who will retrieve it for repair. *(E. J. Creek).*

In the early afternoon, 1. Staffel flew a second sortie, escorting Ju 88s looking for a previously-reported convoy. This force ran into Hurricanes of No. 151 Sqn, which hit the Bf 109E-4 flown by Olbt Reinhard 'Seppi' Seiler, the Staffelkapitan. Wounded by the Hurricane's fire Seiler nevertheless managed to fly back to base. Rushed to a naval hospital near Calais, Seiler recovered to eventually return to his unit after the main Channel Front operation was over.

A heavy landing accident at Detmold badly damaged a further Bf 109 while 4. Staffel, temporarily operating from Haamstede in Holland, was subjected to an RAF bombing raid which destroyed one Bf 109 and damaged five more. The Blenheim raid also killed or wounded six pilots as it apparently came just as the Messerschmitts were taking off, a setback that caused the Staffel to be withdrawn from the Kanalkampf order of battle for two weeks.

Such air raids remained a hazard for JG 54 and other units, for the Dutch airfields were given some priority by RAF Bomber Command's 2 Group tactical units. With their backs to the wall, the British had to even the odds against a German invasion, and light bomber squadrons, invariably flying Blenheims without fighter escort, were ordered to carry out their sorties regardless of cost.

On 8 August No. 41 Squadron's Spitfires tangled with elements of II and III Gruppen of JG 54 on a day which saw large-scale combats developing over the Channel. The fighters were primarily tasked with protecting a sizeable force of Ju 87s bent on the destruction of a convoy as it reached a point south of the Isle of Wight. To the defenders, the Luftwaffe effort appeared to herald the opening of a decisive phase in the battle — as it was subsequently to prove to be. JG 54's participation was as part of the strong fighter escort, the action with Spitfires occurring at midday. Two Bf 109s, one from each Gruppe, were damaged in the action, neither of the German pilots being injured.

Comparative figures of available aircraft fluctuated daily throughout the battle but on 10 August Luftflotten 2 and 3 had 702 serviceable Bf 109s, 875 bombers of the three main types, 227 Bf 110s and 316 dive bombers. The

total of 2,165 aircraft was made up by reconnaissance aircraft. Against this force Fighter Command could count on just 235 Hurricanes and Spitfires in 11 Group squadrons, a figure boosted by the supporting 12, 10 and 13 Groups which had 323 aircraft of the two main types operational and ready for combat on that date.

While the RAF moved squadrons into the battle area as conditions dictated, the above figures do show an enormous disparity of strength on one day at the height of the battle. Also, the figures do not take into account the aircraft of Luftflotte 5 in Norway, or indeed the Defiants, Gladiators, Blenheims and Fulmars which added modestly to the RAF's order of battle but which cannot be considered important as far as the main battle is concerned.

JG 54's hectic debut in the battle was some two weeks before the Luftwaffe's massive 'knock out blow' against the RAF, grandly labelled *Adlerangriff*, 'Attack of the Eagles'. This was, from the German standpoint, the true start of the all-out attack on Britain, previous operations being considered merely a prelude. Originally scheduled for 10 August, bad weather caused a three-day postponement.

Two days of small-scale activity followed before 11 August removed another two Bf 109s from JG 54's strength. One aircraft was totally destroyed at Haamstede when Ltn Wagner of 6. Staffel was injured after experiencing engine failure. A take off accident at Campaigne resulted in thirty-three percent damage to a second machine, the pilot escaping unhurt. Both these sorties were non-combat missions, and typical of the attrition rate recorded by most of the units participating in the battle. Operationally, the Jagdflieger had concentrated their effort that day in the Dover area, trying to draw the British fighters away from a heavy bomber attack on Portland.

Finer weather on 12 August saw attacks on several RAF airfields and radar stations, the thirty-one Luftwaffe casualties including the first JG 54 pilot fatality and the first to become a prisoner of war in the Battle of Britain. Oblt Albrecht 'Bonifatius' Dress was one of the two III Gruppe losses that day. An eye-witness stated that Dress dived vertically out of cloud in the vicinity of Margate in Kent. His Bf 109E was seen to circle the destructor chimney of a refuse dump behind the town and drop towards Hartsdown Hill. The fighter finally made a wheels-up landing at Hengrove.

Following the direction of the aircraft on his bicycle, the witness observed Dress climbing out of the cockpit. He reached behind the seat and removed a small attaché case which he placed on the wing. Dress was then seen to light a cigarette, having walked up a short footpath from the field where his aircraft came to rest. Dress stood as though waiting for someone and soon a lorry and a staff car arrived, followed by a group of civilians attracted by the crashing 109.

The Oberleutnant spoke to an RAF officer who translated what he said to his colleagues and although the witness was not near enough to hear exactly what passed between the two men, it appeared that Dress had admitted that he had 'had enough'. The witness did manage to see that the German pilot's case contained a shaving kit and a change of clothes — which may have confirmed at least a little pessimism about his chances of getting home after a cross-Channel sortie! A further minor mystery in the story was the apparent lack of combat damage suffered by the Bf 109E flown by Oblt Dress; it was later collected by an RAF Queen Mary transporter and moved to Manston for examination.

As well as having Olbt Schon and Ltn Eberle injured in accidents as Guines-Sud, the worst III Gruppe casualty that day was Gefr Stabner. He was listed as missing presumed killed when his aircraft went down in the Channel or waters of the Thames estuary — the first of at least ten JG 54 pilots who were to meet a similar fate.

Engaging Hurricanes and Spitfires in combat so that they could be destroyed in high numbers continued to be the principle duty of the German fighter force, a fact succinctly summed up by Theo Osterkamp, Kommodore of JG 51 and one of the Jagdwaffe's most experienced 'old eagles'. Addressing his pilots early in the battle, he had said,

'Our enemy is the British fighter. Be as cunning as a fox . . . wait patiently . . . then strike like lightning and get out as fast. We have now got a hard battle against a particularly obstinate enemy — good luck in your fight against the "lords"'.

Those sentiments were echoed by all the other *Geschwaderkommodoren* to their pilots; destruction of the RAF fighters would indeed be the deciding factor. If it could be achieved, it would eventually enable the Luftwaffe bomber force to attack targets unmolested, thus preparing the way for the invasion to take place.

But if the Jagdflieger understood their task well enough, the British in their turn quickly realised that combatting free hunting German fighters was a waste of precious resources. Only the destruction of bombers in substantial numbers would save English targets — particularly their own forward airfields — from extensive damage.

As the RAF proved more than capable of shooting down bombers, the Luftwaffe was forced to provide closer fighter escort to the large formations of Dorniers, Heinkels and Junkers. Also, the relatively poor showing of the Bf 110 Zerstorers in fighter versus fighter combat led to an even greater call on the single seaters to offer them some protection as well. The Bf 110s, so promising over Poland, had not been heavily engaged during the French campaign and only now was it fully realised that they were not manoeuvrable enough to escape the attentions of Spitfires and Hurricanes. Only if their heavy battery of nose guns could be brought to bear did the Zerstorer crews have much chance of scoring kills. A Bf 109 escort was deemed more expedient.

But there simply were not enough Bf 109s to carry out all these tasks adequately, most of which reduced the tactically sound free hunt patrols which were responsible for so many British fighter losses. Even so, on most good flying days between 700 and 800 Bf 109s plus 100-150 Bf 110s could be airborne and assembling over Cap Griz Nez to await the enemy — in full view of British radar. . .

Adler Tag finally got underway late on 13 August and although the aircraft of both sides were heavily engaged, the Luftwaffe came off worst: at the end of the day, thirteen fighters had been destroyed in combat — but forty-six aircraft were lost. Some redress for the men of the *Kampfgruppen* was the fact that their raids on a number of airfields had written off

When JG 54 entered the Battle of Britain in August 1940, an early loss to the Geschwader was Oblt Albrecht Dress, whose strikingly-marked Bf 109E came down at Hengrove in Kent. Even by that early stage of the battle, JG 54 had begun using paint to tone down the light blue fuselage sides of its Bf 109s. *(D. G. Collyer)*.

another forty-seven RAF aircraft. Only one fighter was amongst them.

JG 54's Adler Tag task was to provide close escort to KG 3's Dornier 17s bombing Rochester and Eastchurch airfields. The Bf 109 cover proved on this occasion to be all but impregnable and this *Kampfgeschwader* suffered the loss of only two aircraft over England. But in other units, the crew rosters had numerous gaps at the end of the day. In more than 2,000 sorties the Germans spread their attacks too widely and once again, bombed relatively unimportant airfields.

With large bomber formations to protect, the Jagdflieger found less and less opportunity to mount free hunts against RAF fighters, but a high cover, over the lower elements flying in sight of the bomber crews, was usually maintained. Fighter pilots could not communicate by radio with their Kampfgeschwader comrades and orders were emphatic that the crews should see their own fighters. This was undoubtedly a morale booster, but it was highly frustrating for the eager young Turks of the Jagdflieger.

The high formations of Bf 109s were often well placed to attack RAF fighters engaging bombers at lower altitude, although it did

happen that the long climb to height drained the Messerschmitts' tanks at such a rate that by the time the enemy was spotted, there was scant time for combat before the dreaded red low fuel warning light started its blinking and the Germans had to disengage. For their part, RAF fighter leaders stressed time and again the danger of being bounced by the 'Hun in the sun'.

Two days after the indifferent conclusion of Adler Tag JG 54 suffered heavily — as indeed did the Luftwaffe in general. In the heaviest fighting yet seen, the RAF's defence of its vital airfields resulted in the loss of seventy-five German aircraft for thirty-four British fighters. Even the additional strength of Luftflotte 5 from Scandinavia could not swamp the defenders with odds of as many as twenty to one.

It was the first of three occasions when the Geschwader lost four pilots in one day. Combat was joined with Hurricanes during the morning of 15 August and an afternoon sweep in company with JG 26, JG 51 and JG 52 found the Bf 109s of JG 54 high above the Straits of Dover covering the bombers. Fw Schnaar and Ltn Gerlach, both from 2. Staffel, were respectively involved in combat with Spitfires of

39

No. 266 and Hurricanes of No. 615 Squadrons. Schnaar managed to nurse his crippled machine back to France only to crash fatally at Courtrai, while Gerlach was posted as missing when his aircraft went down into the Channel.

Uffz Hautkappe of 5. Staffel was also lost in the Channel, while Uffz Niedermaier ended his last sortie over the southern outskirts of London. His Bf 109E-4 came down at Cranbrook in Kent after combat with British fighters.

Lost to 3. Staffel on 16 August was Fw Knedler, whose Bf 109 went into the sea. Although Knedler was the only fatality suffered by the Geschwader on 16 August, two more Bf 109s were written off and a third damaged. In all three, the pilots were injured. It was the Spitfires of No. 54 Squadron which caused Knedler's demise when the two sides engaged at 12.45. Flying escort to KG 2's Dorniers, the Messerschmitts were engaged in a running fight back across the Channel. Three Do 17Zs were also shot down and JG 54 failed to score any victories over the Spitfires from this particular squadron. A routine test flight of a 7. Staffel replacement aircraft from Guines-Sud ended in a crash which totally destroyed the Bf 109 to round out an eminently dismal day for JG 54.

There was a notable lull in the fighting on the 17th, the Luftwaffe all but standing down even though the day brought fine flying weather. RAF fighter patrols over convoy shipping met no enemy aircraft. It was to be a very different story on the following day.

On 18 August the Germans launched three heavy raids on southern England, air combat resulting in heavy losses on both sides (seventy-one German aircraft and twenty-seven RAF fighters destroyed or damaged). JG 54 participated in two of the operations, the first of which took place at 13.30, and the third, late in the afternoon. Concurrent with strikes on Kenley, a substantial force had been sent to attack the sector station at Biggin Hill, JG 54 putting up about forty Messerschmitts to shepherd the sixty He 111s of KG 1. The latter carried out a textbook attack — enemy fighters otherwise engaged, no flak worthy of the name and no casualties to aircraft or crews before the target was reached. From 12,000 to 15,000 feet, the Heinkels rained bombs on the Kent fighter station. A number of bomber crewmen could hardly believe their luck.

Despite the lack of opposition, many bombs fell short and exploded in woods bordering the airfield, or hit the landing ground rather than the buildings which the crews were presumably aiming for. Very slight damage was therefore done considering the weight and circumstances of the attack. Even the often-hazardous dash for the coast saw KG 1's good fortune holding. One He 111 was shot down and one was damaged, with one member of each crew being killed.

On an occasion when JG 54's escort was hardly stretched, the Geschwader suffered just three damaged aircraft and no pilot injuries. Two of these were machines of II Gruppe which were some way from the main battle area — namely Vlissingen. Both Bf 109s were damaged by bombs dropped when a solitary Blenheim appeared over the airfield. In addition, a 7.Staffel aircraft was damaged on take off from Guines-West — non-operational attrition was an ever-present hazard.

When it became clear that Adler Tag had failed to achieve air superiority Hermann Goering attempted to blame the Jagdflieger, conveniently disregarding the fact that responsibility stemmed from his own direction of operations via his local commanders. Although his display of outrage was an embarrassing, disgusting slur on courageous, able men, the Reichmarschall's pique did bring some benefits. His view that the fighter units were not being led 'aggressively' enough resulted in the replacement of a number of Kommodoren by younger individuals who, presumably by some miracle about to be unleashed by German genius, would soon force a favourable conclusion to this annoying setback to Hitler's plans. Thus the leadership of JG 54 passed from Martin Mettig (who was then thirty-seven) into the hands of Hannes Trautloft, who was at that time still serving with JG 51. At twenty-eight he was one of the most experienced fighter leaders the Luftwaffe had.

With the new blood at the head of the fighter Gruppen, a move was initiated that would bring all the single-seat fighter units under the control of Luftflotte 2 in the Pas de Calais, leaving Luftflotte 3 with the responsibility of bomber operations. This, the German commanders believed, would offer the Jagdflieger more freedom to knock down RAF fighters. But the orders to protect the bombers remained in force and the fact that fighter availability was not being greatly improved left a number of questions as to how the main task was to be achieved. Nobody had an adequate answer.

Even when bad weather forced a decrease in bomber sorties, as on 19 August, Jafu 2 sent fighter patrols out in an increasingly optimistic attempt to find enemy fighters. This 'coat trailing' continued throughout the battle, but the Jagdflieger were invariably identified and often totally ignored by Fighter Command. This served both to mystify and frustrate some pilots, particularly younger men who could be forgiven for thinking that the non-appearance of the RAF meant that the number of Spitfires and Hurricanes had reached a critically low point.

Although this was certainly the case in terms of trained pilots, to believe that the British could not put up any defensive fighters was to seriously misread the overall picture. The reaction shown by the enemy to heavy Luftwaffe bombing raids was proof enough that the RAF knew exactly what it was doing. . .

Knowing that any period of inclement weather gave the enemy a chance to reorganise his battered defences, the Germans were obliged to maintain the pressure with small numbers of bombers, even single machines. These sorties were intercepted where possible, fighter escort not being mounted in all cases. The Jagdgeschwaderen were nevertheless placed on alert, and routine local flights continued. On 21 August, JG 54 experienced another two crashes, neither of which involved pilot injuries.

During this period, when the Luftwaffe instigated a number of base moves for its fighter and bomber forces in France, part of II./JG 54 moved to Xaffevilliers. A further aircraft loss by the Geschwader on 24 August was an Arado Ar 66, one of a number of liaison and courier aircraft maintained by most front line units. Despatched to Schipol, the Arado was written off during an RAF bombing raid on the airfield.

Trautloft's appointment as Geschwaderkommodore was effective from 25 August, by which time JG 54 had lost six pilots killed, missing or made prisoner when their aircraft came down in England. And throughout the battle, the waters of the hated English Channel were to close over the wrecks of ditched Bf 109s and their pilots, some of whom were destined to remain 'missing in action'. The same fate was of course to befall a number of RAF pilots, whose view of the Channel was nevertheless more benign. They knew, as did most of the British population, that the natural water barrier between England and France was serving in 1940 in the same way that a moat had served the occupants of a medieval castle. . .

It was Hannes Trautloft who gave Jagdgeschwader 54 its famous name, perpetuating the green heart marking he had first used in Spain. While each Jagdgruppen had long made a practice of applying colourful badges and often the emblems of component Staffeln to their Bf 109s, the heart marking was very rarely applied to JG 54 aircraft until after the end of the large-scale daylight operations against England. Some sources state that a small number of machines were so decorated before the unit left the Channel coast and it is logical to assume that Trautloft applied it to at least some of the Bf 109s he flew. But only later was JG 54 to be widely known as the 'Grünherz Jagdgeschwader'.

During the Battle of Britain period JG 54 and other units employed a degree of locally-applied tactical camouflage to marginally increase the pilots' chances of survival. If a disruptive paint pattern gave a small advantage in combat, it was very welcome. A Bf 109 so camouflaged observed from above over England's patchwork of fields, roads and rivers, or low over the Channel, could cause momentary hesitation in the mind of a British fighter pilot at a time when aircraft recognition was not the art it was later to become. Friendly aircraft had been shot down by mistake before and each side had to be sure that it was indeed the enemy in the gunsight. It took only seconds to make the difference between being the quick or the dead.

There was also the desire on the part of certain pilots to fly a more 'personalised' aircraft. This had advantages in action, particularly when formation or flight leaders became separated from their colleagues. After combat it was necessary to reform the Staffel as quickly as possible for mutual protection and a highly visible leader was tactically sound. JG 54 made something of a name for itself in individualistic approaches to standard fighter paint schemes, some of which first appeared in the summer of 1940.

Adlerangriff continued unabated and it seemed to the Germans that the RAF fighter squadrons still had ample numbers of aircraft; that the British saw the situation as growing increasingly desperate, particularly in terms of pilot losses, was not a fact that the Luftwaffe was party to. To German bomber aircrews, the enemy's strength appeared to be more than sufficient.

That the RAF had already suffered grievous fighter losses might have been questioned by the younger men of the Kampfgeschwaderen when their aircraft were raked with machine gun fire from the darting brown and green fighters with their huge 'peacock's eye' markings, forcing bombs to be jettisoned and, often, the formation to break up in disarray. With crew members dead or wounded and the aircraft probably damaged by enemy fire, simple survival became paramount. Bombs and everything else to lighten the aircraft would be released, even if the target had not been reached. Then it was a nerve-wracking, preferably low-level, dash across the Channel, with the throttles firewalled to get out of the storm of fire from Spitfires and Hurricanes which to some individuals seemed to be everywhere. One of the biggest problems for the Jagdflieger was that *they* could not be everywhere, although bombers were protected to the best of their ability.

Although the defensive armament of the principal Luftwaffe bomber types had been increased since the earliest days of the war, without exception gun positions on the Ju 88, Do 17/215 and He 111 were unpowered. Most were equipped with single, hand-held weapons. The majority of machine guns were of light, 7.9mm calibre and were less than adequate to defend the aircraft from any quarter. If bombers were caught alone by British fighters, their fate was probably sealed.

With such light armament it was imperative that formations be maintained if anywhere near a mutual screen of defensive fire were to be put up. But under sustained fighter attack, there was a natural human tendency to break away. If damage resulted from the fire, it was equally understandable to want to make a run for home — but individual crews needed a fair degree of luck on their side if they chanced it alone. As numerous bomber crews were to learn the hard way in World War Two, their salvation was vested largely in good fighter protection.

With Trautloft at its head, JG 54 continued the grinding war of attrition against the RAF throughout the rest of August. Experienced men led each of the three Gruppen: von Bonin (I Gruppe), Hrabak (II Gruppe) and Hptm Fritz Ultsch, who had taken over III Gruppe on 10 July. Among JG 54's Staffelkapitans during the battle were Hans Philipp (4.Staffel), Hans Schmoller-Haldy (3.Staffel) and Ekkehard Bob (9.Staffel).

On 25 August, Oblt Held was killed in action when the Bf 109s fell foul of Spitfires of No. 54 Sqn. P/O Gray fired at Held's machine and it was later believed to have come to earth at St Nicholas at Wade. Once more the Luftwaffe struck 11 Group's airfields and the Jagdflieger were primarily occupied with protecting the bomber formations. Apart from one Bf 109 suffering slight damage on the 26 August, JG 54 emerged unscathed from another gruelling round of escort duty.

Between the 28th and 29th there were more accidents although these resulted in only minor damage and no pilot injuries. Still hammering away at British airfields, the Luftwaffe also launched a number of fighter sorties which sought their own targets. Two more pilots were lost in such forays on the 28th, II Gruppe's Uffz Kleeman going down into the Channel. Slightly better fortune attended Fw Schottle of I Gruppe — although the result for the Geschwader was the same. Schottle was attacked and shot down by Sqn Ldr Denholm of No. 603 Squadron over Dungeness. It was a late sortie, the combat taking place at around 19.15.

His aircraft crippled, Schottle attempted to make an orderly forced landing but failed to see HT cables stretched across the field he chose. His Messerschmitt ploughed into these, which brought the fighter down in flames, the pilot being lucky to escape with his life and become a prisoner.

Although most operations against England in those generally fine summer days were hotly challenged, the Germans occasionally met with success. One such occasion was 30 August, at a time when Fighter Command's sector stations had taken a beating far worse than the Germans ever realised. Had they done so, Goering's ill-judged view that there was little point in continuing such attacks — coupled with Hitler's belief that London offered a more lucrative target — could have been altered, with far more serious consequences for the defenders.

The day began badly for JG 54 when two Bf 109s were lost in a collison during combat. That morning the Luftwaffe sent over bombers in three massive, separate waves, timing the attacks to give the defenders little respite. Among the escorting Bf 109E-4s were the machines flown by Ltn R. Ziegler and Oblt Hans Roth of II./JG 54. Having been engaged by RAF fighters, both pilots failed to see each other in the melee and at 11.55, two Bf 109s were quickly out of the battle and spiralling down to impact in different areas of the Surrey countryside. Both Ziegler and Roth managed to bale out, the former's aircraft coming to earth in Chelsham, the latter's at Oxted.

There is considerable evidence to suggest that the collision occurred while Ziegler and Roth were shooting at Pilot Officer D.N.O. Jenkins of No. 253 Squadron, then descending by parachute. His Hurricane had been shot down to crash at Redhill at 11.20 and an official listing and an eye witness state that he was 'killed by enemy fighters'.

Later in the day, fate played a hand. An electrical mains failure suddenly blacked out all the south east radar stations. No warning could therefore be given that Biggin Hill, the most important sector airfield in 11 Group's carefully planned defensive chain, lay naked to attack by a single Staffel of Ju 88s. Having penetrated the Thames Estuary under cover of early evening haze, the bombers, well protected by JG 54, turned south and in a few minutes were over Biggin Hill.

Watched by the Bf 109 pilots, the Ju 88

crews dumped their loads on Biggin Hill's hangars and technical site buildings. Explosions wrecked the main telephone cable, effectively cutting the station off from the outside world, and sixty-five people were killed or wounded. The raid temporarily removed the airfield from the order of battle; its squadrons had to transfer to Hornchurch. And that same day, Hitler gave the order for the main weight of the Luftwaffe's attack to be directed on London. Few Germans realised that a few more raids like the one suffered by Biggin Hill could have been all but fatal.

As September began, the Jagdwaffe continued to find 'Indians' present on most forays across the Channel. On other occasions the fighter pilots could be forgiven for thinking that their efforts of the previous weeks had finally paid off. On 1 September Trautloft was leading his Geschwader in company with JG 52 and JG 53, escorting just eighteen Heinkel 111s of II./KG 1 briefed to bomb the docks at Tilbury. The lack of fighter opposition to this particular raid led to a report stating that,

'Slight enemy fighter resistance easily countered by own escort.'

Despite this, JG 54 lost Oblt Stangl from III Gruppe, who apparently collided with either a German or British aircraft and was forced to put down at Ashford, Kent to become a prisoner. No KG 1 bombers were lost although two suffered damage from RAF fighter attack. Elsewhere the bombers again raided the British sector stations, the various combats resulting in closely matched losses — fourteen Luftwaffe and fifteen RAF.

The ever-present spectre of middair collison haunted every pilot and on 2 September, II./ JG 54 lost Oblt Elsing and Uffz Faruendorft whose Bf 109s came together while assembling over Calais. Both pilots were killed.

Including these early casualties the Geschwader lost no less than twelve pilots in the first nine days of September. They included Fritz Ultsch, Kommandeur of III Gruppe, who was killed when his aircraft was shot down by Hurricanes of No. 17 Squadron over Essex on 5 September, the Geschwader's worst day of the Kanalkampf. Hauptmann Scholtz, then leading 7. Staffel, took over as Kommandeur.

The loss of five Bf 109s, coming so soon after

the four that failed to return on the 2nd, was a hard lesson in the futility of Hitler's gamble. In just over one week, three pilots had become PoWs and two had been rescued by the Seenotdienst but the rest were either killed or posted as missing.

The relatively unusual occurrence of a British fighter coming down almost intact on the French side of the Channel took place on 6 September and JG 54 was able to 'meet the enemy'. Spitfires and Bf 109s had tangled over the Channel off Manston, P/O J.R. Caister of No. 603 Squadron at Hornchurch being unfortunate enough to slide into the gunsight of Hubertus von Bonin's aircraft. The Spitfire fell away with damage. Over France, Caister looked for a suitable field and carried out a good wheels-up landing.

As September dragged on, it became increasingly obvious that daylight operations against England could only bring more losses to the Luftwaffe; Hitler had postponed Operation Sealion indefinitely and it was now decided to rotate individual Gruppen away from the main battle area. Pilots were exhausted and the instances of *Kanalkrankheit* (Channel sickness) were increasing. Manifesting itself in chronic stress symptoms as a result of fatigue, the condition led to stomach cramps and vomiting, a loss of appetite and extreme irritability. It was also obvious that pushed to their limits, more than a few pilots were turning back at the slightest hint of malfunction in their aircraft. . .

I./JG 54 withdrew to Jever on 27 September after the middle weeks of September recorded more losses for the Geschwader, albeit at a

That the Allies were not alone in testing the fighters used by the other side is evidenced by this view. Dispersed with a partially-stripped Bf 109 of I./JG 54 at Campagne-le-Guines is a Spitfire Mk 1 of No. 603 Sqn forced down by Hubertus von Bonin, the Gruppenkommandeur. *(Alois Riebl)*.

Extricated from his machine, he was entertained in the mess at Campagne-les-Guines by JG 54's pilots and introduced to the Gruppenkommandeur who had shot him down. Caister was moved to a PoW camp and his aircraft which had landed very near Campagne, was repaired on the airfield and painted in German markings. Both sides maintained examples of enemy aircraft which, after yielding details of the latest modifications, provided fighter pilots with a chance to fly the first line equipment of their main adversaries — an invaluable aid to improving combat tactics to use against them.

slightly slower rate to reflect the reduced level of operations. One of the casualties was Fw Fritz Schweser of 7.Staffel. His experience on 9 October served to offset the occasionally vicious treatment of helpless enemy flyers meted out by both sides. His oil radiator pierced by the fire of a Spitfire of No. 222 Squadron flown by F/O Thomas following an earlier combat with aircraft of No. 41 Squadron, Schweser's engine promptly seized. He had no choice but to put his Bf 109 down and his White 6 was soon bumping over the grass of a field on Meridan Hunt Farm, west of Hawkinge.

It was 16.00 when the bucking Bf 109 came to rest. Schweser, somewhat dizzy from the thumping his head had received from the rough ride across the field, nevertheless jumped out, keeping a wary eye on the farm workers and troops converging on his aircraft from different directions. He rapidly switched on a fuel cock, screwed up his maps and other papers and stood back, striking a match in cupped hands. In seconds the fuel ignited and his Bf 109 went up in flames.

Schweser, standing a suitable distance from the blaze, took out a white handkerchief and waved it above his head. He could not have failed to spot the Spitfire circling ominously above and the Spitfire pilot, F/O Thomas, later reported that he had witnessed the entire incident. At any time he could have strafed the German pilot. Instead he executed a perfect victory roll to the delight of the civilians, and flew off. Schweser was captured, satisfied that his aircraft would yield no useful information to the enemy.

There was one other JG 54 casualty on 9 October, Ltn Eberle of 9. Staffel being killed in action with enemy fighters. II Gruppe's GeschwaderStab lost Ltn Malischweski on the 11th when he was involved in combat with No. 92 Squadron. F/Lt Tuck brought down Malischewski's machine, the German pilot being taken prisoner, unhurt. And on the 13th, 7.Staffel lost Ltn Behrens, who disappeared into the Channel.

Without large bomber formations to escort, the Jagdwaffe reverted to Frei Jagd sorties in weather that can best be described as 'changeable'. In reality some days were foul, with rain and fog reducing operations to the barest minimum, but increasing the risk of accidental loss. Heavy night raids were conducted against London and other British cities.

Fighter bomber operations were now deemed to have some merit in keeping pressure on the enemy in daylight and on 20 October, large formations were observed by the defenders, the escort maintaining extreme altitude, alert for RAF interceptors. If they were intercepted, such sorties could be costly; fourteen aircraft failed to return on this day, the casualties including Fw Iburg of 9./JG 54. Caught by F/Lt McKeller of No. 605 Sqn, Iburg's combat

career ended at 10.20 when his Bf 109E-4 made landfall at New Romney and he went into captivity.

During the Kanalkampf, JG 54's *Erganzungsjagdstaffel* (replacement training unit) maintained a flow of fresh pilots to the front line Gruppen to make good losses. In a unit that was no stranger to mishaps with the Bf 109, there was the occasional disaster, such as on 24 October. Taking off from Bergen for a routine local training flight in a Bf 109E-1, Fw Brixel crashed and was killed.

On the following day Oblt Schypek of 5. Staffel joined the growing list of JG 54 prisoners in England when he was shot down during a *Jabo* escort sortie. He came down on the coast at Lydd in Kent, a location that for a short time became all too familiar to Arno Zimmermann of 7. Staffel the following day. Damaged in combat his Bf 109E-1 slid ignominiously up the shingle beach at Lydd after he was obliged to force-land.

Zimmermann thus became the last JG 54 pilot to become an unwilling guest of the British during the Battle of Britain, the 'cut-off' date of which the RAF set as 31 October. This reflected very much reduced Luftwaffe activity against the British Isles compared with the high summer weeks. Even so, fighter losses remained high at 104 destroyed plus twenty-four damaged.

In common with the bulk of the Luftwaffe fighter force, JG 54 then withdrew from the Channel Front; German records showed that each Jagdgruppe had scored an average of fifty-five confirmed victories during the Battle of Britain, a figure that correlates with known RAF losses. The combined score for III./JG 54 was, for example, sixty-seven. Few participants who had survived the battle needed reminding of how tough the job had been or how many flying hours the average Staffel pilot had spent in the far from comfortable confines of the Bf 109 cockpit; Hannes Trautloft, who kept a diary throughout that summer, found that he had flown across the Channel no less than 102 times.

Exhausted and perhaps bewildered at the outcome of the war against England which had signally failed in its objective, the pilots of JG 54 pulled back to Holland and Germany, to rest and rebuild strength. For some of them,

The last JG 54 pilot to be lost in combat during the main period of the Battle of Britain was Ltn Arno Zimmermann, who was forced down on the shingle beach at Lydd in Kent on 27 October. The Luftwaffe made no similar distinction between the phases of the battle, but increasing bad weather and withdrawal of forces meant an inevitable reduction in operations against England.

cross-Channel operations were far from over but there was a little time to recuperate or, sadly, to reflect on the loss of good friends and comrades. The fate of hundreds of fighter pilots who had failed to return to their bases in France was initially unknown, although the Red Cross in Geneva provided the German authorities with the names of those pilots known to be prisoners.

It was all but impossible to state categorically that pilots listed as 'missing' had been killed if no trace of man or machine had been found, although the assumption was realistic. A great deal depended on the circumstances and location of the crash site. The stark debit balance, diligently compiled by the Luftwaffe Quartermaster General, put the loss of Bf 109s at 177 for August and 187 for September, plus forty-one damaged.

Teams of RAF specialists did examine all known wartime crash sites with the express purpose of removing any human remains. The majority of wrecks were either removed for more detailed scrutiny, while others were broken up and buried. As the number of Luftwaffe aircraft to make their last landfall on British soil increased, so sizeable dumps began to appear in south-east England.

In the main, aircraft wreckage was melted down for other uses, although less badly damaged examples were placed on display in various parts of the country to raise funds to 'buy' RAF aircraft through public subscription. Other Luftwaffe aircraft made their longest journeys by sea to be both tested and put on display for a similar purpose in the United States.

Since the end of the war, numerous 1940 crash sites have been excavated by members of aviation archaeology groups and museums which have occasionally yielded evidence to confirm the last resting place of a German pilot as well as his aircraft. The most difficult crashes to investigate are those of aircraft that went down in the English Channel — where numerous pilots from both sides remain entombed.

The Jagdwaffe, although it had grown appreciably since the years of peace and the period of the Condor Legion when many of its number had first met was, in 1940, still a close-knit organisation in which numerous firm friendships had been made. Most of the old heads, particularly those who had risen through the ranks to command Staffeln and Gruppen, knew one another and during the time on the Channel Front, they had kept in touch to discuss tactics and exchange news of mutual colleagues and comrades in arms. By the autumn these exchanges were increasingly laced with apprehension over the probable fate of men last seen going down over England or the dreaded stretch of water that separated them from their adversaries.

Staffelkapitan Oblt Hans Schmoller-Haldy had special cause to rue the attrition rate of the summer months — he had begun the campaign with twelve NCOs and commissioned pilots in his 3.Staffel and now only himself, Oblt Kinz-inger and Obfw Knippscheer remained of the original personnel, which had included Uffz Kranz; Uffz Windisch; Fw Knedler and Leutnants Witt and Angeli.

The surviving pilots had flown the Staffel's last sortie of the battle at 10.00 on 23 September. At that time, there were three of them — Schmoller-Haldy, Kinzinger and Knippscheer. To make up the required Schwarm of four, a young replacement pilot joined the veteran trio for a Frei Jagd.

Flying at 10,000 feet in the vicinity of Ramsgate the Messerschmitts were attacked by Spitfires of No. 92 Squadron and Knippscheer was shot down in flames. His aircraft fell at Barham in Kent at 10.20. When the Bf 109s returned the fire, it was small compensation that one of them could have filed a victory claim for the aircraft flown by P/O Pattinson. Hit in the thigh, the RAF pilot was forced to crash-land his Spitfire, which was a write off. Pattinson survived.

That evening the Staffelkapitan and his wingman left Campagne and headed for Wilhelmshaven. On landing Schmoller-Haldy was asked where the rest of his Staffel pilots were. The rejoinder was succinct, with horrifying implications for the elderly colonel who was the Wilhelmshaven station commander.

'Sir, there are only two pilots left of the former Staffel and they are in your front office. The rest are either killed, drowned in the Channel or in England in a prison camp.'

At least thirty-five JG 54 pilots are known to have gone down in the battle, thirteen of whom were made prisoner when they either crash-landed in England or bailed out on the wrong side of the Channel (see appendix). German sources state that a total of forty-three pilots were lost to strength, the breakdown being: eighteen killed in action; two killed in accidents; thirteen missing in action and ten made prisoner.

Notwithstanding Goering's tirade against their lack of courage at the height of the battle, numerous Jagdflieger were to be decorated for their outstanding contribution to Channel front operations. In JG 54 they included the *Ritterkreuz* for Dietrich Hrabak for his sixteenth victory (awarded on 24 October); Hans Philipp for his twentieth (4 November) and Arnold Lignitz (8 November).

The Jagdflieger were in no way to blame for the outcome of the Battle of Britain; rather, they learned as did many others in World War Two and other conflicts, that it is exceedingly difficult to force a conclusion in battle solely by the use of airpower. Too many factors mitigate against the attackers, who fairly rapidly lose the initiative, provided that the defenders are well organised and equipped. Without any participation by ground forces to divide their effort, the defenders are offered flexibility; they are able to pick the time and place of joining combat, while the opposing forces are obliged to fly on fairly narrow and known routes to their principal targets.

As the Luftwaffe bomber force found to its cost, its aircraft were unsuited to the task of reducing England's defences to the point where a Cross-Channel invasion would have had any chance of success. Their bomb loads were too small, they were individually poorly defended against fighter attack and the importance of their primary targets was not stressed strongly enough. Apart from a number of occasions when it achieved success, the bomber force was poorly used. It approached too high, it could not fly fast enough and it drained the freedom of the fighters to attack on their own terms.

Even if this latter factor had been more positive, and day after day the Kampfgeschwaderen had hammered away exclusively at Fighter Command's airfields and the RDF stations, their casualties would have been appalling, with the defenders having little difficulty in positioning the maximum number of interceptors. As the RAF and USAAF were later to find, it is hard to mask intended bomber targets for long. The German policy of spreading destruction through 'terror bombing' and thereby hoping to keep the RAF guessing, resulted only in a watering-down of bombs on each target which was essentially futile. All it achieved was a marginal lessening of aircrew casualties on certain days of the battle. Laudable enough in itself — although aircrew casualties were never of great concern to the Luftwaffe hierarchy — this could not bring the Germans success.

A further factor in the outcome of the Battle of Britain was Hitler's lack of enthusiasm for the entire venture. Well before the Luftwaffe assault began, he had set his mind firmly on the great crusade against Bolshevism. Many believe that this, rather than the subjugation of Britain, so dominated the German leader's conduct of the war in 1940 that even if the Luftwaffe had created the conditions for an invasion to take place, he might still have considered it a time-consuming and costly undertaking. It is not impossible to envisage that the military conquest of Britain would even then have been postponed or abandoned if the Führer had feared that too many troops needed for the invasion of Russia would have been tied down fighting a war of attrition on British soil.

Obfw Kless of II./JG 54 smiles for the camera in the cockpit of Bf 109E-3 'Black 4' in 1940. *(Roberston)*.

Chapter 3

BALKAN MISADVENTURE

Concurrent with the policy of maintaining a night bomber offensive against England, Hermann Goering had in the autumn of 1940 ordered that all Jagdgeschwaderen allocate one Staffel for conversion to the fighter bomber role. Such cross-Channel sorties would extend the Luftwaffe's activities during daylight hours, the domination of which had infuriatingly passed to the enemy. The Reichsmarschall was doubtless inspired by the often spectacular sorties against England by *Erprobungsgruppe* 210, which had begun flying Bf 109 Jabobomber sorties as early as July.

However, Epr 210's activities, primarily with the Bf 110, had been completely different and a good deal more specialised than those of a regular unit, and the idea was not greeted with great enthusiasm by the Jagdgeschwaderen; the pilots generally believed that the flying characteristics of the Bf 109 would suffer appreciably if the aircraft was loaded down with bombs. They had little knowledge of the technicalities of accurate bomb aiming, and there was no special equipment designed for a fighter aircraft which would make the job easier. And those who had been in action against the RAF knew that they would stand a slim chance of survival should they be bounced over England with their bombs still attached.

Nevertheless, a number of Bf 109Es were adapted to carry a single SC 250 500-pound bomb under the fuselage centre section. As was standard practice in the Luftwaffe, such a modification garnered an identifying suffix to the designation. Thus Bf 109E-4s modified as bomb-carriers became E-4/Bs.

JG 54 and other Jagdgeschwaderen thus embarked on fighter bomber attacks, the Jabos being heavily escorted and offering some limited scope for Frei Jagd sorties. The deteriorating weather offered a degree of protection from the defences, which were, by 1 November, more than adequate. No less than twenty-seven RAF fighter squadrons were available for operations in 11 Group alone, the majority being equipped with Hurricanes and Spitfires.

A further twelve squadrons were under 10 Group, and 12 Group had sixteen more, each of which had a Blenheim squadron with some Beaufighters on strength. Last, but not least, there were fifteen squadrons in Northern England under the control of 13 Group. One, No. 263, was then flying the long range Whirlwind fighter bomber.

A strong German bomber force remained under the command of Luftflotten 2,3 and 5 to undertake night sorties during the grim winter Blitz of 1940-41 and, although there would be some rotation of Kampfgeschwaderen, it was the day fighter force that had been reduced most drastically. When large-scale daylight bomber operations over England all but ceased, these were no longer required for escort duty and by 1 November, although a total of twenty-six Gruppen remained, most of these had, or were about to get, orders to move.

As previously mentioned, the bulk of JG 54 had flown to airfields in southern Holland, the exception being III Gruppe which remained in northern France. All Gruppen, plus pilots drawn from the *Erganzungsstaffel* (operational training unit), were to supply pilots for the phase of Kanalkampf operations during the last two months of 1940.

At midday on 2 November a Rotte of II Gruppe Bf 109s were intercepted at 30,000 feet over the English coast by a solitary Spitfire of No. 41 Squadron. In the ensuing combat, Ltn Otto Gothe of 4.Staffel was lost when his aircraft came down near Dungeness; it was presumed that the Spitfire, flown by F/O E.P. Wells had shot him down.

II Gruppe filed two victory claims (for Hurricanes) by Oblt Philipp and an Oberfeldwebel acting as his wingman, but overall the day went badly for the Jagdflieger, which lost a total of five Bf 109s and their pilots, all of whom were killed or captured. The fighter

A number of Bf 109Es were adapted to the fighter bomber role, the ETC 500 belly rack of the E-7/U2 being able to accommodate either bombs or a fuel tank. In this view groundcrew get down to changing a mainwheel, the Bf 109's oleo having been supported on a makeshift trestle. *(Petrick)*.

forces on both sides suffered a number of accidents but no RAF fighters were reported lost in combat.

This period was inevitably punctuated by curtailed or very limited operations due to bad weather, both sides being obliged to scale down the number of sorties that could be flown. RAF Fighter, Bomber and Coastal Commands flew cloud cover sorties, as did the Luftwaffe. Small numbers of aircraft could thus seek some degree of natural protection to mask their vulnerability if the enemy was airborne. It was a period when a large-scale air battle could develop on a certain day, with activity falling to almost nil twenty-four hours later.

Apart from the by now usual rotation of new pilots into the front line Gruppen to replace losses, there was one command change in JG 54 in November. On the 4th Arnold Lignitz

replaced Hptm Scholz at the head of III Gruppe.

With bases, not to mention potential targets, shrouded in mist or fog it was pointless for the Luftwaffe to risk losing pilots and aircraft if the weather was particularly bad. At that stage of the Kanalkampf, few commanders at operational level really believed that the Germans were going to achieve much more than annoyance to the British with small-scale 'hit and run' fighter bomber raids. But orders were orders. . .

Bomber Command's long gruelling campaign with slim resources and obsolete aircraft, continued unabated — as it would until the end of the war. On 6 November, a not atypical small force of six unescorted Blenheims was sent to attack port installations in north-west Germany. Six more followed bound for a familiar target — Haamstede airfield. The outcome of these operations was equally not atypical for the period. Out of twelve aircraft despatched, ten had aborted. One of the remaining machines was intercepted by III./JG 54, and promptly shot down by Gefr Anton Wubke.

Further success against RAF bombers came for the Grünherztrager on 8 November, when Feldw Wilhelm Schilling of III Gruppe destroyed a Blenheim near Bergen. On the 9th it was reported that a PRU Spitfire had failed to return and it was claimed (perhaps somewhat optimistically!) that this aircraft became the victim of Oblt Eckerle of II Gruppe. A skilled proponent of Jabo attack, Eckerle flew numerous such sorties against England during this period. III Gruppe saw more action on 10 November, Unteroffizier Zweigart shooting down a Blenheim from No. 114 Sqn in the vicinity of De Kooy, then a secondary JG 54 base in Holland.

Having somewhat boldly reinstated operations across the Channel by *Stukageschwaderen*, the Luftwaffe high command gave the fighter force the invariably difficult task of protecting the vulnerable dive bombers, which were easy prey to interceptor fighters. On 11 November, JG 54 was part of a strong escort to Ju 87s of StG 1.

During the earlier phases of the Battle of Britain, Ju 87s had drawn British fighters like a magnet and this was no exception. A sizeable air battle ensued as Hurricanes took on the Stukas while the Jagdflieger had their hands full with Spitfires. In company with JG 3, 51 and 53, the Grünherz became embroiled in dogfights, Oblt Hans Ekkehard Bob claiming a Spitfire. No JG 54 Bf 109s were lost.

Hans Philipp claimed a Hurricane on 14 November, but a period without casualties was broken for the Grünherz on the 15th when Ofw Paul Hier of 4.Staffel went down into the sea off Shoeburyness after being bounced by Hurricanes of No. 605 Sqn. His Bf 109 was one of four lost that day, the other machines belonging to JG 2 and 26.

With the combat casualties of some days of autumn 1940 matching those of the summer, JG 54 and other Jagdgruppen were finding fighter bomber sorties a hazardous business. Numerous targets, including shipping, were hit but the scale of damage inflicted on the enemy never approached the point where the loss of any more well trained pilots was justified. The attacks did however tie down a considerable number of RAF fighters and from the point of view of the Luftwaffe high command, the war against England was still going on around the clock.

On 17 November JG 54 was again involved in combat with Spitfires which tried unsuccessfully to bounce the Bf 109s from out of the sun. The enemy fighters were seen in time and the German high cover dived to head them off. The ensuing dogfight resulted in casualties on both sides as the Spitfires and Bf 109s traded fire. The Jagdflieger decided that discretion was the better part of valour and made a run for home.

The melee resulted in three losses from the Grünherz formation, including Obltn Roloff von Aspern, the Staffelkapitan of 5./JG 54. Also reported missing was Oberfeldwebel Wilhelm Donninger, another member of 5.Staffel. A third Bf 109 was damaged when a pilot from 2.Staffel had to put down near Ostend with his aircraft out of fuel.

The 18th saw very little fighter activity over the Channel, but 1.Staffel's Uffz Hans-Helmut Habermehl was injured when he had to make a forced-landing at Langeoog. His aircraft was practically written-off, the resulting damage being put at eighty percent.

Throughout the final weeks of 1940 and into 1941, the Luftwaffe occasionally sent very small numbers of fighters and bombers across to England, these often recording little or no combat with the RAF. Few days passed without some contact being made however, and even if operations were 'off', aircraft still had to be air-tested, particularly after repair.

Such flights, often completed without any kind of mishap, could be frustrating when individual Bf 109s were damaged in hard landings — with the enemy nowhere to be seen. In a lot of cases only the pilot's pride was harmed. One such incident occurred on 20 November, when a 3.Staffel Bf 109E-1 sustained ten percent damage in a crash-landing at Jever. On consecutive days (22-23 November), 5.Staffel had to report similar accidents when two machines were damaged in crash-landings at Jever.

A worse loss for II./JG 54 on 23 November was Ogefr Simon Helmberger, who was posted as missing after a wild running fight with a number of RAF squadrons. A second Grünherz Bf 109 was damaged from the cumulative effect of enemy fire and a resulting forced-landing at Ostend.

Less risky action took place for JG 54 in the last week of November. A dawn alert on the morning of the 25th brought Uffz Albrecht into contact with a Hampden of No. 49 Squadron returning from a night sortie. The British bomber came down on Dutch territory at St Maartensvlotbrug, the crew being captured. Yet another forced-landing, this time by an aircraft of 2.Staffel, occurred on 1 December.

A persistent bout of bad weather followed, giving the Jagdflieger a break from operations — in fact JG 54 personnel were destined to enjoy about two weeks of limited flying by the Geschwader, apart from the regular patrols. The period passed without any reports of success against the RAF, or any casualties. Reconnaissance flights and cloud cover sorties were the order of the day for the bomber units and although a few more Frei Jagd sorties were flown, few of the Grünherz Messerschmitts were involved.

Incursions by British bombers continued to cause alerts at the Geschwader's Dutch bases, although no reports of successful interceptions appear to have been filed during the latter part of November. Among the almost inevitable non-operational casualties was Uffz Bauch of III.Gruppe who was injured when he made a nasty crash landing, virtually writing his aircraft off, on 22 December. On Christmas Eve JG 54 suffered what is believed to have been its last loss of 1940 when a domestic flight by Fw Werner Kruger of the E-Staffel ended in disaster. Kruger was killed when his Bf 109E came down at Cazeaux.

A quiet Christmas period heralded the virtual end to Luftwaffe cross-Channel daylight operations by forces of any size, and for JG 54's fighters particularly, the long war of attrition against England was all but over. Henceforth, most of the activity by single-engined Gruppen would be Jabo sorties without heavy escort — indeed so small did the effort become at times that the RAF had to contend with as few as two Bf 109s. Approaching low and fast, 'under the radar' these raiders often proved extremely

hard to catch and widespread damage was caused. None of this could be in any way decisive and was unlikely to deter the British from carrying on the war, but nuisance raids were deemed to be a way of showing the opposition that the fight went on, however little such air raids could achieve.

In the winter of 1940/41 the German night Blitz intensified and London, Liverpool, Coventry, Manchester and a long list of other cities and towns were attacked. Their nocturnal ordeal was to last well into the spring of 1941 — by which time the Jagdgeschwaderen remaining on the Western Front had to contend with British fighter sweeps over France and the Low Countries. Having consolidated its strength the RAF prepared to mount a long term offensive of its own against targets in occupied Europe. Many sorties were ostensibly to protect medium bombers, but the main purpose was to tempt the Jagdflieger up to do battle — tactics very similar to those of the Luftwaffe in 1940. The price, for both sides, was to be high, in terms of both pilots and aircraft.

New battlefront

With I./JG 54 based at Jever on the German North Sea coast, one Schwarm from each Staffel was temporarily placed under the command of the resident JG 1 — which in turn received its orders from *Luftgau Kommando Holland* — JG 54 sent detachments to Wesermunde, Westerland (Sylt) and Groningen in Holland during the remaining weeks of October 1940. Delmenhorst was the new home for II Gruppe from 3 December, while III Gruppe, having vacated Guines on 21 October, also spent a period on air defence duty in Holland before returning to German soil on 4 December to occupy Dortmund. It was to remain there until 15 January 1941.

The bleak, far less hectic autumn and winter months of 1940/41 permitted some respite from operational flying and most personnel took leave. The pilots enjoyed the facilities at Kitzbuhl, where the ski slopes demanded all their skill and energy. Despite their dedication to the sport, some JG 54 men suffered broken bones. Uffz Norbert Pfeiffer was widely recognised as the unit's champion skier. . .

Among the new blood transferred to JG 54 at this time was Wolfgang Späte. Having built an enviable reputation as a pre-war glider pilot, Spate had spent the early part of the war as a reconnaissance pilot. He joined 5.Staffel on 1 January and was to rise to command it in the autumn of the year before being posted to Rechlin, where he became deeply involved in the Me 163 rocket fighter programme. He would subsequently see further service with the Grünherz.

The winter pause ended on 15 January when orders came transferring the greater part of JG 54 to Le Mans. The GeschwaderStab, plus II and III Gruppen, stayed in France for about two months, their Bf 109s using Cherbourg as a forward base. Briefed to defend the Normandy area against incursions by the RAF, the Geschwader found little activity, although the period was valuable for further operational training, especially for new pilots.

Fledgling fighter pilots, posted to an opera-tional Jagdgeschwader like JG 54 found, even in an air force not yet a decade old, a reverent regard for tradition and ceremony. While this was largely inherited from the fighter elements of the German Air Service that had fought so well during World War One and given the world the name of Manfred von Richthofen, arguably the most famous war pilot ever, the Luftwaffe of the 1940s was in no way a backward-looking force. While honouring the names and exploits of pilots who had fought the Great War, the Luftwaffe added the trappings of regalia, fine uniforms, orders and decorations and an impressive, inspirational system of military ranks and honour titles, the latter perpetuating the names of some of Germany's most famous warriors.

The whole was overlaid with Teutonic order and fearsome obedience to Hitler and the ideals of the Nazi creed. Not that this latter was particularly apparent in any fighter unit; pilots were generally concerned with more immediate

Behind the headlines, the Luftwaffe trained new pilots. Uffz Hans Hermann of JG 54's E-Staffel was photographed in this Bf 109E-1 at Neukuhren, East Prussia in June 1941. *(Crow)*.

matters connected with flying and administering an operational unit than politics — indeed when such things were discussed, they were often treated in a superficial, even irreverent way. Thus far, the war that Germany had started seemed to be going well enough. Few questioned the implications, or tried to predict what the future held. Like air force personnel the world over, the men and women of the Luftwaffe were first and foremost fighting for their country; the implications of political decisions were usually far outside the brief of the operational units, with only a peripheral bearing on their day-to-day existence — if such matters intruded at all.

By early 1941, JG 54 had had considerable combat experience, the early war successes being tempered by the disastrous operations over the Channel. There was little choice but to accept the latter with equanimity; combat, whatever the outcome, was invaluable experience. It invariably created a fund of stories spiced with first-hand observations and rules for survival to hand down to the newcomers who had the heavy responsibility of filling the shoes of those who had fallen.

Among the ceremonies Luftwaffe fighter units held to welcome new blood into the hierarchy was the 'knighting' whereby all new pilots were presented with a scarf by the Kommodore, at a 'pilots' evening' dinner. This was an unforgettable occasion for young men imbued — indeed awed — by the strong esprit de corps established by all Jagdgeschwaderen that had seen action, particularly one with the reputation of Hannes Trautloft's Grunherz.

Any speculation as to where the war would next take pilots of the Grünherz was diminished with the news of Yugoslavia's courageous defiance of Hitler. Announcing, on 26 March, that the country rejected the Axis and instead sided with Britain under a monarchy, Yugoslavia suddenly represented a potentially dangerous threat to Germany's southern flank which could threaten the imminent invasion of the Soviet Union. If the Allies attempted to launch offensive operations from Yugoslavian territory, the Germans could be put under pressure at a time when this was highly inconvenient. Consequently, under Directive 25, Hitler set in motion the subjugation of Yugoslavia and

Greece, and on 29 March 1941 JG 54 was ordered to Austria to prepare for operations in the Balkans.

Flying across the Alps, the Geschwader's Bf 109Es made an en route stop at Salzburg before occupying Parndorf and Graz. Ground echelons meanwhile undertook an exhausting 1630km drive to be on hand at the forward airfields by the time the fighters arrived to begin a new series of operational sorties during the first week of April.

The black men and their equipment duly arrived on time, flyers and other ground personnel alike marvelling at the consistent ability of the unit's truck drivers to bring their vital loads across difficult, ill-paved roads, often at long distances from their previous location, with almost clockwork reliability. And although battles are not won by truck drivers, JG 54 and other Luftwaffe units fighting a highly mobile war would have been sorely pressed if these men had not shown such dedication to duty.

Hitler's Balkan invasion was launched when time was of the essence if the attack on Russia was to start on the scheduled date of 22 June; it opened with armoured thrusts by the 12th Army through Bulgaria's lower Struma valley. A three-pronged advance was made into Yugoslavia which aimed simultaneously at capturing the towns of Skoplje, Bitolj and Strumica, these representing the northern, central and southern thrusts respectively. The Luftwaffe's task was to neutralise airfields, military installations and lines of communication in support of the Wehrmacht.

Luftflotte 4 under Gen Obst Lohr undertook responsibility for directing operations, with two Fliegerfuhrer and VIII Fliegerkorps subordinated to it. JG 54's contribution was split between Fliegerfuhrer Graz, which in turn came under the orders of the Kommodore of StG 3, with II Gruppe, minus 4.Staffel, flying operations with I./JG 27. These fighter units supported the Ju 87Bs of Stab/StG3 and II./StG 77, all components being based at Graz.

Both III./JG 54 and 4.Staffel came under Fliegerfuhrer Arad, under the Kommodore of StG 77, based at Arad in Rumania. This division had more fighters than dive bombers, the Bf 109Es of JG 54 being grouped with the

A well-known view of II./JG 54 aircraft ostensibly taken in Russia, although the eighteen plus Bf 109Es visibly lack the yellow Eastern Front recognition markings. This, and the presence of JG 77 machines in the background, indicate that the photographs was taken earlier, probably during the latter stages of the Balkan campaign. The likely location was Zemlin-Belgrade, during the transfer of aircraft from JG 54 to JG 77 prior to Barbarossa. *(via Hans Obert).*

Stab and two Gruppen of JG 77 and the Bf 110s of I./ZG 26. While both the Bf 109s and 110s would carry out their own attack sorties, the BF 109Es were primarily responsible for keeping enemy fighters away from the Stukas, the Stab and two Gruppen of StG 77 also flying Ju 87Bs.

Opposing the Germans was a miscellany of fighters belonging to the *Jugoslovensko Kraljevsko Ratno Vazduhoplovstvo* (JKRV), among them being almost exactly the same type of Messerschmitts Me 109Es (the Yugoslavs identifying their aircraft by the 'Me' prefix rather than 'Bf' as for German-flown machines) as those used by the Luftwaffe. Yugoslavia had made rapid pre-war progress in modernising her airpower and had purchased equipment from abroad as well as initiating production of indigenous designs.

As far as defence of the country was concerned, there was one fighter and two mixed air brigades, these comprising some sixty Me 109s, thirty-eight Mk I Hurricanes, thirty Hawker Furies and a handful of Rogozarski IK-Z and Ikarus IK-2 monoplane fighters. Of these, the former was the most modern; a single-engined fighter design with a marked similarity to the British Hurricane, it had excellent handling qualities and performance. The IK-2 was an older, gull-winged design which while very manoeuvrable, was hardly up to the task of defending territory against superior numbers of Bf 109s.

In the early hours of 6 April dive bombing attacks, well covered by fighters, had initiated the now-familiar opening moves of Blitzkrieg. The first enemy aircraft the Luftwaffe met in aerial combat were the Furies. Such obsolete biplane fighters could do little against the onslaught of Messerschmitts and there were heavy casualties among the defenders. Others were destroyed in the opening round of ground attacks of Yugoslavian airfields, which also succeeded in reducing the meagre bomber force available to the JKRV.

Small numbers of German aircraft were destroyed by the defences, but the Yugoslavs rapidly found themselves in desperate straits. Concurrent with the Army support strikes on tactical targets, Luftflotte 4 mounted a massive attack on Belgrade. The defences were not however taken by surprise and thirty-four fighters, Me 109s and IK-Zs, together the most modern Yugoslav fighters available, flung themselves on successive waves of He 111s and Do 17s totalling 160 bombers. There were also seventy-four dive bomber sorties against the Yugoslav capital, the armada being escorted by Bf 110s and Bf 109s, the latter flying top cover at 15,000 feet.

As the JKRV fighters made their inital interceptions of the bombers, the Jagdflieger pounced. In the dogfights which followed three Yugoslavian fighters were shot down, with six others being so badly damaged that they were either destroyed in crash landings or subsequently written off. Ten Luftwaffe aircraft were claimed shot down in these opening attacks.

Follow up interceptions by JKRV Me 109s and IK-Zs exacted more German casualties, but their own ranks were further thinned by the Luftwaffe escort fighters. A peripheral danger to the Yugoslavs was their own flak, which not surprisingly, had extreme difficulty in distinguishing friendly single-engined Messerschmitts from those of the invaders. It was during the two afternoon raids on Belgrade that JG 54's pilots scored confirmed victories. Three Me 109Es were shot down by three different III Gruppe pilots, these being Oblt Hans-Ekkehard Bob, Staffelkapitan of 9./JG 54, who scored his twentieth victory, Ltn Max-Hellmuth Ostermann for his ninth and Oblt Gerhard Koall, who opened his score.

Early on the second day of the campaign, German tactics changed. Mass bomber raids were replaced by sorties by small formations which made extensive use of cloud cover to carry out their attacks and leave the area quickly. Later in the day, more large formations were noted by the defenders, who made valiant attempts to intercept them all. At 16.00 Yugoslavian Me 109s bounced twenty-six Ju 87s covered by nearly double that number of Bf 110s and Bf 109s, among the latter being

aircraft of 4.Staffel, JG 54. In a series of dogfights, the pilots claimed four, two by Hans Philipp for his twenty-fourth and twenty-fifth victories; one by Max Stotz for his sixteenth and one by an unidentified Grünherztrager

Further success was to follow. Heavy snowfalls on 9 April hampered defensive air operations, although the German 12th Army made good progress towards Bitolji, well supported by VIII Fliegerkorps. The Panzers began to threaten the very airfields from which the JKRV operated. Nis had to be abandoned that morning.

Despite bombing raids, the German column rolled inexorably towards Bitolji. The bad weather held retaliatory attacks to a minimum, while in the north Luftflotte 4's Fliegerfuhrer Graz and Arad elements carried out attacks on Yugoslavian troops and lines of communication.

The Stukas also continued the pressure on enemy airfields, heavily escorted by Bf 109s. At around 14.00, aircraft from two Staffeln of III./JG 54 were in the vicinity of Rovine airfield, base of the JKRV's 8th Bomber *Puk*. Two IK-2s were about the land as the Bf 109s came on the scene, and one took on the German formation. A hectic dogfight ensued lasting some seven minutes, the Yugoslav pilot throwing his aircraft all over the sky to evade the fire of the Grünherztrager. In this he succeeded and made good his escape.

In the meantime, five 108 *Eskadrila* Hurricanes had arrived, followed by some 106 *Eskadrila* machines and IK-2s. A third Staffel of Bf 109s also joined in. That the two sides gave little or nothing away in flying skill was eventually reflected in the respective victory claims. The Yugoslavs lost two Hurricanes and an IK-2, the JKRV pilots claiming two Bf 109s.

When the German fighters broke off, low on fuel, Hans-Ekkehard Bob, Staffelkapitan of 9./JG 54 could claim one IK-2 and Oblt Gerhard Koall a second for his second victory of the campagn. Ltn Erwin Leykauf's single victim, identified as a Hurricane, was his sixth victory to date.

Confusion over the finer recognition points of enemy fighters was a problem not confined to Yugoslavian AA gun crews. The Hawker Hurricane was very similar to the IK-2, leading to German combat claims confusing the two.

Gefr Fabian was reported missing when JG 54's fighters had landed, although he turned up some days later, possibly a victim of enemy fire during this combat.

On 10 April, the 12th Army entered Bitolj and fighting in Yugoslavian Macedonia was all but at an end. Simultaneously, the 14th Panzer Division took Zagreb, free of interference from the air. The bad weather over the fighting fronts persisted, keeping the Yugoslavian air force on the ground: the flights that were made mostly involved reconnoitring safer airfields to the west, a task hampered by low cloud. When squadrons did attempt to take off in appalling conditions, accidents inevitably occurred and the JKRV suffered more losses that could not be replaced. Yugoslavia was clearly doomed.

Bad JKRV communications as to exactly where the German forces were led to the premature demolition of aircraft that could have been used for some further raids, even if these had caused only temporary setbacks. Chaos quickly resulted. By 12 April the weather prevented VIII Fliegerkorps from flying but previously, the non-appearance of the enemy air force had permitted free hunt sorties by fighters which included strafing attacks on trains, vehicular traffic and airfields. Dive bombing continued to take its toll of Yugoslav equipment and, in no small measure, the nerves of the hard-pressed defenders, who had not only German, but Italian and Hungarian airpower ranged against them.

Even before all resistance had ended, JG 54 and other Luftwaffe units moved from forward

When the war in northern Europe reduced in intensity in the winter of 1940, Hitler geared up for the invasion of Russia, but anti-German moves in the Balkans saw the Luftwaffe occupied there before the great crusade began in the East. At the end of another lightning campaign, JG 54 passed many of its Bf 109Es to JG 77, pending delivery of the new Bf 109F. Here, pilots enjoy the fine spring weather before the start of Barbarossa. Behind them the Bf 109E, 'Black 10' of 2.Staffel has the insignia of both Jagdgeschwader, the badge of II Gruppe and a personal marking, the name 'Lilo' under the cockpit. A black triangle on the aircraft in the background indicates a ground attack unit, probably SG. 2. *(E. J. Creek).*

airfields in Rumania and Hungary to occupy bases in Yugoslavia. Grünherz ground crews flew up in Ju 52s, staging through Arad, Deta, Pancevo and Belgrade-Semlin. At Bjeljina, some 100 miles west of Belgrade, the Luftwaffe had created conditions for a daring coup. Heavy bombing and strafing attacks were followed up by the arrival of troop-laden Ju 52s which landed even while the defenders were still manning their guns. Grünherz ground crews were among the passengers in the transports and they subsequently had to double as airfield guards against partisan attacks. Some casualties resulted, although the Luftwaffe black men were supported by their own pilots, who made numerous strafing passes on enemy positions until the airfield was finally declared safe.

The remnants of the surrounded Yugoslavian army surrendered at Bosna on 17 April and the Luftwaffe was again free to commandeer airfields in a newly-conquered country. By mid-April JG 54's entire strength was dispersed at Semlin, although once again, the Geschwader did not remain in its new home for long; it was ordered to pass most of its Bf 109Es to JG 77 to make good attrition suffered during Yugoslavian operations and reinforce that Geschwader for forthcoming combat over Greece and Crete, for which JG 54 was not required. Instead the Geschwader moved to Stolp-Reitz in Pomerania to re-equip with the Bf 109F and by 12 May most personnel had arrived there. Some Bf 109Es were retained, for JG 54 had by no means finished using the Emil and was to fly this Bf 109 sub-type for some time in its new area of operations.

Leaving aside the possibility of a transfer to the Mediterranean, where the Italians were not faring well against the British, it was almost certain now that JG 54 would be heading Eastwards. With the Balkans campaign over, the Geschwader's tally of aerial combat victories had risen to 376 since the war began; the Jagdwafffe's pride had been restored — the Balkans had been reminiscent of Poland, France and the Low Countries and had resulted in similar success for German arms. With his southern flank now secured, Hitler could finally launch his great crusade against Bolshevism — the Luftwaffe's greatest test was days away.

Chapter 4

BARBAROSSA

Having partially re-equipped with early production models of the Bf 109F, JG 54 moved to airfields in East Prussia to become part of Luftflotte 1 under the command of *General-Oberst* Alfred Keller for Operation *Barbarossa*. It joined the tactical sub-division I Fliegerkorps, (General der Flieger Helmut Forster) which was tasked with supporting Army Group North's drive on Leningrad and the capture of that city — Operation *Rentier* (Reindeer). A parallel task codenamed *Silberfuchs* (Silver Fox), was to capture the port of Murmansk.

Together with Stuka, bomber and reconnaissance units, JG 54's strength was boosted by the aircraft of JG 53 and overall there were

twenty-one other fighter Gruppen under the command of Luftflotten 2 and 4. On the eve of Barbarossa the Grünherz Geschwader was dispersed on four forward airfields: Lindental (I.Gruppe commanded by Hptm Hubertus von Bonin); Trakehnen (Maj Hannes Trautloft's GeschwaderStab and II. Gruppe under Hptm Dietrich Hrabak) and Blumenfeld (III. Gruppe led by Hptm Arnold Lignitz). In addition was the operational training unit E./JG 54, under the command of Hptm Eggers. Htm Heinz Bretnutz commanded II./JG 53 at Gerlinden.

As the combined twenty-six divisions of XVI and XVIII Armies, supported by IV Panzergruppe, which comprised Field Marshal Ritter

Poised on the outskirts of a Polish airfield, JG 54 prepares to support the Luftwaffe bomber force in the early stages of the Russian campaign in June 1941. Still largely equipped with the Bf 109E at that stage, the Geschwader would receive ample numbers of Bf 109Fs and early G models with weeks. *(Bundesarchiv)*.

von Leeb's Army Group North, crossed the border in the early hours of 22 June 1941 to begin a headlong race over the parched Russian steppes towards Leningrad, JG 54 awaited orders for its first sorties. These came at 03.05 and Grünherz Messerschmitts were among the total of 231 fighters to make the first penetration of Russian airspace.

The Grünherztrager's task was primarily to put a solid shield of fighters over the tanks and men of Army Group North and to cover the Junkers Ju 88As of KG 1, 76 and 77, themselves the spearhead of 637 bomber sorties flown on that first day. These early morning sorties systematically bombed the Russian airfields at Kowno, Kedainal, Pomiawesch and others in one of the most devasting pre-emptive air assaults in history.

There was little the Russians could do either to stop the German tank columns or prevent the Luftwaffe gaining air supremacy all along a 175-mile front. Despite the fact that two Red armies, also with twenty-six divisions, including six of armour, directly faced Army Group North, the suddeness and pace of the invasion achieved almost complete surprise. The Red Army was either swept aside, or as often happened in the North, simply bypassed, allowing the Germans to thrust deep into Soviet territory. In eighteen days, the Wehrmacht advanced 400 miles.

In the fifty years or so since the start of World War Two, historians have questioned whether the Russians were as unprepared for war as the events of June 1941 appeared to indicate. Stalin had ample advance warning from agents in the West but these were apparently dismissed as false by the Soviet leader. But the recent declassification of some Soviet war records appear to make a very strong case that the Russians, although pre-empted by Hitler, fully intended to make their own attack on Germany in mid-1941. Stalin, evidently fearing that Hitler's territorial gains would continue, was at least prepared to safeguard his borders by neutralising his Eastern European flank and establishing a broad buffer zone which, in any conflict with Germany would hopefully contain the fighting in these bordering states rather than the Soviet Union proper.

The Germans fully realised that their numerically inferior air forces (it was estimated that the Russians then had around 7,000 aircraft in service with twenty-three air divisions) had quickly to gain ascendency over the *Voyenno-vozdushnyye Sily* (VVS) if the advance was to continue its momentum and succeed in capturing key objectives, prevent counter-attacks and consolidate territorial gains. And this had to be done before the inevitable pause to establish supply bases deep inside Russia.

A huge logistical effort was required behind the lines: there was for example the need to overcome the different rail gauges in use in Germany and the Soviet Union; trains could not simply roll from depots in the Reich, through Eastern Europe and into newly-captured territory to deliver the vast amounts of supplies required by the army on a daily basis. A great deal of material had therefore to be moved by road, and there were relatively few good ones in existence in the sparsely-populated regions of Russia at that time. This placed many calls on the Luftwaffe transport force to move priority items up to a front line that got further from Germany with every passing day.

The advance covered ground at a staggering rate, all but unhampered by air attack — and often without a sign of the Red Army. Extraordinary luck afforded the Germans in those early days, their forces meeting little or no opposition in some sectors, which represented huge chunks of territory.

The Luftwaffe, although spread thinly, succeeded in neutralising much of the enemy airpower based in the western part of the Soviet Union before it even had a chance to get off the ground. Luftwaffe bombers attacking airfields did a great deal of damage with small fragmentation bombs, liberally seeding these over dispersal points, maintenance areas and flight lines. Such live munitions had to be cleared before air operations could be undertaken; even if the aircraft themselves had not been destroyed, this task took time — time enough for the Germans to have passed well out of range.

On numerous airfields the Germans were surprised to see little evidence of dispersal or even of camouflage paint having been used to

Ltn Heindl, Adjutant of II./JG 54, flying a bomb-laden Bf 109E-7 over the Eastern Front. Of note is the way that the original camouflage pattern shows through the washable yellow distemper on the engine cowling. This aircraft is the subject of one of the colour side views shown in the end papers. *(Petrick).*

hide Russian aircraft from the air — all this despite Stalin having been reliably informed that a German attack was imminent. In fact, warnings had been sent to outlying bases, but communications over such vast distances were often poor and many a Soviet airfield commander received orders to go onto a war footing only when his fighters, bombers or ground attack aircraft were already going up in flames.

Just how high the cost of Russian unpreparedness for a German attack was is reflected in the figure of 1,811 aircraft lost on the first day of Barbarossa; 322 shot down by fighters and flak and 1,489 destroyed on the ground. In total the Luftwaffe raided sixty-six airfields in the border regions, some of which housed units which had recently been equipped with the newest Soviet fighter types, the Yak-1, MiG-3 and LaGG-3, plus the Pe-2 light bomber and the soon to be infamous *Schturmovik*, the Ilyushin Il-2. In the main however, the VVS was still equipped with a selection of obsolete types which gave it a significant disadvantage, particularly in fighter strength.

The German assault was not without cost, the total number of aircraft lost on 22 June being thirty-five. Ltn Kinzinger was one of the casualties from JG 54's 3.Staffel, which apart from the Staffelkapitan, Hans Schmoller-Haldy, had now lost all its original pilots since the war began.

With their ground crews making Herculean efforts to keep up, flogging their vehicles over miles of dusty, ill-prepared roads, JG 54's fighters blazed a trail through Lithuania, Estonia and Latvia, their pilots using the call signs 'Bruno', 'Hildegard' and 'Leopold' for the three respective Gruppen. Pausing briefly at airfields at Dunaberg, Pleskau, Ostrow and Luga, the Geschwader pushed on towards the Gulf of Finland, sweeping all opposition aside. Until the ground advance slowed and more permanent base facilities were secured, the Geschwader's fighters were refuelled and re-armed by small working parties flown in by transports to the nearest available Russian airfield or airstrip.

Russian attempts to defend their territory, though courageous, were often futile and poorly organised in the face of battle-hardened

A rural idyll at Windau catches a Bf 109F, 'White 2' of the E-Staffel during a break from operations. The wooden slats helped the Bf 109s' tyres get a grip when taxying out of soft earth dispersals and the pig, albeit looking rather pleased with life here, was no doubt destined for the cooking pot! *(Petrick)*.

German ground and air forces. Although numerically strong, the Red Army lacked experienced leaders, many of whom had perished in Stalin's notorious pre-war purges of all levels of Soviet society, up to and including the armed forces. Outgunned and lacking modern equipment and communications, the Russians had little choice but to fall back. And to keep falling back. More than once the Germans executed fast pincer movements to surround entire armies while overhead Russian troops had to contend with rapid air attacks by Stukas and medium bombers which destroyed defensive positions, rail junctions, river crossings and concentrations of troops.

The Red Air Force seemed equally powerless against the Jagdflieger who initially appeared invincible. So many aircraft were caught on the ground by the early morning raids, that there was next to nothing that the pilots of units equipped with the diminutive I-16 Rata monoplanes and I-153 Chato and I-15bis biplanes could do to stop their designated defence areas being overrun. Those that did manage to take off faced daunting odds.

Air battles during the opening weeks of the Russian campaign were, at times, unbelievably one-sided. The German fighters were frequently able to employ text book tactics against Russian bombers, the hapless crews of which often maintained straight and level flight with no attempt at evasive action even as streams of cannon shells and machine gun bullets chopped their aircraft to pieces.

On 30 June JG 54 claimed no less that sixty-five kills over the town of Daugavpils. Desperately flinging themselves at two recently-captured bridges over the tactically-vital Dvina river, Soviet bomber crews attempted to stop the Panzers continuing their north-westerly advance. Given their lack of fighter cover, it was a valiant but futile gesture. The inexperienced Russian flyers were driven off with heavy losses in personnel and aircraft. Similar near-suicidal assaults were made by VVS bombers on other sectors of the front — usually with the same result.

Flying in support of the next German bridgehead at Ostrov the tally of JG 54's kills rose to 109 between 4 and 7 July. Numerous staff conferences were necessary to keep the Luft-waffe commanders up to date on Wehrmacht progress, enabling them to provide the maximum possible air support. Such was the pace and scale of air fighting that the Geschwader was able to celebrate its 1,000th kill on 1 August by Max-Hellmuth Ostermann, who then led 7.Staffel. In the circumstances, this young Leutnant had a very apt name!

But the very fruits of victory contained sour implications for German airmen over Russia: hard on the heels of the regular army units were the notorious liquidation squads, bent on turning the Soviet Union into a wasteland inhabited only by those acceptable to Nazi racial ideals. When the news of the handiwork of these barbarians spread, merciless revenge was taken on any German unlucky enough to be captured by the Russians. Hitler's deliberate policy of wholesale murder, torture and deportation of Russian civilians took no heed of the retribution that would be meted out to captured Germans, many of whom were shown no mercy at the hands of hate-filled soldiers and civilians alike. All Luftwaffe units were to experience personnel losses directly attributable to this cause and JG 54 was no exception.

Russian reaction

Although it was initally caught badly off-balance and suffered accordingly, the Red Air Force had so much territory at its disposal that it was able to keep up a steady pressure on the Germans. And with massive reserves of manpower, the Russian armed forces could withstand the loss of whole divisions — and indeed complete armies — without being defeated, much less forced into a position where surrender was the only option. And the massive migration of workers to new factory sites beyond the Ural mountains, safe from the German Wehrmacht or Luftwaffe, meant that there was little or no question of capitulation.

On each front there were terrible Russian defeats in 1941, but neither the air or ground forces were ever completely destroyed. The Germans remained in awe at the numbers of aircraft the enemy had lost on the ground and in the air — and yet the Russians still returned to the fray. Even by their own admission, these attacks were often clumsy, uncoordinated and ineffectual. The important point was that they were made at all.

It had been estimated by the Germans that

Commanding Luftflotte 1 for Barbarossa, GenOberst Alfred Keller made flying visits to front line units to maintain an up to date picture of the overall progress of the army and the degree of Luftwaffe support. Having disembarked from his Heinkel He 111 transport Keller greets officers of II./JG 54, including Hannes Trautloft (right). *(Petrick)*.

Army Group North faced 1,155 Soviet aircraft (570 bombers and reconnaissance types and 585 fighters) under the command of the Leningrad Military District, plus a further 630, including 315 fighters, which were directed by the Baltic Military District. Operations on the Northern Front opened with an attack on bases in Finland and Norway on 25 June, aimed at nullifying the forces available to Luftflotte 5 and the Finnish Air Force. In seven days of raids, the Russians partially succeeded in their objective.

Fighter units defending Leningrad entered combat on 23 June, their initial objective being the destruction of German reconnaissance aircraft. Individual pilots did not shy from ramming enemy bombers to bring them down and a number were successful in this most hazardous form of combat. By 10 July the Northern Front units had 837 aircraft at their disposal.

Hampered to a considerable degree by the obsolescence of many of their combat aircraft, the Russians nevertheless learned from their mistakes. Fighters began to fly high cover as well as close escort to bomber formations, the crews of which made every effort to stay together for mutual protection and resist attempts by the Jagdflieger to break up their formations and destroy small flights of bombers piecemeal, as they had frequently done while surprise still lay with the invaders. Better tactical deployment helped to overcome the performance disadvantages of the I-153 and I-16 and exploited those of the newer Yak-1 and MiG-3. So manoeuvrable were the diminutive Russian biplanes that many a Jagdflieger grew very frustrated in his repeated attempts to keep them in his sights long enough to fire a telling burst.

Elements of Army Group North's component forces reached Lake Ilman on 31 July and were on the Gulf of Finland by 17 August; although the south-western encirclement of Leningrad had not gone entirely to plan, there being considerable hold-ups to progress due to difficult terrain and Russian counter-attacks, not to mention the beginning of a long series of 'temporary' dilutions of strength to reinforce other areas of the front threatened by enemy resistance, it looked likely, against all odds,

A quartet of JG 54's Experten pictured shortly after an awards ceremony. (left to right) Dieter Hrabak, Hans Phillip, Gotthard Handrick and Joachim Pohs. *(Petrick)*.

that Hitler would indeed achieve his 'six week victory' in Russia. On all fronts, progress was being made: Smolensk had been taken on 16 July; the attack on Kiev opened on 19 September, two weeks after the advance on Moscow had started, and the drive into the Ukraine to the Caucasus had made excellent time.

In the air, German success also continued apace. On 19 July, a young Leutnant named Walter Nowotny, who had joined 9./JG 54 on 23 February, shot down three I-153s over the island of Osel before he was forced to ditch his Bf 109 in the Baltic. For three days Nowotny paddled his dinghy with his bare hands to reach dry land.

Oblt Hubert 'Hubs' Mutherich, Staffelkapitan of 5./JG 54 was one pilot who built up his personal score in the early days of the Russian campaign and by August he had claimed twenty-seven. Hannes Trautloft's Ritterkreuz for twenty kills had been awarded on 27 June.

August 1941 brought its share of honours as

well as setbacks. Two more pilots, Joseph 'Joschi' Pohs and Mutherich, were awarded the RK for twenty-eight and thirty-one kills respectively on the 6th and on the 24th, 'Fips' Philipp received the Eichenlaub to the RK for sixty-two victories. He was the first of JG 54's pilots to become the recipient of the prized Oak Leaves.

The fortunes of war turned against JG 54 on the 30th when Arnold Lignitz, victor over twenty-five enemy aircraft, was shot down over Leningrad, his aircraft breaking up as it plunged into the beleaguered Russian city. Although he managed to bail out, Lignitz was never seen again.

The ring closing around Leningrad was temporarily slackened by stronger enemy resistance, including air attacks. No attempt was made to capture the city, which had always been of a secondary importance in the original plans for Barbarossa. Instead a long, bitter siege began. Another victim of the Leningrad defences was Ltn Mutherich, killed in a forced-landing near the city on 9 September, with his score at forty-three.

Four days before this tragedy, JG 54 had occupied Siverskaja airfield which, together with Kragnogwardeisk, Staraja-Russa and Rjelbitzi, was to remain its base for nearly two years. Siverskaja was a large, purpose-built Red Air Force base located with the others in a rough arc around Leningrad. From these bases, JG 54 flew numerous sorties in support of dive bomber attacks which were working in conjunction with the Wehrmacht's attempt to shell the city into surrender, and imposing a blockade on the Russian Fleet.

In order to appreciate the prevailing situation at first hand, Trautloft flew up to Leningrad on 22 September. Ensconsed in a bunker overlooking the city, the Geschwaderkommodore peered through a powerful periscope at the devastation even then being carried out by artillery and Stukas. The latter had the important task of trying to neutralise the Russian Baltic Fleet and Trautloft knew that two anti-shipping strikes had already been carried out that day.

As the Kommodore watched the third Stuka attack get underway, he grimly noted the flak put up by the defences — flak that had for

some two weeks now kept his own fighters at high altitude over the city. At that moment there came an urgent warning that the command post was under attack — Russian fighters were strafing. Trautloft and the artillery officers dived for the floor as the bunker splintered around them and although he was unhurt, the commander of the Geschwader could not help an angry question in the heat of the moment. 'Where in hell', he demanded of an army officer lying nearby, 'are our fighters?'

It was ironic that such a question should have been put by one of the very Luftwaffe officers in a position to know the answer and the army officer was amused. He said, 'You should know Herr Major, that all available machines have been ordered to confine themselves to escorting Stukas.'

Hannes Trautloft, the man largely responsible for JG 54's early success in combat, pictured in one of his personal Bf 109s.

Trautloft had seen the fighters, circling high above the Ju 87s and, perhaps, realised that they had already been tied too closely to escorting pin-prick attacks on strategic targets by small numbers of bombers. The fighters could still do their job with extreme efficiency — but they could hardly be expected to destroy cities.

It was now that the German belief that Blitzkrieg could dispense with a long range bomber force, even as a back up to the much vaunted dive and medium bombers, was being show up for the folly it was. After an initial series of raids with 100-plus medium bombers on Moscow, the number of aircraft that could be spared in such strategic attacks fell off drastically. And even in Russia, the day of the Stuka was waning as Soviet fighter strength increased.

In the meantime, Operation Taufin, the capture of Moscow, had belatedly restarted on 2 October. Hitler's indecision over the relative importance of capturing the capital, as against Leningrad or Stalingrad, plus the three-pronged 'broad front' adopted for Barbarossa, was running into difficulties, not only from the enemy, but the weather. By 20 October, although the foremost Wehrmacht units were just forty miles from Moscow, the first cold rains of winter had turned to snow. Now the conditions, which had been so favourable at the start of the campaign in the East, went from bad to worse.

Fighter operations for JG 54 over the Leningrad front included escort to tactical bombers pounding Red Army positions and Leningrad's supply lines across the now-frozen Lake Ladoga, free hunts and long range ground attacks to disrupt Russian reinforcements. With the only good road into Leningrad in German hands, the defenders were forced to resort to unconventional means to supply a small proportion of the daily needs of the starving city. But neither JG 54 or any other Jagdgeschwader was called upon to fly the kind of close escort sorties to bombers pounding an enemy capital, as they had done in the past, for no similar pattern of operations developed. It was not only the Jagdwaffe that became the fire brigade of the Eastern Front — the bomber force found its strength similarly depleted by the

number of important targets that had to be attacked. When bomber sorties were flown, there were sufficient fighters to cover them, but there simply were not enough Dorniers, Heinkels and Junkers with which to mount attacks anywhere near the scale of those made against London, for example.

In a period marked by a slackening of air activity due to the appalling weather, the Grünherz fighters flew whenever possible. There were numerous targets for their guns and some pilots became increasingly adept at train strafing. On 1 October Hauptmann 'Seppi' Seiler took over I Gruppe in place of the downed Lignitz, his place at the head of 1.Staffel in turn being filled by Oblt Heinz Lange. Up to 8 November the Grünherz had lost twenty-seven pilots and seven groundcrew since the start of Barbarossa.

Although Russian air attacks on Luftwaffe bases had been sporadic and had not achieved widespread destruction of aircraft or installations, there were personnel casualties on the ground. Among them was Oblt Ruland of 3.Staffel, a very promising pilot who was fatally wounded during bombing raids on 1 and 2 August, and Ofw Braden from the same Staffel, who was badly injured.

As the Russian winter deepened and the ground fighting around Leningrad tailed off, JG 54's area of responsibility remained little short of awesome: from the Gulf of Finland to Demansk it covered 400km of territory. It was all but impossible for the already stretched Luftwaffe to police an area of that size adequately and it was the Russians rather than the Germans who now tended to take the initiative. Well used to their unbelievably cold winters — the barometer went on dropping until temperatures as low as minus forty-five degrees Centigrade were recorded on 5 December — crews of the Red Air Force not only continued to fly but gradually to become a great deal more than an irritation. Able to rebuild their strength on bases now beyond the range of German bombers, the enemy showed that although they had suffered grievous losses, they still had vast reserves of manpower and centres of industrial output that the Germans could not touch. . .

By the time Hitler ordered a renewed attempt to take Moscow on 15 November, time

The ever-deeper drive into Russia brought a problem of range to single-engined fighter units and to the normal hazards of war was added the risk of running out of fuel. This happened to an 8.Staffel pilot on 30 March 1942 at Romanowa when the winter snow still provided some cushioning effect. The pilot of the Bf 109F, 'Black 1' was either Erwin Leykauf or Rudolf Patzak. *(Crow)*.

was rapidly running out. Rostov was taken on the 26th, but progress towards the capital was slow. A three-pronged assault began on 1 December and within four days, the troops were able to see the spires of the Kremlin. But that same day 'General Winter' stopped the Wehrmacht in its tracks. Then, on 6 December the Red Army began a counter attack. Limited in scope and similarly slowed by the prevailing conditions, it nevertheless edged forward along a front stretching for 200 miles. The Allies, and indeed the world, watched and waited. . .

On 20 December there were more changes in JG 54's leadership. I Gruppe lost its Kommandeur, Hauptmann von Sella, who was posted, his place being taken by Hptmn Franz Eckerle, Staffelkapitan of 6./JG 54. Obltn Sattig now took over command of the Staffel.

While the Russian front was widely believed to be a marginally easier hunting ground for the Jagdflieger than combatting the daylight American bomber formations in the West, numerous pilots had to wait some time before they could put into practice what they had learned in both flight training and on many operational sorties. For some men the chance to score a personal victory simply did not materialise for months on end, despite their colleagues being in the right place at the right time to do so. Erich Hartmann of JG 52, later to become the world's leading combat pilot, experienced this phenomenon, as did a young Unteroffizier who had joined I./JG 54 in the summer of 1941. The fact that Karl Schnorrer could not claim a victory was compounded by the difficulty he had in controlling the Bf 109 during landing. He had 'cracked up' no less than three early in his career.

Nevertheless, with some sense of frustration, and good-natured acceptance of the nickname 'Quax' after an accident-prone cartoon character, Schnorrer persevered to score his first victory on the last day of 1941. During 1942 he proved to be a very able fighter pilot, so much so that he, Anton Dobele and Rudolf Radamacher teamed up with Walter Nowotny to become a highly-efficient Bf 109 Schwarm.

With the rank of Feldwebel, Dobele had also joined the Geschwader in mid-1941, Unteroffizier Rademacher arriving later in the year.

67

Karl Schnorrer preparing to fly an E-Staffel Bf 109F that has, judging by the degree of exhaust staining, already seen considerable service with 8.Staffel before being passed on for training duties. At the time JG 54's training unit was based at Meukuhren in East Prussia. *(Crow)*.

Dobele too experienced a slow start to his score, managing to shoot down only four enemy aircraft in a year of operational flying. Rademacher's first kill came sooner, on 9 January 1942, but it was to be 1943 before the Nowotny Schwarme really began to make its presence felt.

One result of the Russian rally at Leningrad was that on 2 January 1942 JG 54 was caught on the ground at Siverskaja. Soviet bombers swept in, taking the defences by surprise and destroyed ten aircraft. By that time, some of the Grunherz' pilots had flown the Fw 190A-1, a few examples of which had been issued to II Gruppe the previous November. However, operational evaluation of the potent 'Butcher Bird' had proved disappointing. Numerous cases of engine trouble had kept the 190s on the ground for extended periods and by late January all remaining examples were returned to maintenance units while the Gruppe reverted entirely to the trusty Bf 109F and the first of the G models.

Franz Eckerle's leadership of I Gruppe was to last less than two months, as he was posted missing on 14 February, to be replaced by the redoubtable Hans Philipp. Eckerle had scored a total of fifty-nine victories, all of them in the East and was last seen going down for a forced landing in the Welikije Luki area behind the Russian lines. On 12 March Philipp became the first recipient of the *Schwertern zum Ritterkreuz* in JG 54 and, on the 31st of that month, the fourth Luftwaffe fighter pilot to claim 100 kills, following Werner Molders, Gunter Lutzow and Walter Oesau.

Casualties recorded by any air force unit naturally included a number of men who were wounded, either in action or as a result of accidents on both non-operational and front line flying duties. On 23 February 3.Staffel's Hans Schmoller-Haldy was injured badly enough to have to pass his command over to Hptm Gerhard Koall.

March also brought slightly higher temperatures which were, if anything, worse than the bitter cold. Warmer air turned the previously iron-hard earth into a glutinous quagmire that all but stopped movement of men and vehicles. On the airfields, ground crews had to lay log taxiways to enable aircraft to be moved at all and unless runways were well drained, take-offs by heavy fuelled and armed aircraft were very hazardous — when they were attempted at all. One consolation was that the weather affected forces on both sides to much the same degree, and for days air activity all along the front was reduced drastically. The stalemate situation had to prevail until a weather improvement enabled either side to make any substantial gains.

This came in the fullness of time and 4 April 1942 recorded the Geschwader's 2,000th victory as increased Russian activity presented the Jagdflieger with a plethora of targets over the front. On the 30th, the Germans renewed their offensive against Leningrad in line with Hitler's Directive No 41 which reaffirmed the intention to take the city and break through to the Caucasus — with the capture of the oil-rich region taking operational priority. He also wanted Stalingrad taken or destroyed, and to pursue these objectives, thousands of Axis troops arrived in the Soviet Union to make good the German losses in the first year of Eastern Front fighting.

Among the fighter pilots who increased their personal scores at this time was Max Ostermann, whose 100th victim fell on 12 May. For this feat, Ostermann received the Swords on the 17th. The Geschwader's success was to be reflected in numerous such decorations, with many individuals rapidly passing the fifty kills

mark during the period when the Germans were on the offensive. May also saw the Ritterkreuz awarded to Ltn Horst Hannig of 6.Staffel — no relation to Norbert Hannig, who also flew with JG 54 — for achieving a total of forty-eight victories.

Although the siege of Leningrad was renewed with increased ferocity, no German breakthrough materialised. The city continued to hold out and in June the Russians, with some desperation, began making supply flights on moonlit nights. JG 54 mounted patrols to intercept these and met with considerable success. On the night of 22/23 June Ltn Erwin Leykauf of III Gruppe shot down six Polikarpov R-5 biplanes and was subsequently to claim two more. II Gruppe's Hptm Joachim Wandel doubled Leykauf's score with sixteen and JG 54's night kills, in aircraft that were hardly equipped for this form of combat, eventually reached the impressive total of fifty-three.

As with most air forces at various periods of the war, the Jagdverbande's air combat success continued to be tinged with sadness at the loss of good pilots; JG 54's time on the Eastern Front was increasingly to offset the pride derived from the accolades of victory with tragedy, particularly when those who failed to

A well-decorated Bf 109F flown regularly by Oblt Max Ostermann, who was killed in August 1942. *(E. J. Creek).*

return were men whose experience and inspiration was thus lost to younger pilots, many of whom strove to emulate the Experten.

An example of this phenomenon came on 4 August when Nowotny shot down seven Russian aircraft to increase his score to fifty-four. Just forty-eight hours later the Geschwader was stunned by the news that Ostermann, victor over 102 enemy aircraft, nine of them before the campaign in the East began, had been killed in combat with a substantial force of Russian fighters over Amossowo. On 10 August Ritterkreuztrager Karl Sattig, Staffelkapitan of 6./JG 54, was also lost in action, with his personal score at fifty-three, two of which had been at night. Reported missing near Rshew, it was assumed that Sattig fell into Russian hands and died in captivity. Karl Beisswanger took over 6.Staffel.

Pilot strength of JG 54 on 26 May 1942 was 140, comprising of forty-seven officers, seventy-eight NCOs and fifteen airmen grade personnel. During the year the Geschwader's mix of operations included escort to renewed bomber attacks on Russian naval units in Leningrad harbour and to transports supplying the Cholm 'fortress', operations in the latter area having begun on 21 January. The fighters also flew in support of the besieged XI Army Korps in the Demjansk 'cauldron', an action that started on 9 February and was to last until 21 October; army support during the battle of Volchov (13 January to 27 July) and low level Jabo attacks on merchant shipping using the now ice-free Lake Ladoga to get vital supplies through to Leningrad.

Detachments in Finland

By the autumn of 1942, I./JG 54 led by Oblt Heinz Lange, 2.Staffel (Obltn Count Matuschka) and 7.Staffel (Obltn Waldemar 'Hein' Wubke) were well used to operating from bases in Finland, allied to Germany since her 'Winter War' with Russia had terminated in March 1940 with annexation of some eleven percent of her territory. Although Luftflotte 5 had the main responsibility for conducting the war against Russia in these far northern latitudes, Luftflotte 1 provided substantial support units during the inital offensives of Barbarossa.

When the German XXXVI Army Korps reached Kirkenes and pushed northwards from the Baltic up the Gulf of Bothnia and along the western borders of Finland, the Russians reacted with air attacks on Finnish territory, thus precipitating the 'Continuation War'. Although the Finnish Air Force and the Luftwaffe flew entirely separate operations, German aircraft used bases in Finland, which considerably shortened the ranges over which operations had to be flown in support of the most forward Army units.

Luftflotte 1's subordinated *Fliegerfuhrer Baltic* co-ordinated operations in the region, these including coastal and sea reconnaissance and anti-shipping and submarine patrols over the Gulf of Finland and ground support sorties on a line Riga-Tallinn-Leningrad up to the White Sea. The demarcation between German and Finnish spheres of operations was established on a line Oulujoki-Oulujarvi-Kuhmo-Nuokkijarvi.

Luftflotte 1 operations against the supply route across Lake Ladoga began on 25 November 1941. But such was the extent of these roads, which snaked over extemely thick ice, that air attacks could not hope to cut all of them and Luftwaffe activity was soon reduced to mounting little more than small-strength nuisance raids as other sectors of the front required support in the ever-harder conditions of the Russian winter. As the new year also brought vigorous Russian counter-attacks, Luftflotte 1 became preoccupied with support for supply flights (primarily by He 111s) attempting to sustain German troops surrounded at Demjansk and Cholm. Fighter escort strength was increased accordingly and JG 54 was among the Jagdgeschwaderen that sent individual Staffeln for duty in the far north.

At times, the forces deployed in Finland were extremely modest: 1.Staffel for example escorted eight Ju 87s, a Bf 110 and a Ju 88, the latter flying armed reconnaissance, during the occupation of Suurasaari Island in the Gulf of Finland on 27-28 March 1942. The Grünherz Staffel then had a nominal eight operational Bf 109s out of a maximum strength of eleven. The nature of the sorties remained much the same as before — bomber and transport escort or fighter bomber attacks on Russian shipping

White camouflage, probably fairly recently applied judging by the continuity of the paint, on a Bf 109F 'Yellow 4' of II Gruppe. The Germans found the Russian 'General Winter' a terrifying enemy. (*MBB*).

and the provision of air cover for armed Siebel ferries.

Occupying Patajarvi and Viipuri, JG 54's fighters did what they could to ensure that German air and ground units carried out their operations without interference from the enemy, but despite all their efforts supplies continued to get through to Leningrad. Against all odds, the city continued to hold out. Its situation was dire, with thousands of inhabitants starving. For many, the meagre supplies that did manage to get through came too late.

Command Changes

In September 1942 a reorganisation of the Luftwaffe in Russia culminated in the creation of a new command, *Luftflotte Ost*, which combined Luftflotten 1 and 2. It encompassed JG 54's three Gruppen, the four of JG 51, two from JG 77 and II./JG 3. At a time when German fortunes were beginning to wane on all fronts there began what turned into a desperate and increasingly wasteful switching of fighter Gruppen from theatre to theatre to act as fire brigade forces to combat the Red Air Force.

Already receiving adequate numbers of better replacement aircraft from its own factories, the VVS was now being further bolstered by Lend-Lease supplies from Britain and the US, fed through the principal ports of Murmansk and Archangel. Notwithstanding this regeneration of front line units with much improved aircraft, there was seemingly little the Russians could do to stop the runaway attrition rate exacted by the Luftwaffe fighter pilots out of all proportion to their numbers; on 14 September Ltn Hans Joachim Heter could claim the traditional laurel wreath for shooting down the Grunherz' 3000th enemy aircraft. His own score had then reached fifty-three, including six at night. Such success was invariably recorded for the cameras, photographs of the pilots and their aircraft making excellent propaganda for the German national press and the pages of *Signal*, the Luftwaffe's own magazine record of war operations.

For the time being, JG 54 avoided the necessary rapid re-climatisation and different operational demands of an unfamiliar front, which was the lot of units that were, for example, rushed from the East to fight in the Mediterranean, and stayed in Russia. Even so, the area over which the Geschwader operated was so large that, depending on the season, the pilots could experience virtually every kind of weather condition within a relatively short period of time.

The GeschwaderStab and I Gruppe had begun in late 1942 to receive examples of the improved Fw 190A-3 and A-4 and by early 1943 the Geschwader was flying a mix of Fw 190s and Bf 109Fs and Gs. The arrival of new aircraft (although the supply of Focke-Wulfs remained generally poor) and postings brought changes to JG 54 at this time, but there was no slackening of pace and success in aerial combat.

Before the year was out, Nowotny had become Staffelkapitan of 9./JG 54 (on 25 October), II Gruppe had lost Dieter Hrabak to JG 52 two days later and gained the sixty-eight-victory Experten Hans 'Assi' Hahn from JG 2. Ofw Max Stotz not only reached his 100th victory on 29 November, but single-handedly destroyed no less than ten enemy aircraft on the 30th. Nowotny had shot down 1.Staffel's 300th victim in November.

This group of pilots of 5.Staffel in Russia around mid-1942 included Ltn Horst Hannig (seated, far left) Staffelkapitan Joachim Wandel (seated, centre) and W. Kretschmer (seated, far right). *(Crow)*.

Chapter 5

WESTERN FRONT

By the end of 1941, only two complete Jagdge-schwaderen, JG 2 and JG 26, plus one Kampf-geschwader, KG 2, remained in France. As fighter bomber operations against England were to continue, on 10 November the start of a rationalisation took place with the formation of 10.(Jabo)/JG 2. This activation was followed shortly afterwards by forming 10.(Jabo)/JG 26, both these units being specialised fighter bomber Staffeln. It was the latter that was to be part of the history of JG 54 for a short period of time, the operational career of the *Grünherz* and *Schlageter* Jagdgeschwaderen being closely interwoven for much of the war.

Equipped with Bf 109Fs and Gs, these units continued to carry out small scale hit and run raids on shipping and targets on the English coast. Although anti-shipping strikes took some precedence, the fighter bombers would go after any worthwhile target within range, particularly the huge gasholders located around most towns of any size. Unmistakable from the air, these were relatively easy to hit, sometimes with spectacular results. Evidently believing that the Jabos were achieving useful results, Luftflotte 3 ordered a second Staffel in each Jagdgeschwader converted to the Jabo role on 10 March 1942.

JG 2 and JG 26 could rarely muster a combined total of more than thirty Jabos, but they succeeded in tying down a far higher number of RAF fighters tasked with their interception. And when in 1942 the Fw 190 began to replace the Bf 109, the job was often impossible for pilots flying Spitfire MkVs. The Butcher Bird was superior on almost every count and could evade easily in a shallow dive.

So began the long and far from easy struggle to provide the RAF with a better low altitude interceptor, a programme that eventually resulted in the mighty Hawker Typhoon. An aircraft fraught with technical problems, the Typhoon owed its later success partly to the fact that the Luftwaffe continued to send Jabo sorties across the Channel. When the Typhoon went operational in September 1941 (at almost the same time that the Fw 190A entered service with JG 26), there were high hopes that the German sneak raiders would be defeated.

In the event it was more than a year before a Typhoon shot down its first 190, and throughout their operational span the raiders proved hard to destroy. But once the Typhoon reached a level of reliability the writing was on the wall for the Luftwaffe. The British fighter's four-cannon armament proved lethal to the lighter Focke-Wulf and a good many were shot down by the increasing number of squadrons that kept a watch on the Jabo menace.

Although the German attack on Russia involved almost all of JG 54, its unit number was allocated on a temporary basis to the Jabo Staffel of JG 26 early in 1943. Officially this unit was part of the Grünherz order of battle from 17 February and as 10.(Jabo) JG 54 it was technically under the command of Geschwader-kommodore Hannes Trautloft. While based at St Omer-Wizernes, its pilots even removed their *Schlageter* uniform cuffbands to indicate their allegiance to JG 54 rather than JG 26.

The Jabo unit remained under the tactical operational control of JG 26, which was led at that time by Major 'Pips' Priller, and any casualties it suffered were reported against the JG 26 inventory. Sadly, during the two months or so that the unit carried the JG 54 number, it had such to report. On 24 March 1943, Staffelkapitan Oblt Paul Keller was shot down and killed by British anti-aircraft fire during an attack on targets at Ashford, Kent.

It had originally been the intention to exchange JG 54 with JG 26 in its entirety, although the switching of the Grunherz to the Western Front was only partially completed by February 1943 and the plan to move the rest of the Gruppen from the Eastern front was eventually abandoned. Only III Gruppe under Maj Seppl Seiler (now recovered from the

The partial transfer of JG 54 to the West in 1943 brought further success and disaster on a fighting front that was widely recognised as the toughest there was. Based at Schwerin in October that year, 9.Staffel was then equipped with the Bf 109G as shown by this view of Fw Gunter Wrobbel in 'Yellow 6'. *(Fritz Ungar)*.

wounds he had received in combat during the Battle of Britain), plus Obltn Graf von Matuschka's 4.Staffel, made the long journey westwards by train, travelling via Smolensk and Krasnowardiesk to arrive at Vendeville near Lille, on 12 February.

Flying Bf 109s, these four Staffeln initially operated as an independent unit, but were subsequently placed under the command of JG 26. Priller himself made a formal inspection of the intake of JG 54 personnel soon after they arrived from Russia.

With the creation of SKG 10, the former 10.(Jabo) JG 54 became 11.(Jabo) JG 26, although the unit was still alternatively identified as belonging to JG 54 for a time. On 5 May 1943 the Jabo order of battle of JG 2, JG 26 and SKG 10 included seventeen 11./Staffel Bf 109G-6s, ten of which were serviceable on that date.

The Grünherz pilots from the East included some who were in a position to compare the two fighting fronts and these men were to find

that the war in the West had changed, the only similarity with Russia being that the enemy no longer showed much sign of being cowed by the quality of German arms. Numerical superiority was becoming a thing of the past as the Luftwaffe's war effort increasingly changed from offensive to defensive in the face of burgeoning Allied might on the other side of the English Channel.

For the fighter force, the problem was not one of replacement aircraft, despite the intertuptions to production and repair through Allied bombing, but of adequate numbers of well trained pilots. From 1943 onwards, every experienced Jagdflieger killed in action created a gap that could still be filled — but not by men of equal calibre to the Staffelkapitanen and Gruppenkommodoren who had gone. The high command, having failed to plan for a long war, arrogantly assuming that *Lebensraum* for the Third Reich was simply there for the taking, had not initiated training programmes that could cope with the demands of protracted combat operations and an almost inevitable high attrition rate. Germany's military forces were now beginning, albeit slowly, to reap the whirlwind of those erroneous assumptions, none more so than the Luftwaffe fighter force.

Not that the Luftwaffe fighter force in the West was by any means a spent force; it was poised to offer combat to the RAF and USAAF bomber offensive by night and day and would exact a terrible price for the continuation of such operations by both Allied air forces.

JG 54 found that whereas two- and four-fighter elements had been adequate on many sorties in the East, these had to be flown in Staffel or even Gruppe strength if they were to have any chance of scoring victories, particularly against American four-engined bombers. They now faced these heavily-armed B-17 Fortresses and B-24 Liberators in increasing numbers over continental Europe. And it appeared that the Allies could and would sustain any number of casualties to continue the pounding of centres of German war production and population.

Luftwaffe pilots tasked with inflicting such heavy losses on USAAF B-17 and B-24 formations that the Americans would find daylight bombing raids prohibitive in terms of both men and machines, found the bombers tough opponents. Bringing down *Vermots* required a special kind of nerve, every ounce of skill and not a little reckless bravery, so much so that this category of aircraft was highlighted in the victory lists of individual pilots. To the average German pilot, the number of guns (rarely less than ten and usually twelve in each type) fitted to each US bomber was incredible, and the web of hot metal they were obliged to fly into nothing short of awesome.

Nevertheless the Jagdflieger were shooting down American heavy bombers at a steady rate. And that rate was rising, to the dismay of the US 8th AAF bomber commanders in England, who had staked a good deal more than their collective military careers on the gamble that their Fortresses and Liberators could prevail over Germany by day and not suffer the appalling loss rate of RAF bombers much earlier in the war. Although the comparison was hardly valid, the Americans believed that their heavies had enough guns

to deal effectively with fighter attacks, and that fighter escort would not be needed. To prove that the AAF had a serious stake in the Allied policy of defeating Germany before channelling resources into the war with Japan, daylight precision bombing almost had to succeed, whatever the cost. The offensive opened on 17 August 1942.

From 27 March 1943 JG 54 operated within the Central European sector which covered the German coast and adjacent areas. Combat with the USAAF brought further casualties and changes, Ltn Rupp and Hptm Fink going down on 15 May while attacking Fortresses briefed to hit a variety of targets, including industrial installations at Emden.

It was the 8th's 4th Bombardment Wing that bore the brunt of the fighter attacks while seeking targets of opportunity when their primary, Wilhelmshaven, was covered by cloud. III./JG 54 initiated a running air battle over Heligoland, Dune and Wangerooge Island. Combined casualties in the 1st and 4th Bomb Wings amounted to six B-17s. It was an occasion when the bombers gave better than they received, for the German loss for the day totalled eight Bf 109s.

Exactly one month later Maj Seiler was transferred back to the East to take command of I./JG 54, his place as Kommandeur of the Grunherz in the West passing to Maj Siegfried Schnell. 'Wurm' Schnell was no stranger to the air war in the West. He had been one of the most successful pilots of JG 2 during the Battle of Britain and had scored his seventieth victory in August 1942. More had been added by the time he took over III./JG 54.

American heavy bombers were not of course the only adversary facing the Jagdflieger at this time. Daylight raids by the RAF had gradually increased in size and scope since the early days of the war when the damage they caused was relatively light. By mid-1943 2 Group RAF was building its strength for an all-out assault on tactical targets built around a substantial force of light bombers. An influx of more modern US types, particularly the Douglas Boston, had seen far less reliance on the older, vulnerable British aircraft with which the group had cut its teeth. Not all the American types pressed into service were capable of surviving the conditions

In a Geschwader where regulation markings were more often the exception than the rule, Ltn. Erwin Leykauf's Bf 109G has his personal insignia on the cowling, forward of the III Gruppe badge, heart and single chevron of an Adjutant. Note the external bullet-proof windscreen. *(Bundesarchiv)*.

then prevailing over Europe. The Lockheed Ventura proved terrifyingly easy to shoot down, and was soon dropped from the inventory.

But the Boston, and subsequently the North American Mitchell, did an outstanding job; with a good medium to low altitude performance the British-flown mediums, covered by strong formations of fighters, primarily Spitfires, attacked a wide variety of targets in the occupied countries including airfields, industrial complexes, power stations and lines of communication. The Jagdwaffe made every effort to make these raids as costly as possible, although the fighter opposition was invariably heavy.

On 15 May, fighters were ordered up to meet a Circus raid on Drucat airfield by two elements of No. 107 Squadron, flying Bostons. Having duly plastered the dispersals and runway, the light bombers came under repeated attack from German fighters. Mixing it with the British escort, Obltn Horst Hannig's aircraft was hit.

Badly injured, Hannig managed to bail out of his crippled Bf 109 but his parachute failed to open. He was one of two casualties suffered by the Jagdflieger in this air battle and was then the Staffelkapitan of 2./JG 2, having transferred from JG 54 early in 1943. Hannig had joined 6./JG 54 on the Eastern Front in the autumn of 1941 and scored thirty victories as a Grunherztrager.

The German fighter losses of 15 May 1943, although not high, serve to illustrate how the force was increasingly to be obliged to divide its strength between British tactical and American strategic attacks. The problem for the Germans was that while their own fighters were only gradually updated to meet increasingly stringent operational demands, the Allies were bringing into service their most modern fighters and bombers. The Germans began to be faced with a multiplicty of excellent new warplanes, including the de Havilland Mosquito,

North American Mustang (albeit in early PR form flown by RAF squadrons) and versions of the Spitfire which through progressive development nullified any advantage the Fw 190 had enjoyed over the earlier marks.

Mounting losses gradually forced a change of US policy regarding escort fighters for 8th Air Force heavy bombers, although initially Republic P-47 Thunderbolts were too short-ranged to cover their charges right into Germany, and those groups equipped with P-38 Lightnings were more than preoccupied with a host of technical malfunctions which depleted their numbers and reduced mission effectiveness. The Luftwaffe fighter force could afford to bide its time until the bombers from England came to them without escort over the Reich.

It was questionable whether these tactics were sound — had they attacked the US fighter escort over the French coast, thus forcing pilots to jettison their extra fuel tanks early, the Jagdflieger would have had more opportunity to shoot down the bombers, which anyway were obliged to fly over enemy territory for anything up to three hours.

But for those wishing to accept the implications of how the air war in Europe might effect Germany in the next six to twelve months, the portents were clear enough. On 22 June the 8th AAF delivered a heavy raid on the synthetic rubber plant at Huls — the first such foray against an important target in the Ruhr. It would by no means be the last. And on 28 July 1943, Thunderbolts flew the first mission with belly tanks in the European Theatre of Operations. It was a date of even grimmer significance to the Jagdverbande, although it was hardly realised at the time. Due to production and operational problems with the early external fuel tanks, American fighters would not be able to reach the major German target areas for some months, the first penetration of Reich airspace by P-47s not taking place until 27 September 1943.

In the meantime most 8th AAF raids were intercepted and harried across France, the Low Countries and the Reich, the same fighter units often attacking the bombers on their way into the target and having subsequent tries to knock them down as they made their way back to their bases in England. Ably supported by the German flak units, which hotly defended all important targets, the Jagdflieger invariably found the AAF heavies to be tough adversaries because unlike most other bombers they had had to face, the American crews stayed in formation so that their heavy ·50 calibre guns could put up walls of mutually protective defensive fire. Only by tearing holes in the formations could the fighters despatch the tough Forts and Liberators, but they rarely, if ever, succeeded in breaking up the carefully worked out combat boxes, stacked for miles upwards and horizontally.

Individually, an experienced German pilot could usually achieve the demise of a B-17 or B-24, a fact not lost on the American formation leaders. They continually stressed station-keeping despite the risk of collision and damage from bombs dropped by combat boxes flying above those which drew the low, more vulnerable position.

In its turn, the Luftwaffe studied the defences of the US bombers, both from pilot observation and examination of shot down examples, became thoroughly familiar with their respective weak points and issued comprehensive instructions as to the best method of deploying available forces to bring down the maximum number. A comprehensive set of attack angles and ranges were fully illustrated in such literature, which was required reading in every Jagdgeschwader crew room.

In 1943, the Americans noted to their cost that the Jagdflieger often favoured head-on attacks which if opened from close enough ranges, could knock out engines, smash flight deck controls and bombsights and worst of all, kill or incapacitate lead crews, navigators and bombardiers. Even if such intercepts did not ruin the carefully briefed target run, they could reduce its destructiveness by having the mission pass into less capable hands. At that time both the B-17 and B-24 were marginally less well protected from straight ahead than from other quarters and a good many were lost in this way. But it took great courage on behalf of the German pilots to hold to the head-on intercept, as the combined speed of fighter and bomber was in the region of 500mph plus. It was often difficult to judge the closing speed, open fire close enough to cause damage and time the

A group of 9.Staffel pilots at an in-the-field tactics conference at Schwerin during early 1944. *(Ungar)*.

break-away correctly, for the target had a relatively small area from dead ahead. But the pilots who favoured such tactics had plenty of time to hone their technique and throughout the summer the US loss rate gradually rose.

JG 54 contined on home defence duty well into August 1943, operating under Luftflotte 3 control and using the bases at Deelen, Schipol and Arnhem. It was at this time that JG 54's ski champion, Uffz Pfeiffer, was shot down and Ekkehard Bob, commanding 9.Staffel, was posted to take over IV./JG 51. A unit that was constantly on the move, JG 54 operated from Schwerin, Ludwigslust and Luneburg in the turbulent remaining months of 1943.

By August, 8th Bomber Command had been flying combat missions over continental Europe for a year and on the 17th it laid on an ambitious 'anniversary' raid to Schweinfurt and Regensburg. The staggering loss of a total of sixty B-17s on one raid resulted in a reduction of effort that lasted until early the following month.

Then, on 8 October the 8th Air Force sent 170 B-17s and B-24s to Bremen and Vegesack. Waves of Bf 109s and Fw 190s met them in the now familiar relay of interceptions into and out of the target area. Elements of JG 1, 3, 11 and 54 were engaged as were ZG 1 and ZG 26. It was the start of three successive days of carnage in which the Zerstorers suffered particularly grievous losses. The Grünherz came off comparatively lightly. On the 8th Heinz Schulz of 9.Staffel was wounded and the following day, when the Americans flew a long range mission to various targets in Eastern

Germany and Poland, Emil Hecker, also of 9.Staffel, was similarly wounded in action. Although then not flying with JG 54, Hans Philipp was killed on the first of these operations. The third, a devastating strike on Munster, did not involve JG 54.

This trio of bombing missions cost the 8th another fifty bombers and four fighters, while the Luftwaffe lost at least twenty single-seat fighter pilots and twenty-two destroyer crewmen killed. In addition, thirty-one pilots and crewmen were wounded. AAF fighters claimed a total of thirty-one victories, all of them on the 8th and the 10th — and bomber gunners filed claims of 308 German fighters shot down. Such inflated figures of enemy casualties were commonplace. Most of them were made in the sincere belief that high numbers of fighters had indeed been destroyed as they attacked the bombers. They came about because every gunner thought his shots to be the ones that did the damage and in the heat of an air battle, there simply was not the time to verify the claim. Fighters also passed quickly beyond the vision of most of the gunners. Similar inflated figures were totalled up after virtually every big mission and many people must have wondered just what sort of industrial miracle the Germans had created to sustain such losses over a period of fourteen months.

Nevertheless, on the grounds of sustaining morale in the bomber groups, the claims were solemnly registered and recorded for posterity. Had they known about the figures, many Luftwaffe pilots might have ruefully reflected that they would have liked such numbers of aircraft to lose!

That is not to say that many of the Jagdflieger did not meet their end at the hands of bomber gunners; the ·50 caliber machine gun was a nasty weapon to face, particularly en masse. A fighter making a three-quarter rear attack on a formation of fifty B-17s, for example could be exposed to the fire of up to six guns on each bomber — 300 in all. On numerous occasions the Americans found their turret and hand-held guns to be more than adequate to destroy German interceptors.

Events were now moving towards a climax in the air war over Europe; by the autumn of 1943 the Jagdflieger were barely able to contain the enemy bomber offensive. The US fighter escort, pushing further into Germany than anyone would have believed possible a year earlier, was systematically wearing down the fighter force. The intensive efforts made to develop reliable drop tanks had borne fruit and on many missions they enabled the Thunderbolts and Lightnings to take their charges 'all the way'. And late in 1943, yet another fighter type made its debut in the European Theatre.

German fighter pilots and American bomber crews alike initially had difficulty in distinguishing this new type from the Bf 109, which it closely resembled. That it was superior to the German type on almost every count soon became grimly obvious: the Jagdflieger came to loathe the very name of the North American Mustang. And had they known about it, the Allied plan to make their aircraft, airfields, servicing and supply centres the priority target in the first few months of 1944 would have shocked every member of the Jagdwaffe — for it was little short of a death sentence.

At the close of 1943, the fighter units of *Oberbefehlshaber Mitte* (High Command Central) had a total of 1,223 single-engined and twin-engined fighters on strength. The figure included the inventories of both day and night fighter Gruppen, and neither branch of the Luftwaffe would find the numbers anywhere near high enough. The factories were still maintaining a steady flow of replacement fighters and behind the scenes new weaponry was being tested in order to make the single-seaters more effective bomber destroyers — but the training schools could not give their student flyers the necessary experience to replace those who had gone down. Pilot shortage began to seriously affect the Luftwaffe fighter force. . .

1944 — Year of disaster

Siegfried Schnell left III./JG 54 early in 1944 to return to the East to take over command of IV Gruppe, effective 11 February. This move temporarily left the Gruppe without a leader, pending the arrival of Hptm Rudolf Sinner from Russia. Acting Gruppe Kommandeur at this time was Oblt Rudolf Patzak, Staffelkapitan of 8./JG 54, who was to go down in February. Sinner duly arrived from the East, but he too was destined not to remain operational for long.

Having instigated the Pointblank plan, the systematic destruction of the Luftwaffe fighter force and those sections of the aero industry that supported it, the 8th Air Force, which was to be the primary instrument of this phase of the air war, was forced to postpone the start of the all-out assault until early 1944. In the meantime, a new strategic bomber force had been created in Italy when the 15th AAF became part of the new United States Strategic Air Forces in Europe. Encompassing strategic 8th and tactical 9th Air Forces, this was a major command step towards the Allied plan to invade Europe in mid-year.

Meagre response to this mighty force in embryo was the Luftwaffe's 'Little Blitz' on targets in England. Beginning on the night of 21/22 January, bombers attacked London and various targets in the south-east. The scale of these raids, which lasted until April, paled into

insignificance alongside what the AAF was doing to Germany by day and RAF Bomber Command at night.

The 8th Air Force initiated a round of heavy attacks on 19 February 1944 following a period of winter bad weather that had restricted bomber operations. At that time, the Luftwaffe fighter force in the West comprised fifteen Gruppen of single-seat fighters, totalling approximately 750 aircraft, and seven flying about 180 twin-engined Zerstorers. Every pilot and crewman of these aircraft now had a huge responsibility, faced as they were by twenty-eight US heavy bomber groups when the first mission of 'Big Week' unfolded. By the end of that short period the number would rise to thirty groups.

On the 29th, the heavies were briefed to attack a dozen targets in Germany; employing sixteen combat wings of B-17s and B-24s, that force represented a total of 689 bombers and 835 fighters despatched from bases in England.

Ofw Emil Hecker in a Bf 109G marked as 'Yellow 12' of 7.Staffel at Ludgwigslust in February 1944.

The Bf 109 manufacturing complex at Erla near Leipzig was included on the target list and 7./JG 54 was among the fighter units that intercepted. The Staffel was then based at Ludwigslust in Schwerin, about halfway between Hamburg and Berlin.

Part of the intercepting force was led by Staffelkapitan Hptm Rudolf Klemm. At around 13.00, the German fighters made contact. The Bf 109s plunged through the fighter screen to get at the bombers, Klemm himself despatching one from the target formation of about sixty. In concert with Fw Gerhard Raimann, he made at least two firing passes before the bomber fell out of formation, by which time the US escort was hot on the tail of the Bf 109s.

Klemm yelled a warning to Raimann, but was then fully occupied with his pursuers. He last saw Raimann's machine in a vertical dive trailing smoke. It was lost to sight in cloud and Klemm sustained a slim hope that the young pilot had parachuted. It was not to be, and forty-five years later, the wreckage of Raimann's Bf 109G was unearthed at Duingen, a village some forty kilometres south of Hanover.

It was the American escort fighters which deprived III Gruppe of one of its most able Experten of 6 March. That day the USAAF mounted a massive raid on Berlin, an operation that resulted in many casualties on both sides — including eighty-one German aircraft claimed as destroyed in air combat. A flight of P-51s of the 357th Fighter Group, furnishing withdrawal support for the B-17s, went down to rampage their way across Germany, expending all their remaining ammunition on any worthwhile target that presented itself.

One of the American pilots, Lt John Carder, had previously carried out a strafing run across Wunsdorf airfield as part of a flight led by Maj Tom Haynes. Pulling off the target and climbing south of Bremen, Haynes spotted a lone Bf 109G. Lt John Howell, with Carder as his wingman, went down after it.

Opening fire from 300 yards out, Howell observed hits. He closed to 100 yards and the German fighter flipped over, still taking hits from the P-51's guns. The Americans saw the Messerschmitt pilot cut his throttle and pull up to about 2,000 feet altitude. The canopy opened and Oblt Gerhard Loos attempted to make a safe descent — but his assailants saw that as the parachute opened the harness broke apart. The 92-victory Experten of III./ JG 54 fell to his death near Rheinsehlen. While most of his victories had been achieved in the East, Loos had claimed fourteen since his Gruppe had been operating in the West.

Nor was Loos the only casualty suffered by the Grunherz that day; five other Bf 109Gs were destroyed and a further two were damaged. Rudolf Sinner's aircraft was hit by return fire from a straggling B-17 he was attacking. Forced to bail out, JG 54's Kommandeur was seriously wounded in the action. Less fortunate were Unteroffiziers H. Rosenburg, W. Straub and E. Louis, all of whom were shot down and killed, while Fw Fritz Ungar suffered a wound to one of his feet during combat with a P-47 of the 56th Fighter Group and was forced to put down in a field near Homfeld. Uffz E. Muller, who was also wounded, similarly force-landed, his Bf 109G coming down at Aumuehle. On 14 March Hptm Schroer became the new III Gruppe Kommandeur, Oblt Patzak's place at the head of 8.Staffel being taken by Ltn Zweigert.

Such carnage as that inflicted on the Grunherz on 6 March — and on other Jageschwadern which experienced even higher losses — was not at all untypical, with the German fighter losses exceeding the number of enemy bombers brought down. The spring 1944 air battles, with the resultant loss of Experten and novice alike, reached staggering proportions as the flower of the German fighter force was systematically decimated. In an effort to provide some tangible defence against the US daylight formations, the Luftwaffe high command had little choice but to implement further moves of Jagdgruppen from other theatres — but all of them were now urgently in need of more, not less fighters. By denuding one sector, the situation there quickly deteriorated, leading to yet more fire brigade bolstering and further losses among the ranks of pilots fresh from training schools. It set a pattern that was to last more or less for the duration of the conflict.

In May 1944, a special composite unit to combat the Allied bombers was formed as Jagdeschwader z.b.v. under Maj Walter Dahl. Converted to the Fw 190A-8 at Illesheim, III./

'Yellow 1' a Bf 109G-6 fully marked with the badge of 9.Staffel and the green heart decorated with Gruppe badges, also bears the blue Reichsverteidigung band allocated to aircraft of JG 54 as well as the III Gruppe vertical bar at Luneberg in the spring of 1944. (*Ungar*).

JG 54 was part of this new formation, as were four other fighter Gruppen. The unit undertook its first anti-bomber intercept on 23 May, and a second on the 27th.

Representing a considerable improvement over earlier versions of the Fw 190, the A-8 variant was the last of the A-series to be built in quantity. A reliable indication of the type of flying that now occupied the Jagdflieger was the fact that this machine, primarily intended for the destruction of heavy bombers, became more numerous than any other model, over 1,300 examples being produced.

Utilising the all-cannon armament of the Fw 190A-7, the A-8 had additional cockpit and engine armour protection and was powered by the BMW 801D engine fitted with MW50 methanol-water injection to boost output to 1,700 horsepower for take off. Force of circumstance began turning the fast and manoeuvrable Fw 190, once a thoroughbred amongst fighters, into a sluggish bludgeon, good only for the ever-more urgent task of bringing down bombers and providing a degree of self-protection for the pilot.

Always it was a case of 'get the bombers': everything became geared to that end. But the bombers were now better protected by their own guns and those of the swift and deadly Mustangs — no bomber force ever had so much firepower to ward off the desperate attacks of the defenders.

On 24 May, JG 54's Fw 190A-8s joined combat with one of the 8th Air Force's crack Mustang units, the 4th. The target for the B-17 element of the total 1,106 heavies sent out was Berlin, while Liberators went to Luftwaffe airfields in France. The 4th FG was part of a 280-strong P-51 force briefed to protect the bombers heading for the Reich capital. In addition, there were 178 P-47s and 144 P-38s flying escort.

At 10.25, III./JG 54's Fw 190s were part of a forty-plus attack formation flying between Hamburg and Lubeck. The Jagdflieger split their formation into two attack waves and were about to peel off to make their runs on the bomber boxes when the 335th Fighter Squadron plunged down on them from 36,000 feet.

Uffz Gunther Schonwaldt of 9.Staffel was unlucky that day. On his tail as he concentrated on the bombers was a P-51B flown by one of the 4th's aces, Ralph 'Kidd' Hofer. Schonwaldt threw his Focke, yellow 9, into a turn as Hofer's fire came dangerously close. The American pilot's object had been to distract the Fw

190 from the bombers and he now closed in. The Focke-Wulf began to smoke as Hofer found the range, and Schonwaldt broke away, slightly wounded. He jettisoned the canopy and jumped.

In the meantime Hofer and his wingman, Lt Thomas Fraser, went after more targets. Both pilots succeeded and two more Fw 190s went down. Back at Debden, they claimed ten for the loss of one of their own. Schonwaldt spent the night in the reserve hospital at Wittenberg before rejoining his unit.

JG 54 somehow continued to absorb the astronomical attrition rate, which could, short of a miracle, only get worse. Even a straightforward transfer from one airfield to a new base brought JG 54 disaster: taking off from Luneburg, a transport allocated to the technical staff crashed, killing twenty-five men. Virtually all of 7.Staffel's highly trained groundcrew were wiped out.

This was the crescendo: almost on a daily basis, the Jagdgeschwaderen lost the initiative. They found operations in the West almost totally defensive. They now faced massive Allied formations of medium and heavy bombers with their fighter escort, as well as devastating fighter bomber attacks by squadrons of Typhoons, Spitfires, Mosquitos, Thunderbolts and Lightnings. While individually the better Luftwaffe pilots could still emerge victorious over all these types if they enjoyed any tactical advantage, the situation was rapidly worsening, as the level of skill enjoyed by their Rottenflieger was slowly but surely decreasing.

Those terrible months were marked not only by losses in aerial combat, but widespread devastation on the ground; pilots returning home from the increasingly rare successful sortie (one on which they scored victories and suffered minimal losses to make the whole exercise worthwhile) could never be sure of finding their home base intact. Chances were high that even if the enemy Jabos had not left their calling cards, the airfield would have been thoroughly 'worked over' by the Mustangs, en route home to their bases in England after escorting the heavies over Germany.

When the Allied invasion of France was launched on 6 June, there was little the Luftwaffe could do to prevent the Normandy bridgehead being established. At the height of the landings, just two Bf 109s made a strafing run over the crowded beaches. But in the days immediately following the launching of Operation Overlord, a picture of Allied intentions began to emerge, allowing the Germans to make limited plans for counter-attacks with slim resources. Allied air superiority was terrible to behold; it meant that fighter units were poured into the invasion front more or less piecemeal to occupy those remaining French airfields and make what amounted to a token defence of German-occupied territory.

This dispersion to yet another fighting front — the one most dangerous to the German homeland — spelled the end of Walter Dahl's JG z.b.v. But even the limited success of this special unit pointed the way towards the probable logic in forming the so-called *Sturmgruppen*, the very existence of which hung on the number of bombers their pilots were able to bring down, even to the point of ramming themselves into a Fortress or Liberator in a final, invariably fatal gesture of defiance.

By no means all units were involved in such desperate measures and the 'regular' Jagdgeschwaderen carried on, albeit with some reduction in the number of component Staffeln, some of which had all but ceased to exist — there were other, more conventional ways to commit suicide than deliberately ramming enemy bombers. Daily operations brought more than enough visits from the Grim Reaper.

To partly make good recent losses, 2./JG 54 was withdrawn from the Eastern Front to be based at Chartres as part of III Gruppe. Initially commanded by Ltn Forbig, it was retitled 12.Staffel on 10 August, having moved location to Oldenburg. A Gruppe change of command also occurred at this time when Hptm Robert 'Bazi' Weiss became Kommandeur, Schroer being posted to instructor duties.

An energetic and well-liked leader, Weiss continued to lead the Western Front element of JG 54 as the Allied armies gained a foothold in Normandy. There was next to nothing the German pilots could do to even slow the advancing enemy ground forces, although Luftflotte 3 achieved what was possible with the meagre forces at its disposal. Based for a short period at Villacoublay, III./JG 54 carried out free hunt sorties over the invasion area, flew bomber interceptions interspersed with Jabo attacks on Allied forward and rear ground echelons and made a number of reconnaissance flights.

On a typical scramble from Villacoublay in answer to an urgent called from Primadonna — the codename for the central fighter control station for that sector of France, situated near the Eiffel Tower in Paris — 'Bazi' Weiss had barely got his fighters airborne when he saw the airfield's 2cm flak guns open up. Suddenly a dozen P-47 Thunderbolts were attacking Villacoublay. Naturally feeling that their own base now needed their protection, the Gruppe pilots reluctantly complied with ground control's order to climb to 16,000 feet to attack an incoming bomber formation.

Setting a course of 340 degrees, the 'Raven' aircraft (Callsign for III./JG 54) received the message, 'Strong four-engined units in flight to your garden fence. Now in square E-F-4. Verstanden?' Weiss acknowledged and grimly led some forty Fw 190s onto the new course. He was, to put it mildly, furious.

'Thanks Primadonna!', Weiss called. 'You have driven us into a damned wild boar wallow this time. But Rube Anton attacks. Out.'

The Paris controller was aghast. He radioed, 'Wait till other cyclists (friendly fighters) can come to help.'

Weiss refused. He knew that every second wasted orbiting would bring the American heavies closer. He snarled back,

'The enemy won't wait any longer. My last request to you is to shut up and play a good record. With hot music we can bank better!'

Trying his best to calm down, Weiss led his aircraft into the attack. The B-17 formation appeared to be escorted by Spitfires as high cover, while thirty P-51s bored in from the furthest side of the bomber formation to place themselves between the Luftwaffe fighters and their charges.

Weiss chose a rear-quarter attack, the 190s diving through the Fortress formation to wing-over and come back, head-on. This initial pass caused some of the American crews to jettison their bombs before the target had been reached.

Climbing hard to get out of the range of massed ·50 calibre machine gun fire, the Grünherz fighters went up straight into the glare of the sun. Above them, Thunderbolts waited. Someone yelled for a defensive circle, warning the others about the Indian ambush. Hptm Bully Lang took his 9.Staffel up to cut off the diving Thunderbolts.

The ensuing combat was one-sided. Seeking the safety of the French capital and its defensive guns, the surviving Fw 190s later returned home to find the airfield unscathed. But a quick count showed only fifteen Fw 190s available for the next operation.

Such evidence as reconnaissance flights brought back was sobering in the extreme; the Allies were pouring men and material into France and their air forces were providing a solid umbrella over the beachhead areas. Life now became a matter of basic survival against overwhelming odds.

Nevertheless, orders went out to attack the invasion shipping, now heavily congested at the mouth of the River Orne. There was almost a mutiny on one such occasion. The Jagdflieger heard the orders in disbelief. They were to attack with guns and bombs. At the briefing Bully Lang protested strongly.

'This is suicide. In a few days you can shut up shop and sing a funeral song for III./JG 54.'

Although knowing Lang was right, Robert Weiss had little choice but to stress the importance of trying to disrupt the Allied bridgehead. Orders were orders. Lang still protested.

'Our efforts will be only gnat bites. With our few crows we can't do much harm to them.' Resignedly, Lang led his pilots out. 'Come along boys, let's have another drink so we don't appear too sad when we meet St Peter.'

Lang's apprehension was not misplaced. When two hours later 15 Fw 190s with a Bf 109 escort swept out over the North Sea at 16,000 feet and executed a wide turn to come in on the mouth of the Orne from seaward to give just a small element of surprise, the Allied flak was appalling. Every gun in the invasion fleet seemed to be firing and casualties were predictably heavy.

Luftwaffe bases in Northern France became more untenable with every passing day. Ground attack sorties were cutting swaths through the remaining strength and in about three weeks,

The typically nomadic existence of a Luftwaffe Jagdgeschwader saw elements of JG 54 back on its old stamping ground in Holland in 1944. A fully kitted-up pilot is perched on top of the Fw 190's cowling while two colleagues use the wing for a seat. *(Petrick)*.

nearly 1,000 German aircraft were destroyed. For JG 54 it was time to withdraw and III Gruppe received orders to pull back to Germany. A short time was spent in Belgium beforehand.

Despite the odds, JG 54 had achieved another 100 victories while it was based in the West and was widely acknowledged as the most successful fighter unit during the initial invasion period. Even so, the cost had been high: in two weeks of operations over Normandy III Gruppe was whittled down from eighty pilots to around four or five per Staffel — twenty or so.

June 1944 was a month most Luftwaffe personnel in the West wished to put behind them as rapidly as possible, JG 54 perhaps more than most. Having previously suffered the loss of almost all 7.Staffel's ground specialists at Luneburg, the same unit was under the post-invasion bomb carpet being laid across all types of military target in France. On 25 June sixty-three B-24 Liberators poured 168 tons of bombs onto Villacoublay, decimating the repair shops and aircraft dispersal areas.

Faced now with a vast arena crawling with ground targets, the Jagdflieger was obliged to divide its efforts between attacking bombers and trying to make some inroads against the Allied advance through France. Hard-pressed Wehrmacht commanders in some sectors almost gave up hope of ever getting the air support they needed from the Luftwaffe, the rare appearance of which began to turn into a sick joke, not least amongst the frustrated and increasingly cynical pilots themselves. The harsh reality was that there were precious few units able to provide such support. The slaughter of the Bf 110 and Me 410 Zerstorer units in the previous months led to surviving crews being converted onto single-seater fighters — otherwise, the Jabo task was handed to the Jagdflieger.

With a dwindling number of aircraft available for each operational sortie, it was seen — far too late as it transpired — that the punch available to each fighter should be as lethal as possible. To supplement the heavy cannon

85

An Fw 190A-8 Fighter bomber of III./JG 54 pictured in 1944, a year in which advancing Allied ground armies presented a plethora of targets. Ground attack sorties were flown in the face of extremely heavy opposition.

already carried by the Fw 190 series, the 21cm Werfer-Granate 21 single-round rocket launcher was introduced as an interim anti-bomber weapon. With only two rounds per aircraft, these missiles were hardly as effective as the batteries of at least eight rocket projectiles carried by the Allied fighter-bombers, but they were quite widely used. III./JG 54 received examples of the Fw 190F-9 fitted with the rocket tubes in late July.

Tests showed that provided a group of fighters launched their rockets simultaneously, a good concentration could be achieved. The RLM conducted tests at Rechlin that showed that at 2,187 yards range, fifty per cent of the projectiles would hit within a ninety-seven foot diameter circle. If the attacking fighters bored in closer, to 1,859 yards, the rockets would still be well concentrated over a circle of roughly 144 feet diameter. With a little adaptation the standard Revi C 12d gunsight could be used for rocket attacks, although marginally better results were achieved by the improved Revi 16F sight.

Over a chaotic, constantly fluid front line, the Jagdflieger now had to contend with their own forces in headlong retreat. Their sacrifice in the weeks since the first Allied troops set foot on the beaches of Normandy had been terrible, and German troops, so used to seeing and hearing enemy fighters rather than their own, grew increasingly jumpy and opened fire on any pretext. More than a few members of the Jagdwaffe had cause to rue the fact that Panzer and motorised infantry units failed to recognise their Bf 109s or Fw 190s until it was too late. . .

Action in France was left behind by IV./JG 54 for a few weeks in July when it was ordered to the East, but so bad had the situation become for the Germans that this unit was soon to return to the defence of the homeland for the duration of hostilities.

For the defenders, the pace hardly slackened once the Allies had broken out of their beachheads at Normandy. On 3 August III./JG 54's pilots flew three separate operations, their targets being troops concentrated to the west of Caen, which the British advance had reached that day.

Trying desperately to support their own

Panzers by shooting up Allied Shermans, the Grunherz pilots used W.Gr 21 rockets for the first time that day. Their efforts did hamper the Allied push, which nevertheless succeeded in all but wiping out the SS Panzer Division *Hitler Jugend*. While making their attack runs, the Jagdflieger had always to keep a wary eye out for enemy fighters, particularly Spitfires, a type JG 54's pilots had developed a particular aversion to!

The same went for the P-47, which was reckoned to be a tough opponent, mainly on account of its superior diving speed. Pilot recollections do not, surprisingly enough, reflect over-much respect for the Mustang or Lightning, both of which the Germans reckoned their Fockes were equal to — unless they were met in substantial numbers. This was increasingly to be the case. . .

Whereas the Allied fighters and bombers had always had to contend with German flak over the continent, anticipating anti-aircraft fire from their own side was an extreme annoyance for the Luftwaffe. Fighter formation leaders carried coloured flares to fire if there was any danger from this quarter, but their reactions to the hazard were sometimes too late, particularly if the fighters were flying at very low level. This is exactly what happened on one of JG 54's 3 August sorties.

Willi Heilmann's 9.Staffel was making all speed from Caen when friendly ground fire chopped down one of their machines. Despite discharge of a red flare to stop the gunners putting up more murderous fire, the damage was done. Fortunately, the pilot of the stricken aircraft managed to break his onrush in the branches of trees before it dropped and skidded into a small copse. The limping pilot was back on the roster the following day.

After a few more weeks of blood-letting over France, III Gruppe was given a temporary respite from operations at Oldenburg, where it was placed under the command of Luftflotte Reich for home defence duties. Even though this seemed like jumping from the frying pan into the fire, the pace was definitely a little less hectic than trying to penetrate the solid Allied air umbrella over Normandy.

While based at Oldenburg JG 54 became, in late October, the first fighter Gruppe to receive examples of the Fw 190D-9, the potent *Langnase Dora*. While the unit was working up on the new type, it received a visit from Professor Kurt Tank, the Fw 190 designer.

Answering pilots' questions about this latest, much-improved 190, Tank showed much enthusiasm for his brainchild, but there were sceptics among his audience. When Tank told them that from his point of view, one of the keys to German success in the air, even at this late stage, was his as yet unrevealed Ta 152, he found himself the butt of some grim but honest aviator's humour. The pilots agreed that even more improvement to the faithful Focke would be welcome — always provided there was still time left for anyone to fly it in combat. Willi Heilmann, who was present at the briefing, was none too impressed. He had the distinct feeling that industrialists like Tank were seeing the world through rose-tinted glasses and in common with others who had been much favoured by contracts from the Reich's military budget, had indulged himself accordingly.

Nevertheless, a fly-off between two of the early Fw 190Ds appeared to show that the aircraft had much to offer — more speed, better altitude performance and heavy armament. In Heilmann's words, the old Focke-Wulf, nicknamed 'The Strangler' had undergone a bit of a change: 'The old pot-bellied gentleman had become a slender, pretty lady'.

New aircraft for the Jagdflieger could come none too soon: a further portent of how close the Allied armies had pushed towards the German border came on 25 September when Goering issued an order that forbade the Jagdflieger from undertaking anything but fighter-bomber sorties. This order, circulated at the height of the Allied Arnhem operation, remained in force only for a short time, as indeed it had to if the bomber fleets were not to fly over Germany unmolested. The luxury of deploying Gruppen on specialist tasks had gone — the same units were attempting to carry out a range of different duties, a fact which tended to dilute the effectiveness of any given type of operation, most of which brought further pilot deaths or injuries. Specialist Jabo Staffeln were, however, maintained as long as possible.

More Staffel renumbering had changed the

composition of JG 54 and by September Kommandeur Robert Weiss had four Staffeln in III Gruppe under his command — 9./JG 54 led by Oblt Willi Heilmann; 10.Staffel by Ltn Prager, 11.Staffel by Ltn Crump (who was succeeded by Hptm Hans Bottlander) and 12.Staffel, which was commanded by Ltn Hans Dortenmann.

It was also at this point of the war that the Grünherz pilots were in for another nasty surprise — if they had been more than unnerved at the 'bulldog tenacity' of the pilots flying Spitfires, they were about to be faced with something a good deal worse — Tempests. On 28 September 2nd Allied Tactical Air Force had finally released the first Tempest units for duty on the continent and Nos 3 and 56 Squadrons flew to Grimbergen, near Brussels. It would not be long before the British fighters would clash with JG 54 — with fatal results for both sides.

First blood went to Willi Heilmann, who claimed the distinction of shooting down the first Tempest lost in aerial combat, on 7 October. Heilmann's victim was almost certainly F/O Mears of No. 272 Sqn, a unit making its first sorties with the new Hawker type from Volkel that day.

Tempests became lethal antagonists for the Jagdflieger, as the RAF pilots needed to give nothing away in terms of performance and gun power to the Fw 190D. The high-performance British machines were particularly effective against Me 262 jet fighters, which JG 54 and other Jagdgeschwaderen flying high performance conventional fighters were increasingly tasked to protect.

By the autumn of 1944, the Messerschmitt Me 262, the first practical application of the new 'wonder weapons' nearly everyone in the Luftwaffe had heard about, was very much a reality. Mass production of the aircraft as the fighter it had been designed to be finally got underway after the invasion. A letter from Goering's office received limited circulation on 2 July. It stared that Hitler had on 30 June,

A helping hand with a recalcitrant flying boot offered by a ground crewman to Oblt Bernhard Schulten, who is believed to have succeeded Heindl as Adjutant of II Gruppe. Note the distress flares worn around the top of the boot. *(Petrick)*.

Mechanics pose for their photograph around a Bf 109, believed to have been one of those flown by Hannes Trautloft. *(E. J. Creek)*.

ordered an 'absolute top priority' concentration on fighters to protect the homeland.

Included in the letter were some figures: the inventory of fighters was to be increased to 10,000 and was to include 500 Me 262s, 3,300 conventional fighters, 400 destroyers and 500 night fighters. Despite the need for fighters, Hitler, doubtless inspired by the generally positive results of Jabo operations across the Channel, still clung to the notion that the Me 262 could be useful as a fast bomber. Production of the Messerschmitt jet was to be raised to 500 per month for the remainder of 1944, and thereafter to increase to 1,000 per month. 'At least half of these', the letter stated, 'are to be the fighter version.'

Notwithstanding the extreme optimism behind these and other edicts from the highest authority in the Third Reich, little could be done to improve the flow of pilots to the front line units. Giving the finest fighters in the world to poorly trained youngsters would not alleviate Germany's situation. The plain fact was that the flak units, not the fighter arm, now constituted the greatest hazard to Allied aircraft.

Flak batteries continued to put up deadly barrages over most of the important targets, particularly airfields, and it was the ground gunners who succeeded in bringing down the majority of the top US fighter aces who crashed on the continent, rather than fighter pilots. In the majority of cases, these men were not killed or even badly wounded, 'flyers' luck' staying with them to a remarkable degree.

Casualties to flak were also high in RAF and Allied squadrons, but again many individuals survived to spend a brief period in a PoW cage. This tended to prove that a pilot stood a much better chance of surviving even a crippling hit on his aircraft by groundfire than he did under fighter attack.

This was in marked contrast to the decimation of the Jagdverbande, so many members of which were unable to beat the odds. Such was Germany's current predicament that normal rest periods for exhausted pilots were a thing of the past; Experten and novice alike succumbed to the continual pressure.

Despite the speed with which Germany was crumbling towards the unconditional surrender demanded by the Allied powers, the air commanders knew there was little room for complacency. There would be a few more demonstrations of German prowess before the Third Reich was finally laid to rest.

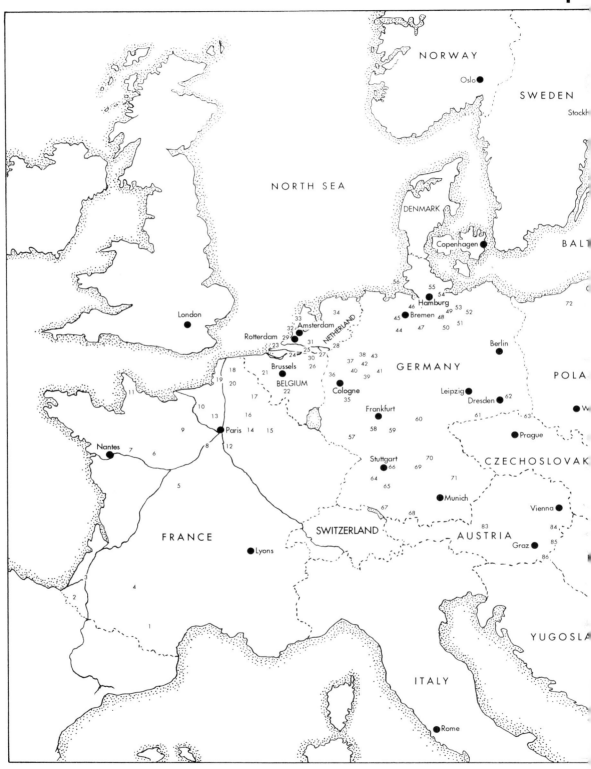

ions Map

With ears muffled against the freezing air, the black men ensure that another I Gruppe Fw 190A has enough electrical power before attempting to start the engine. *(Bundesarchiv).*

Chapter 6

THE LONG RETREAT

Surrounded at Stalingrad, the German Sixth Army was fighting for its very life. As the bloodshed intensified, both Stalin and Hitler increasingly saw the city as a symbol, respectively of victory or defeat. Consequently the Wehrmacht operation to take the city had met unbelievably stiff Russian resistance and as the casualties mounted in the rubble of the once-bustling industrial conurbation on the Volga, an unprecedented disaster was in the making.

Once more the Russian winter seemed to the Germans to side with their enemy, who asked and gave no quarter. Soon 100,000 Wehrmacht troops were trapped at Stalingrad, with little real hope of being relieved by German ground forces strong enough to defeat the enemy in that sector of the front. Near starvation and rapidly exhausting their stocks of ammunition, fuel, food and supplies of all kinds, the men of the Sixth Army were given slim hope by Goering's assurance that air supply could save them.

The Luftwaffe consequently gathered its far from adequate transport force, now critically over-stretched, for a life or death airlift. Only by flying in the vital supplies they needed could the army commanded by General Friedrich Paulus fight on. The Red Air Force and Army vowed that the rescue would not succeed.

The Jagdwaffe similarly shouldered the task of shielding the slow transports from interception and annihilation. Assi Hahn claimed his 100th kill on 26 January, the same day that Max Stotz, depleting Russian airpower at a fantastic rate, notched up his 150th victory, despite the appalling weather.

Throughout its time in the East JG 54 welcomed new pilots who came either from other units, were fresh from training or, in rarer instances, had transferred from other branches of the German armed forces. In January 1943 Hugo Broch arrived to lead II Gruppe. Scoring his first victory in March, Broch proved to be an excellent pilot and often

flew as wingman to Horst Adameit and Bazi Sterr.

Winter brought another spell of harsh conditions that taxed Luftwaffe ground crews to the limit. In ice, snow, freezing rain and low visibility, the fighters of JG 54 were required to fly from first to last light, responding to the need for air support all along the multiple sectors of the front. When the fighters landed they were hurriedly serviced, refuelled and rearmed, ready for the next sortie. Battle damage repairs had to wait until stand-down and by working around the clock, the black men somehow contrived to have the maximum number of fighters on the line for operations the following day.

Despite everything the Luftwaffe could do, just short of sacrificing every transport aircraft it had, not only in the East, but elsewhere, the Russian ring closed around the remnants of the Sixth Army. With hardly anything to fight with and wishing to prevent further battlefield casualties, Paulus, promoted to Feldmarschall by Hitler just before the end on the pretext that no soldier of that rank had ever surrendered, did just that on 31 January. It was an unprecedented disaster for the Germans and an enormous morale booster to the Russians.

After Stalingrad there were signs of a general German withdrawal from forward positions all along the Eastern front. From then on, the name of the second Soviet city would be synonymous with defeat — indeed it was later recognised as one of the true turning points of the war and marked the passing of the initiative from the Axis to the Allied powers. Inspired by this incredible victory over the seemingly invincible invaders, the Red Army flexed its muscles to push the Germans out of the Caucasus region.

For JG 54 and other fighter units, the period was one of sporadic skirmishes with Russian fighters and tactical support aircraft, numerous sorties of a ground support nature and a

Once modifications had been carried out, both in the field and by the manufacturers, the 'Butcher Bird' was to more than prove its worth against the technically improved Red Air Force. This new I Gruppe Fw 190A builds up oil pressure prior to taxying out at Siverskajya. *(Bundesarchiv).*

continuation of long and short range attacks on Russian lines of communication and transport over the centre and southern sectors of the front, the Ukraine and Crimea regions, and Finland.

JG 54 began using the Fw 190 to some effect, although the Bf 109 was still plentiful — it was fortunate indeed for the Luftwaffe that the Messerschmitt factories were still able to produce the aircraft in vast quantities, for although the once primary fighter in the West had not really been modernised sufficiently to meet ever more rigorous operational demands, numerous improvements had been made and it was always on hand.

More changes to the structure of the Geschwader were made in January. Hannes Trautloft was designated *Jagdflieger Inspektor Ost*, a more than fitting honour for the man who had led the Grünherz for nearly three years and was largely responsible for welding it into the

fine fighting unit it had become. Following in Trautloft's footsteps could have been a daunting prospect for anyone, but Hubertus von Bonin shouldered the duties of Kommodore with alacrity. The responsibilities of command held no surprises for him as he had previously led I and II Gruppen.

It was a challenging period for the Luftwaffe on the Eastern Front, as the Germans began to realise just how vulnerable their long supply lines had become in the face of Russian counter-attacks. No more proof of this was needed than the events in and around Stalingrad.

Ltn Wlater Beims of 3.Staffel had the unfortunate distinction of being one of the first JG 54 pilots to lose his life while flying the Fw 190 when his A-4 crashed at Heiligenbeil on 28 December 1942. The Geschwader was to lose another pilot in January 1943, Uffz Helmut Brandt of 2.Staffel becoming a PoW when his

Fw 190A of 1.Staffel piloted by Fw Karl Schnorrer over the Leningrad sector early in 1943. *(Crow).*

Fw 190A-4 was destroyed in an emergency landing SE of Schlösselbug.

By February 1943, JG 54 had flown 21,453 war sorties and on the 19th of that month had achieved its 4,000th aerial victory. Two days later Assi Hahn was lost. An Experten with 108 victories, Hahn became a prisoner. He fortunately survived his incarceration but was not to be released from Russian captivity until 1950.

The ebb and flow of air fighting reached a more positive high point on two days in February when the Grünherz were heavily involved. On the 23rd, I and III Gruppen claimed forty-six kills, following this with forty-three more the very next day.

It was understandable that some pilots preferred the Focke-Wulf 190 to the Messerschmitt Bf 109, but JG 54 was still not receiving sufficient quantities of 'Wurgers'. March began on a low note when Hans Beisswanger, Staffel-kapitan of 6./JG 54, was shot down and killed in combat with ten Russian fighters on the sixth. 'Beisser' was apparently bounced by the enemy fighters and although he managed to shoot down two of them, his aircraft sustained engine damage and he was forced down, his propeller slowly windmilling, near Lake Ilmen.

Spring 1943 brought future Ritterkreuztrager Gunther Scheel in to join 3.Staffel and Eugen-Ludwig Zweigert transferred from 5.Staffel, with which he had served since 1941, to III Gruppe. On 2 May Ulrich 'Pipifax' Wernitz scored the first of his 101 victories on only his second sortie.

Grünherz pilots were by now increasingly operating with other units on other fronts, where the risk of their being killed or incapaci-tated in aerial combat was reckoned to be marginally greater than if they had stayed in the East. One such was Gunther Fink, an instructor who had achieved notable success flying with 8.Staffel when he transferred to operations from the E-Staffel in 1941, including the destruction of nine enemy aircraft over Leningrad at night, was posted as missing presumed lost while attacking American heavies off Heligoland on 5 May.

Summer 1943

Kursk

As the spring months ushered in better weather all along the Eastern front, the German forces planned a new offensive that would, it was predicted, consolidate the front line positions previously taken and enable the offensive to be resumed. A 100-mile wide Russian salient around the city of Kursk, lying between Orel in the north and Belgorod in the south, was to be subjected to a two-pronged thrust aimed at encircling the enemy, just as had been done with such outstanding success earlier in the campaign.

Armoured spearheads, boosted by ample supplies of new and improved Panther and Tiger tanks, were to advance from the south and north, to 'pinch off' Karkov and annihilate the defending Red armies trapped in one gigantic pocket and thereby straighten the German front line. Operation *Zitadel* was about to commence. Hitler personally orches-trated the battle, impatiently waiting until he had assembled the necessary force to prove decisive. When the battle started, he had fifty army and Waffen SS units, over 2,000 tanks and about 1,500 aircraft in range of Kursk to ensure that Wehrmacht operations were not unduly hampered by the Red Air Force.

The Russians were, however, well aware of German preparations and launched an air strike of their own on 5 July, aimed principally at reducing the weight of airpower ranged against them. This attack sparked off one of the largest air battles of the war, although JG 54's part in 'Zitadel' was relatively small, only I Gruppe being withdrawn from the north to participate in an operation that was supported by a total of eight Jagdgruppen.

With better weather, servicing could again be carried out in the open. The large tent behind these dispersed III Gruppe Bf 109Fs is in fact two canvas awnings attached to a mobile workshop. *(Creek).*

Fighter units other than JG 54 therefore took the lion's share of the victories in the aerial side of the Kursk battle, although Walter Nowotny's increasing tally of kills had exceeded 100 during June 1943. His 100th victim had gone down on the 15th and on the 24th the German Experte had made ten claims for the day. Overall, Nowotny claimed forty-one victories for the month. Hogo Broch also scored his first victories out of an eventual eighty-one during the month.

On the day following the big Russian attack on Luftwaffe airfields — which did not find many German fighters waiting helplessly on the ground as these had been withdrawn in time — Hptm Reinhard Seiler scored his 100th victory. He was however, badly wounded in the resulting combat. Withdrawn from front line flying to recuperate, Seiler would not return to JG 54 but would fly again, as the Kommodore of JG 104, in 1944.

Despite ongoing individual air combat successes for the Jagdflieger, the picture on the ground was far less encouraging: the massive clash of the opposing armies at Kursk resulted in the largest tank battles of the war, any losses from which the Germans would be hard put to replace. By using natural features to prepare a massive defence in depth with minefields, thousands of artillery pieces and Katyusha rocket launchers, the Red Army held. Estimates of Russian front line strength at Kursk was put at seventy-five divisions, 3,500 tanks and 3,000 aircraft.

Making slow progress against this wall of steel, Hermann Hoth's Fourth Panzer Army and Walther Model's Ninth Army were forced to withdraw, losing in the process a combined total of about 1,000 tanks and more than 100,000 troops. The largest tank battle took place on 12 July, when 600 of Hoth's Tigers and Panthers slogged it out track to track with 850 T-34s and KV-1s of the Fifth Guards Tank Army near Prokhorovka.

In eight hours of fighting, often over point blank ranges, both sides lost about 300 tanks.

The Wehrmacht could ill afford to lose anywhere near that number, whereas the Russians, after a brief withdrawal from the scene of battle, would return to the offensive not only with all losses made good, but with fresh crews at the controls of their ubiquitous T-34s.

While the infantry and tank crews hardly had any cause to celebrate at Kursk, Luftwaffe fighter pilots' success in the air continued to be one of the brighter military achievements on an increasingly dangerous front. Just how dangerous was demonstrated on 16 July when Gunther Scheel of 3.Staffel went down to crash fatally near Orel, then behind the Russian lines. In combat with Yak-9s, Ltn Scheel rammed one of his antagonists and the Fw 190 plunged 700 feet to earth and burned on impact.

There was a happier conclusion to the fighter sorties made by the Grünherz on the 17th.

Congratulations were definitely in order when Fw Helmut Missner of I Gruppe found that he had scored the Grunherz' 5,000th victory of the war.

Hitler abandoned the Kursk offensive on 25 July, reeling not only from the losses there, but from the deposition of Mussolini and the Allied landings in North Africa. The Luftwaffe too licked its wounds, having thrown into the Kursk battle a large proportion of its strength in the East and sacrificed around 1,000 aircraft.

The fighters' task had included preventing Russian interceptors from hacking down the most deadly German ground attack aircraft, particularly Ju 87s fitted with twin 37mm cannon. Slow but effective anti-tank weapons, these machines were responsible for many Russian losses — when they could force a way through to their targets. However, the Jagd-

Pre-take-off checks are made to Fw 190A 'White 2' on a Finnish airfield as the slow Ju 87s the fighters are to escort form up to head for their target. A small force, Battle Group Kuhlmey nevertheless gave a good account of itself. *(Stenman)*.

flieger had difficulty in protecting the slow and cumbersome converted dive bombers.

After Kursk, the Eastern front became an increasing nightmare for the Wehrmacht as the Soviets countered nearly every move the Germans made with offensives of their own, feeding seemingly limitless supplies of manpower and equipment into the 'meat grinder' that the Eastern Front had become. On the ground and in the air, Russian equipment steadily improved, as did the tactics employed.

The summer of 1943 was also to see further combat reversals for the Grünherz; I Gruppe lost no less than three Kommandeuren in succession between 6 July and 4 August: Seiler's replacement was Major Gerard Homuth who had most recently occupied a staff job in Bulgaria following service with JG 27. Only three days after taking command, he went missing near Orel on only his second sortie as Gruppenkommandeur on 3 August. Oblt Hanz Gotz, (eighty-two victories) Staffelkapitan of 2./JG 54 stepped into the breach — but he too was lost on operations the following day. Going into the attack on a formation of Il-2s near Karatchev. Gotz' aircraft was last seen going down to crash inverted into woods.

Walter Nowotny was named as the new I Gruppenkommandeur but in the meantime, the 'orphaned' Gruppe was led by Oblt Vincent. To fill Nowotny's place at the head of 1.Staffel, there was to be a succession of four pilots — Ltns Helmut Wettstein, Heinz Wernicke and Fritz Tegtmeier and finally, Hptm Erdmann.

II Gruppe's Kommandeur, Hptm Heinrich Jung, who had taken over when Assi Hahn went down, also failed to return from a sortie on 30 July. Having scored eighteen victories by May 1942, Jung had sixty-eight to his credit by the time he went down in a final combat with Russian fighters, near Mga. Ltn Adameit took over III Gruppe. This run of casualties continued when on 19 August, the enthusiastic Max Stotz, whose score had risen to 189, was forced to bail out behind enemy lines near Witebsk after his engine was damaged in combat with a Russian fighter. He was never seen again.

Stotz' place at the head of 5.Staffel was initially taken by Ltn Wohnert and, perhaps to prove that luck had not completely abandoned the unit, Ltn Hermann Schleinhege who succeeded him, remained at the head of the Staffel until the war's end and scored a total of ninety-six victories.

The supply of Fw 190s to JG 54 continued to fluctuate and the Geschwader was obliged to

In order to add weight of fire to the light built-in armament of the early Bf 109Gs, cannon were installed in detachable gondolas under each wing as operational requirements dictated. 'White 7' in the background has the extra guns while 'White 10' nearest the camera, is a standard Bf 109G. Both aircraft bear the markings of 7.Staffel. *(Bundesarchiv)*.

continue operations with the Bf 109G, which was being increasingly outclassed by Russian fighters. Not only were these numerically on the increase over the battlefields; more significantly, Red Air Force pilot skill had appreciably improved in comparison with their showing in the early days — but it was the sheer numbers that the enemy was able to put up, in all kinds of weather, that inexorably wore down the Germans.

In July, Erich Rudorffer had been handed the task of forming a fourth Gruppe of JG 54 near Konigsberg, and when he was recalled to the East to take over II Gruppe, Hptm Rudolf Sinner assumed command of the Bf 109G-equipped IV./JG 54 in the West, until Rudorffer returned early in August. When this change had been implemented, all the Fw 190s on strength were concentrated in I and II Gruppen, plus the GeschwaderStab.

The situation on the Eastern Front during July 1943 saw the rapid transfer of IV Gruppe to the Northern sector, where the pilots mounted free hunt and bomber escort sorties, withdrawing from Siverskaja to Idriza, Dno, Pleskau and Dorpat in the face of a massive Russian summer offensive. The Gruppe's 12.Staffel flew fighter bomber sorties using external bombs as well as their fixed armament for ground attack work, the Grünherz having received examples of the Fw 190 adapated for Jabo operations.

Despite their increasingly difficult position, the Luftwaffe fighter pilots maintained the pressure on the Russians in the air whenever and wherever possible. Superior numbers did not automatically see the Red Air Force sweeping the hard-bitten Jagdflieger from the skies — the reverse was often the case — if the Germans were no longer the spectre of military defeat they had been to the Russians in 1941, many an enemy commander had cause to rue the day his unit ran into the crack Luftwaffe fighter force. August 1943 was a particularly sobering month for the Russians, for they lost ninety-eight aircraft — to two German pilots!

These titans were Nowotny and Eric Hartmann of JG 52, who racked up forty-nine kills each during the month. Nowotny scored nine on the 13th and shot down seven on the 20th — the day after Hartmann was himself shot down

That the Fw 190 soon became an effective weapon in the hands of those Experten who flew it in the East is demonstrated by this view of the traditional scoreboard painted to mark the 300th kill for 1.Staffel by Walter Nowotny in November 1942. Nowotny is perched above the laurel wreath and scoreboard. *(Petrick).*

and captured. 'Bubi' Hartmann, who was eventually to eclipse all other Jagdflieger in terms of aerial kills, was in Russian hands for just four hours.

That there were targets aplenty for an able fighter pilot flying on the German side was demonstrated by Nowotny on 1 September, when he despatched seven enemy aircraft in the space of seventeen minutes during a morning sortie. Building on this feat, he got another three in the afternoon, taking just nine minutes!

By 4 September, Nowotny had scored his 200th kill, his total for the month reaching forty-five.

September saw the momentum of the Russian advance perceptibly pushing the Germans back. On the twenty-second Poltava, subsequently to figure in the USAAF shuttle bombing programme — with disastrous consequences — was back in Russian hands. Lying seventy miles west of Kharkov, Poltava's change of occupancy came three days before the Red Army liberated Smolensk.

With the Germans back on the Dnieper line, there were hopes that some sort of stand could be made, but enemy pressure ruled this out. Almost without pause, Russian forces crossed the tactically important river to the north of Kiev. About the only bright spot in the enforced retreat for the Germans was that their supply lines from the Reich were considerably shortened. . .

Russian success on the ground was well supported by airpower, and the Luftwaffe fighter force had a large number of relatively easy targets on some sorties. On others, the tables were turned, and it was the Germans who suffered casualties, particularly if one of the growing list of Red Air Force aces happened to

be chanced upon. Yet the Germans often found that while the Russians had some outstanding pilots, the rank and file still clung to outmoded tactics. It was relatively easy to spot the difference and many of the novices were not given the chance to improve.

No two days were exactly the same; Walter Nowotny had a comparatively quiet period of operational flying until 5 October when his personal scoring rate resumed its meteoric progress and thirty-two Russian aircraft were downed in ten days. Eight fell on 9 October, one of the unfortunate Russian flyers becoming the Geschwader's 6,000th kill. The tenth brought the sad news that Hans Philipp, then Kommodore of JG 1, had been lost.

The 14th of the month saw Nowotny's 250th victory and he thus became the first Luftwaffe pilot to achieve this feat. He was to add five more before his last kill on the Eastern Front on 15 November. Another quiet period then set in and Nowotny was notified that he would soon be posted back to Germany to undertake important training duties.

Other pilots, doubtless spurred on by the example of men like Nowotny, and JG 52's Gerd Barkhorn and Gunther Rall, added to JG

The aircraft flown regularly by Erich Rudorffer. He came to JG 54 from JG 2 and was one of the outstanding Experten of the war, finishing with 222 kills, winning the Knight's Cross with Oak Leaves and Swords in the process. With the II Gruppe symbol aft of the Balkenkrauz, Rudorffer's rank of Gruppenkommandeur is shown by the chevrons which encompass a small 'Black 1'. *(Stenman).*

While less well-equipped Russian airfields became white wastlelands seemingly in the middle of nowhere when it snowed heavily, the prewar bases occupied by the Luftwaffe at least boasted permanent hangars and admin blocks. Siwerskaja was among them and this scene showing the groundcrew running up the engine of Bf 109G 'Red 12' of I Gruppe appears quite homely. *(Bundesarchiv)*.

54's reputation for shooting down Russian aircraft and brought forth grudging acknowledgement from the Russians that the Grünherz Geschwader had one of the most dangerous groups of young men on the entire Eastern Front. October's successes included the 123rd kill scored by Ofw Otto Kittel since 1941, followed by the confirmation of his *Ritterkreuz* on the 29th.

On the 21st Ltn Emil 'Bully' Lang claimed twelve victories in a single day. It was the start of a three-week run of good fortune that was to net him no less than seventy-two victories, including a phenomenal eighteen in one day. That figure was to stand as a record achieved by a single pilot. By November, Lang's score had risen to 120. Also notching up an exceptional record for lightning fast victories was Erich Rudorffer, who claimed thirteen kills in seventeen minutes on 6 November.

This incredible run of good fortune was not without its grim side and the price included Anton Dobele, who was killed on 11 November, and 'Quax' Schnorrer, wounded on the following day. On the 15th of the following month, one of JG 54's popular old hands, Hubertus von Bonin, was also to succumb to the pace of the fighting. He was killed in combat near

Vitesbk with his score standing at seventy-seven. Oberst Anton Mader, having returned from Reich defence duty, became the new Kommodore of the Grünherz with his personal score then at eighty-six.

Among the men wounded in action during this period was Franz Eisenanch, Staffelkapitan of 3./JG 54, but he would return to the Grünherz in about three months' time. Casualties among the unit's former personnel did not always take place over the fighting fronts, and on the 30th the duty of test pilot of the highly-dangerous Me 163 claimed the life of Josef Pohs when the machine he was flying blew up.

On the ground, the Germans were finding it difficult to replace the terrible losses of the Russian campaign with sufficient trained men. During late 1943, Feldmarschall von Manstein had to accept a shortfall of 100,000 troops even though 33,000 replacements had been sent to the East. Already the Wehrmacht had been forced to give up Dnepropetrovsk, the first town of any size lying west of the Dnieper and, as the winter began to force its by-now familiar slowdown in the pace of the fighting, German occupied territory remained only in the Crimea and south of Kiev.

In the North, Leningrad still held out against

101

the German land, sea and air blockade, but there were signs that the suffering of the city's remaining inhabitants would not last much longer. As the winter closed in to restrict operations on the German side, the Russians prepared for another offensive.

By the closing months of 1943, JG 54's Eastern Front elements had been able to standardise on the Fw 190, as had JG 51, only JG 52 and JG 54 remaining with the Bf 109G. At that time the Grünherz could muster seventy-two aircraft, split between elements of three Gruppen plus the Stab.

In view of the German position, losses of Experten in aerial combat on the Eastern Front were remarkably light — only six of the top pilots were killed between November and June 1944. Small numbers did not however, diminish the degree of loss for JG 54, for half of these men represented a trio of the unit's most able leaders.

Such losses went deep and inevitably had an adverse effect on morale, if only for a short period — there was little time to dwell on the statistical likelihood of survival; whether a man still had good luck or if that intangible asset had abandoned him, or if his combat prowess had lost any edge. In such an atmosphere, any evidence that made the men at the front feel that they had not been forgotten by the people at home, was desirable. Accordingly, Luftwaffe units were 'adopted' by organisations in Germany so that military personnel could write to them and receive news.

Despite the fact that if the individuals concerned lived in one of the big cities, news of the bombing and shortages made increasingly sobering reading, these links were very welcome. In JG 54's case the men of the Geschwader exchanged letters with the employees of the Mercedes office machine concern in Zella Mehlis. When home leave was possible for the pilots, they would keep in touch by visiting company staff. Such moves helped morale to remain high in a war theatre that increasingly did little to inspire confidence in a German victory.

Nowotny bows out

Early in 1944, I./JG 54 which had been switched to the central sector of the Eastern Front under Luftflotte 6, and II Gruppe, then part of Luftflotte 4 in the Southern sector, were both returned to Luftflotte 1 control. Thus the Grünherz were back more or less in their old stamping ground of the North. The Geschwader was therefore able to witness the end of the siege of Leningrad after 890 days. It resulted, not in German occupation, but relief by the Russians, who concurrently opened a massive offensive which would not be stopped. As well as lifting the siege (on 19 January) the Red Army swept onwards to take Novgorod to the south of Leningrad. Army Group North was ordered to fall back to defensive positions in Estonia.

On 4 February Nowotny received specific orders to return to Germany to form the first fully operational Me 262 jet fighter unit. He was succeeded in turn by Hptm Adameit, who was destined to be reported missing on 8 August. When the Gruppenkommandeur's mantle passed to Hptm Franz Eisenach, he was to remain in command until the end of hostilities. His 100th victim was to fall on 14 September.

Next to go down was Hptm Siegfried Schnell, who had received notification of posting to lead IV Gruppe. An Experten with ninety-three victories to his credit, Wurm Schnell was a fine pilot and it was a sad day when he was shot down by Russian fighters on 25 February.

Having filled Adameit's position as Staffelkapitan of 6./JG 54 Ltn Albin Wolf scored the Geschwader's 7000th victory on 23 March. That was Wolf's 135th personal victory, but his subsequent career was to be short-lived; he fell over Pleskau on 2 April with his score at 144, his aircraft taking a direct hit from anti-aircraft fire. It was in March that Anton Dobele's posthumous Ritterkreuz was announced, to be followed in April by the award, under happier circumstances, of the *Einchlaub* to both Rudorffer (on the 11th for 113 kills) and Kittel on the 14th, for 152.

Ltn 'Bazi' Sterr took over 6.Staffel for the time being until he was succeeded by Oblt Helmut Wettstein, who once again was to remain in action as Staffelkapitan until the end. Eisenach's 3.Staffel was taken over in succession by three more pilots — Ltn Fritz Tegtmeier (in August), Ltn Wernitz and Oblt Eberwein.

Of these latter Jagdflieger. Tegtmeier had scored a total of 146 victories in the East and, like numerous other pilots, had an impressive list of operational sorties in his logbook — in this case nearly 700. Subsequently to fly with JG 7, Tegtmeier was apparently nominated for the Oak Leaves, but the award was never made. Ulrich Wernitz had the distinction of destroying his first enemy aircraft on his second operational sortie, on 2 May 1943. He was Otto Kittel's wingman for a period before an illness took him off combat flying. He became Staffelkapitan of 3./JG 54 early in February 1945, a few weeks before he was able to celebrate his 100th kill in late March.

Finland

In the meantime, the Luftwaffe's 'holding war' in Finland continued to occupy elements of JG 54 which assisted the relatively modest forces of Luftflotte 5 to contain Russian ground forces, pound the port of Murmansk to disrupt the unloading of Allied war material, and to mount attacks on shipping on Lake Ladoga and in the Baltic. The main bomber striking force loaned by Luftflotte 1 were the Heinkel He 111s of KG 53, the torpedo-carrying Heinkels of KG 26 having been transferred to the Mediterranean by November 1942.

JG 54's fighters flew escort to the bombers, which attacked rail connections at Tihvina and Bologoje, and harassed Leningrad's still tenuous supply lines. The Grünherz were also very active in covering Stukas tasked with blockading Lake Ladoga, and in carrying out their own Jabo sorties. These were interspersed with routine fighter patrols to prevent Russian bombers depleting German strength in the area.

That additional aircraft were needed in the Far North was evinced by the fact that after the Russians had identified the main German targets in the area, the Northern Air Army had been split into two task forces. Thus by late August 1941, separate air forces for combat on the Karelian and Leningrad Fronts had been established, with a total of some 800 aircraft, including a fighter corps with 270 aircraft.

German reconnaissance noted no less than ninety-four airfields with a total of 1,300

A Bf 109G-2 of III Gruppe in Finland. 'White 1' is highly decorated with the badges of 7.Staffel and III Gruppe and the green heart, the white bars on the rudder denoting twenty kills. *(Stenman)*.

aircraft (drawn from about ninety air regiments) in the area by May 1942. Around Leningrad there were seventeen airfields with 173 aircraft; twenty-six south of Lake Ladoga on the Tihvin and Volkhov Fronts (244 aircraft) and East of Lake Ilmen, a further 606 aircraft had the use of thirty-one airfields.

The majority of these Russian bases remained open either because they were situated beyond the range of available Luftwaffe bombers, or because those attacks that were carried out were far too light due to the low numbers of aircraft deployed. The strength of the opposition, plus low serviceability of the German bomber force, accordingly reduced effectiveness and when the Russians initiated an offensive across the River Neva to strike south of Lake Ladoga and establish a bridgehead at Marino, the Luftwaffe was hard put to prevent it.

Retaliatory attacks were nevertheless carried out; JG 54 pilots had their hands full with the mounting number of Shturmoviks which swept in at low level to pound German positions, their heavy armour making them all but immune to anti-aircraft fire. They were generally tough targets to shoot down in air combat but on January 14 1943 JG 54, widely known in Finland as the 'Philipp unit' destroyed fourteen Il-2s.

The combined force of JG 54 aircraft, drawn from all three Gruppen based in the Soviet Union, was placed under the jurisdiction of one of a number of temporary operational commands, *Gefechtsverband Kuhlmey*. For several weeks the Gruppe flew sorties in defence of the Karelian zone, which encompassed airfields at Helsinki, Petajarvi and Immola. The German pilots scored a number of victories during interception sorties against

Oblt Fritz Gotz of I Gruppe JG 54 chatting with the top Finnish fighter ace, Capt Eino Lunkkanen. Despite sharing a common enemy, the northern allies rarely flew together. *(Stenman)*.

Soviet bomber formations, flying alongside their Finnish allies.

The latter had by then received quantities of the Bf 109G to partially replace some of the motley collection of fighters, both modern and obsolete, that the Finnish Air Force had flown with admirable skill and courage since the Winter War. Numerous pilots rated the German fighter the best they had flown, particularly with regard to the destructive power of its cannon armament. The Luftwaffe on the other hand, received far less potent aircraft. Early in the year, about 100 training aircraft were delivered, these to be used by Luftflotte 1 as night 'nuisance raiders' fitted with exhaust flame dampers and armed with 100kg bombs.

The increasing number of ships reaching Murmansk and Archangel gave cause for concern at Luftflotte 1 headquarters — there simply were not enough aircraft to impose the required sea blockade and to prevent supplies being transported to the fighting fronts. Luftwaffe units were deployed in attacks on both shipping and railway lines using Stukas and Jabos, bombers and torpedo-carrying seaplanes. Every type of aircraft was pressed into service, to the extent that Luftwaffe forces based in the Far North made numerous combat sorties that were unique to the theatre of operations, not so much in the type of operation flown — although these were often unusual — but in the variety of aircraft that were used as a matter of routine. It says much for the tenacity of the Germans, pitted as they were against vastly superior Russian forces, that success was achieved against the enemy in this area right up to the end of the war.

The threat of the summer 1943 Russian offensive on the Central and Southern sectors of the Eastern Front saw JG 54's area of operations moved temporarily away from Finland until June 1944 when in response to a Finnish call for assistance in the face of a strong Russian attack on the Karelian isthmus, some of its Fw 190s returned there.

Luftflotte 1 despatched Gefechtsverbande Kuhlmey to Immola, the airfield nearest to the combat area. Composed of fighters, dive and reconnaissance bombers, the unit staged through Malmi airfield, Helsinki to arrive at Immola on 16 June. The sizeable force was made up as follows:

> I Gruppe and Stab StG 3 with thirty Ju 87s
> I Gruppe SG 5 with Fw 190s
> II./JG 54 with Fw 190s
> NAG 1 with Do 217s and Ju 88s.

In addition, the unit had a total of nineteen Ju 52 and SM 81 transports of *Gefechtsverband K. Lft 5* for general support duties.

By the 16th of the month, twenty-five Fw 190s and an equal number of Ju 87s had arrived at Malmi along with the transports. The majority of these took off for Immola without delay. One JG 54 aircraft was written-off in a crash-landing at the operational base. Three days later, the Grünherz Geschwader sent 1.Staffel to Turku to protect German naval units operating in the northern reaches of the Baltic.

Gefechtsverband Kuhlmey was immediately in action against Russian ground forces, but such was the enemy strength, particularly in fighters, that operations were mainly of a defensive rather than offensive nature. Bad weather was almost as great a hazard to operations as the enemy, as can be seen from the following table of losses from II./JG 54:

> 16 June – 1 Fw 190 (landing accident)
> 17 June – 1 Fw 190 (engine failure)
> 18 June – 1 Fw 190 (weather related loss, Malmi)
> 19 June – 2 Fw 190s (combat damage/engine failure)
> 26 June – 2 Fw 190s (cause unknown)
> 28 June – 1 Fw 190 (shot down by enemy fighters)

In addition, the other units suffered a high rate of attrition, StG 3 losing six Ju 87s between 20 and 29 June and 1./SG 5 four Fw 190s. But these losses paled into insignificance in comparison with what a German fire brigade force had, not untypically, achieved during a short space of time. The fighters had been responsible for the destruction of sixty-six Russian aircaft during the month, including seventeen Yak-9s and twenty-three Il-2s. Another twenty-four enemy machines were claimed by flak units.

Retribution was not long in coming; German tenure in Russia was waning fast and despite further transfer of forces into the area by Luflotte 1, notably five Gruppen from the Italian Front which included Fw 190 fighter bombers, they could not hold the Russians. Daily ground attack sorties rose to an impressive 400-plus, compared with the Red Air Force's 950.

Gefechtsverband Kuhlmey continued to fly dive bomber sorties against armour and infantry in the Tali and Ihantala regions, although Immola was now right in the front line. On 2 July the Germans were taken by surprise by a Russian attack on the base, with Il-2s bombing and fighters, put at sixty-five aircraft, strafing. One of the airfield's large hangars was destroyed and with it four Ju 87s and six Fw 190s.

Combat flying brought further losses, although the Russians paid the price to the tune of eleven aircraft, mainly fighters, from 2-16 July. German targets during this period included a dangerous Russian thrust at Ayrapaa, seaborne landing forces at Uura, the Vuosalmi bridges and troop concentrations at Ihantala.

In total, German losses from the Kuhlmey force amounted to twenty-seven Fw 190s and twenty-two Ju 87s between 17 June and 6 July, plus three Bf 109s from an unknown Staffel. During this period, fifty-two Fw 190s, four Bf 109s and forty-three Ju 87s had been based at Immola and together with the losses in aircraft, seventeen pilots had been killed and sixteen wounded.

After further Stuka losses, the decision was taken to withdraw the remaining elements of the force from Immola. One of the final operations mounted from the base was against the Ayrapaa bridgehead on 16 July. Escorted by sixteen Fw 190 fighters, thirty-five Ju 87s and twelve Fw 190 Jabos swept in to drop their bombs, only four Stukas being damaged by the defences.

The withdrawal from Immola had begun the day before with the departure of the Bf 109s. I./SG 3 followed on the 21st, while Stab. and II./JG 54 undertook a phased withdrawal which lasted from 20-23 July. A handful of Fw 190 Jabos remained, these aircraft flying more sorties using primarily 250 and 500kg bombs. By mid-month 1.Staffel of JG 54, which had not lost any aircraft during its period at Turku, had also returned to German soil.

A front line cameraman works fast as an Fw 190 flashes overhead en route for the front. Finland, and the Northern Front in general, were not entirely overwhelmed by the Red Army and JG 54's sterling effort in the area helped to protect the only German army group which held out until the final days of the war. *(Stenman)*.

Oblt Wilhelm Schilling climbs into 'Black 2 ', an Fw 190A with the name 'Schlange' (snake) painted below the canopy. Schilling scored fifty kills during the war and flew with JG 1 as well as the Grünherz. *(Stenman).*

This general transfer did not however mark the complete end of JG 54's operations under Luftflotte 1's tactical force, for a small number of pilots remained to fly fighter bomber sorties in company with SG 5, using the Fw 190F-8. The situation was now critical; by the end of July, Russian troops had cut all land communication routes between Germany and the Baltic states and surrounded *Heeresgruppe Nord* which encompassed the majority of Wehrmacht forces in the region. Air evacuation of these troops began in August.

On 3 August, SG 5 aircraft moved to Utti airfield to undertake anti-shipping strikes in the Gulf of Finland, while JG 54 maintained the pressure on land bridgeheads. On 4 August the Grünherz Jabos attacked a Russian build-up at Kivijarvi, multiple sorties being made during the course of the day. On 7 August twenty-one Fw 190F-8s attacked the Russian airfield at Lavansaari, having evacuated Immola and moved to Utti the previous day. A shipping strike was made on 8 August with twenty aircaft, and shortly afterwards the remaining elements of the Kuhlmey unit abandoned Utti and moved to bases in Estonia.

In just over one month, from 7 July to 8 August 1943, II./JG 54 had, from the previously quoted list of casualties, lost only two pilots from its strength, neither of them receiving fatal injuries. Aircraft losses had been three aircraft destroyed and eleven damaged.

On the Russian Front, from September to October 1943, the strength of JG 54 was:

GeschwaderStab	3 Fw 190As
I Gruppe	27 Fw 190As
II Gruppe	27 Fw 190As
IV Gruppe	36 Fw 190As

Total aircraft 93

Despite the inevitable losses in combat and accidents, this inventory was not only maintained, but was improved upon during 1944. While the overall figures fluctuated, and always had to take account of serviceability on any given day, the Jagdwaffe was rarely kept short of aircraft for long. Somehow the supply system coped with a fluid situation at the front with operational units now likely to move at a moment's notice.

Leader of the world's first operational jet fighter unit, Major Walter Nowotny died in November 1944 at the controls of an Me 262. He is pictured here in the autumn of 1943 in the uniform of an Oberleutnant. His decorations include the Knight's Cross, worn at the neck, the Operational Flying Clasp above the ribbons on the left breast with the Iron Cross on the tunic pocket. *(Petrick)*.

Chapter 7

GRÜNHERZ JET LEADER

Walter Nowotny, former Kommandeur of I./JG 54, began training on the Messerschmitt Me 262 during the late summer of 1944. Since his return from the Eastern Front Nowotny had, up until February that year, undertaken a spell of duty as the commanding officer of the training Gruppe SJG 101 at Pau. In the meantime, *Erprobungskommando Lechfeld* and EKdo 262 had introduced the jet fighter into action, with some positive results. Both these formations were the first steps towards the creation of 'regular' Jagdgeschwaderen fully operational on jet fighters.

Nowotny was named as the Kommandeur of a new Me 262 unit which would draw some of its strength from these early operational evaluation units. It was to be the final stepping stone, creating a pool of combat experience: no jet training programme had been established at that time and few pilots had had time to fly the aircraft with the degree of confidence that was necessary to take it into combat.

Taking the honour title *Kommando Nowotny*, the new jet unit had been formed from the remaining personnel of EKdo Lechfeld and EKdo 262, at Achmer near Osnabruck. It had an initial strength of between twenty-three and thirty aircraft and these moved to forward operating bases at Hesepe and Achmer, along the Mitteland Canal near Osnabruck, when the unit was declared operational on 3 October.

Despite the vast amount of fighter experience of Nowotny (he then had 255 victories to his credit) and his pilots, the Kommandeur's task was daunting; not only did he have a completely new type of aircraft to bring quickly to operational efficiency, he was, if the jet was indeed to prove its superiority over the enemy's pistoned-engined aircraft, obliged to score a substantial number of victories with it almost immediately his unit had aircraft to fly. And that went for every pilot on every sortie.

It goes without saying that Nowotny had

been handed an all but impossible command, even with an aircraft possessing the undoubted capabilities of the Me 262, which had the potential to out-perform anything in the Allied inventory. But the Me 262A had, like any other new aircraft, particularly one that was nothing short of revolutionary, its share of teething troubles.

In an atmosphere that was hardly conducive to unhampered and thorough test flying to prove its advanced powerplant and systems, the aircraft would take some time to reach the point where it could be deployed operationally with a fair degree of success. That time was no longer available.

Behind the scenes, the advent of a practical jet aircraft had brought its own problems to Messerschmitt. At a time when Germany was in desperate need of fighters to defend her factories and cities from devastation, time had to be spent to adapt the Me 262 to other roles, particularly that of high speed bombing, at the behest of Hitler who could not be persuaded that it was defensive, rather than offensive, operations that, by 1944, the Luftwaffe fighter force should have been confined to.

However, had conditions been different, the concept of mass retaliation against the Allied armies by jet aircraft which were almost impossible to intercept or shoot down, was far from unrealistic, particularly in support of a last ditch Panzer assault on the Allied lines. The problem was that by the time the Me 262 had been adapted and flown tests in the bombing role, the opportunity to use it in the ground attack role had long passed. Early production aircraft did not perform well as bombers due mainly to a restriction that they should not be used at a low altitude and thereby increase the risk of being shot down, and the operational sorties that were flown achieved next to nothing.

But the Me 262 certainly possessed develop-

The operational Me 262 Geschwaderen that saw action were manned by pilots of two widely differing experience levels: on the one hand were the Experten such as JG 54's Nowotny, Schnorrer and Rademacher and on the other the novices to whom the jet fighter was a handful even under ideal conditions. This group of Me 262s is headed by Wr Nr 170059.

ment potential in roles other than those of interceptor fighter and the research programme continued, albeit on a modest scale. A number of fighter bomber units were formed and these performed as well as their modest numbers, aircraft serviceability and the Allied opposition allowed. As with so much of the highly advanced technology developed in Germany, the allocation of the necessary resources was a case of too little, too late.

Even when Nowotny had installed his unit at the forward bases, much time had still to be spent in testing the aircraft to tailor it for combat, and determining the most advantageous way of using it in action. It was found for example, that the 100mph or so maximum speed advantage bestowed by the two Junkers Jumo 004 turbojets over enemy piston-engined bombers, which invariably flew over Germany at less than 300mph, would be all but useless if conventional, piston-engined fighter type firing passes were employed. In that case the target bomber would stay in the gunsight for mere seconds, far too short a time for the jets,

particularly with an untrained pilot at the controls, to inflict substantial damage from their heavy armament of four 30mm cannon. The high closure speed had to be killed off, but not so much as to lose the performance edge the Me 262 enjoyed.

What finally emerged from a great deal of discussion was an adaptation of the proven 'rollercoaster' intercept manoeuver used by conventional fighters to attack bombers, but tailored as far as possible to jet performance. The Me 262s would approach the enemy bomber formation at a substantial height above the target, around 6,000 feet. This enabled the jet fighters to power-dive through the escort high cover to position themselves 1,500 yards behind and 1,500 feet below the bomber boxes. They would then pull straight up to make their attacks, leveling out just as the target came within range. Firing was initiated 1,000 yards from the target.

By the standards of 1944, even these tactics allowed scant time for the Me 262 pilot to sight his target — about two seconds elapsed if he maintained a flying speed of 300mph, which meant he was travelling at 150 yards per second. At 600 to 650 yards he would launch his R4M rockets and open up with cannon immediately afterwards. Only one burst was possible at this closure speed.

Many of the jet pilots found bomber attack to be highly taxing — there simply was no margin for error and a lethal hit on a bomber was often a matter of sheer luck. The 55mm R4M rocket was stabilised by a ring of eight folding fins in the tail, which deployed immediately after firing. Each rocket was tiny at two feet eight inches in length and weighing about seven and a half pounds. The warhead was a little over two pounds in weight.

Those few Me 262s which were modified to carry the R4M had streamlined racks for twelve under each wing. This compensated somewhat for their lack of individual hitting power, although it was clear that the interception of slow bombers by fast jets demanded not only a completely new technique on the part of the pilots, but 'stand-off' weapons. Had these latter been developed in parallel with the aircraft itself and had something akin to what was later called a 'weapons system' emerged, the effect on the Allies would have been traumatic, to say the least.

The Germans quickly realised that the Me 262 could not be really effective without such advanced weapons, and work was initiated on the first air-launched guided missile, the X-4. The less-sophisticated R100 BS unguided rocket with an incendiary shrapnel warhead was also under study before the end of hostilities, but neither this nor the X-4 reached operational status.

That is not to say that the Jagdflieger failed to master the challenges offered by the Me 262. Its battery of four Mk108 cannon pumped out forty-four rounds per second and an average of just three hits was sufficient to blow a heavy bomber almost in two, to wreck an engine or punch fatal holes in flying surfaces. At least twenty-three men became Experten on the Me 262, if the Allied yardstick of Ace (five confirmed victories) is used. Four of them had previously served with JG 54, including the fifth and sixth most successful pilots, Erich Rudorffer and Karl Schnorrer, with twelve and

eleven victories respectively.

Nowotny's Kommando did not have an auspicious combat debut; even before the first sorties were flown, Oblt Alfred Teumer, previously Staffelkapitan of 7./JG 54, was killed on 4 October while attempting to land an Me 262 at Hespe with one engine flamed-out. With seventy-six victories to his credit, Teumer had only joined the jet unit three days previously.

The first aerial victories for Kommando Nowotny were on 7 October, when Ltn Schall and Fw Heinz Lennartz shot down a B-24 Liberator apiece — the fourteenth and fifteenth enemy aircraft to be claimed by Me 262 pilots since the very first victory on 26 July, the majority of the earlier kills being RAF aircraft. Immediately set upon by the escort, three of the attacking Me 262s were shot down. One pilot was killed.

A P-51 fell to the guns of Kdo Nowotny on 10 October, and it was no accident that the balance of the unit's kills were all fighters. Although bombers remained the prime target, it made sense for the jets to attack the escort and force them to drop their external fuel tanks prior to entering combat, leaving the bombers to Fw 190s and Bf 109s. The trouble was that the latter were so outnumbered that their pilots rarely had a chance to shoot down bombers, however many P-51s the Me 262 had drawn off beforehand.

This highlighted the difficulties the jet pilots faced; even if they were ordered to attack bombers (as was frequently the case), they had little choice but to swat the escort fighters that got in their way. The jets' necessarily limited 'loiter time' in the combat area often resulted in their having to break off after sparring with the American escort without getting anywhere near the bombers and in this way, the US piston-engined fighters were effective enough by their mere presence.

The vital need for conventional fighter cover for the Me 262 bases resulted in 9. and 10.Staffeln of JG 54 occupying the airfields at Achmer and nearby Hespe respectively, on 12 October. Three days later 9.Staffel lost six Fw 190s on a single jet protection sortie.

Nowotny had specifically requested air cover for the operation and 9.Staffel, with the bulk of its pilots away from the airfield, responded as best it could. Six aircraft were available. Engines were started at 08.14 and the Fw 190s took off, the sound of their own Jumo piston engines followed a few minutes later by the low rumble of Jumo turbojets as Nowotny's sleek Me 262s taxied out. They also numbered six aircraft, moving slowly along the runway, recently extended to provide the 500 extra yards of take off distance they needed.

Their pilots watching to make sure all the turbos got safely airborne, the aircraft of 9.Staffel split, two taking up station over the airfield to act as spotters. Other aircraft, both jets and Fw 190s, were expected from Achmer, but none materialised. Everything seemed quiet, as it was still very early, too early to expect much interference from enemy fighters — or so the Jagdflieger thought.

At 6,000 foot altitude the German fighters circled; their flight duration would be about six minutes, time enough for the Me 262s to clear the area. Then came a radio message — enemy fighters, numbering about forty had been detected, south of Osnabruck. A sudden flash of sunlight from the metal surfaces of aircraft flying high above made the JG 54 flight leader elect to land, hoping that his small force had not been spotted. It was a vain hope. As the Doras turned north-west to make their run-in for landing, Mustangs of the 78th Fighter Group dived on them.

The Germans had no choice but to fight and a wild running melee ensued, but as soon as they became separated the individual Jagdflieger were all but doomed. Five of the Focke-Wulfs were shot down, the sixth making good his escape and executing a forced-landing at Munster-Handorf when the landing gear refused to lower.

For the rest, only one victory could be claimed from the carnage although one other pilot also survived when he bailed out, hitting the tailplane and breaking a leg as he did so. The disastrous day was not yet over and on an evening sortie another four aircraft were shot down, two pilots being killed.

Wr Nr 170041, an Me 262A-2a, taxying out for take off in 1945. Flown largely by ex-bomber pilots who had undergone a rapid conversion course, the Me 262 had undoubted potential in the ground attack role although Germany's predicament prevented its widespread use. Sharing its unit number with the Grünherz Jagdgeschwader was KG(J)54, although its antecedent was KG 54 'Totenkopf' rather than JG 54.

Contrary to popular mythology, Hitler's order for a proportion of Me 262 production to be given over to bombers was sound enough – when it was made in November 1943. By the time the aircraft was ready in some numbers, the aerial opposition was so heavy that little could be achieved. Jagdgeschwarderen equipped with conventional fighters were thus handed one more task – of covering jet Jabo sorties. Here, the groundcrew prepare an Me 262A-2a bomber during the winter of 1944-45.

An influx of new pilots helped make good the attrition of the summer months although these men were a new breed. The majority were bomber pilots, 'Cab drivers', many of them highly decorated and experienced leaders with enough rank to be at least Staffelkapitans. Plenty of flying hours at the controls of bombers did not however, count for much in a fighter unit, so such men had to be content with learning the exacting art of air combat from their junior colleagues. Everything now required to be done at least twice as quickly as they had been used to — for some it was a difficult if not impossible transition.

When success was achieved by the Me 262s against Allied bomber formations the German pilots delighted in the fact that once again they had an aircraft which was superior in most respects to anything the opposition had —

when the unpredictable turbojets functioned smoothly and they could evade the fighter escort. The Me 262 was a fine aircraft to fly and in the hands of the veteran fighter pilots the Luftwaffe still possessed, albeit in dwindling numbers, the most dangerous of the jet and rocket types the Germans then had in production.

Had they had many more jets in an operational state, sufficient fuel, the necessary skilled ground support organisation and numerous other factors that were then extremely scarce in Germany, the jet pilots may well have devastated the US piston-engined bomber force to such an extent that the war would have at least gone on a little longer. There was no doubt that the Allies were extremely worried that the wily Germans might just manage to achieve something of the sort. Potentially, the

Germans had the means to cause a serious setback to Allied war plans.

Reality quickly showed these fears to be groundless. So overwhelming had Allied fighter strength become that all Nowotny and other highly decorated Experten could achieve were pin-prick attacks when they could penetrate the escort fighter screen. Such intercepts invariably ended with the Germans fleeing home with low fuel gauges, watchful for literally scores of RAF and USAAF fighters that might appear in their area. Although few Allied fighters could catch the Me 262s in the air, the jets were as vulnerable as any other type of aircraft once they were on the ground. It was the intention of Allied air commanders that most of them should stay there.

As the jet airfields were identified, so a close watch was kept on them, to time ground attacks when the German fighters were at their most vulnerable. A great many Me 262s were destroyed by such tactics, rudely dubbed 'Rat Patrols' by the RAF. Despite what JG 54 and other units tried to do to cover the jet bases by standing patrols with conventional fighters their losses continued to be grievous.

Eight Me 262s were lost to all causes early in November and the 8th was remembered as Black Friday. It was one of the worst days in the Luftwaffe's darkest period for it recorded the demise of Nowotny himself. He was shot down while engaged in combat with AAF P-51s in the vicinity of Achmer, his aircraft falling about four miles from the airfield. Considerable doubt remains as to the exact circumstances of Nowotny's death in action. No American pilot claimed to have fired the fatal shots that hit him or his aircraft and there is evidence that the German Experten was killed not by the enemy but by his own flak defending the aerodrome. The fact remained that the Grünherz and the Jagdwaffe had lost one of their greatest fighter leaders.

During its brief introduction to combat, Nowotny's unit had lost twenty-six aircraft. Adolf Galland, who had been visiting Achmer on the day Nowotny was shot down, realised the difficulties surrounding the introduction of the Me 262 to action far too early in its development. He ordered a withdrawal to Lechfeld where on 24 November the unit was redesignated III./JG 7. Fittingly, the honour tile 'Nowotny' was perpetuated for the world's first 'official' jet fighter formation.

Oberst Johannes Steinhoff was appointed Geschwader Kommodore and III Gruppe was placed under the command of Maj Erich Hohagen. Maj Theodor Weissenberger arrived at Lechfeld to lead the GeschwaderStab and subsequently replaced Steinhoff after the latter was badly injured in a crash landing.

Deeply shaken by the loss of their commander, the remaining pilots of Kommando Nowotny returned to Lechfeld, to undertake refresher training with III Gruppe and also to provide a pilot cadre of a second Gruppe of JG 7. This latter was formed under the command of Hptm Horst Geyer, an ex-Zerstorerflieger, who successfully integrated the remaining personnel of his own III./ZG 26, which had in turn been reformed as Erprobungeskommando Lechfeld, with those of Nowotny's test unit.

III./JG 7 was declared operational in mid-December, but it was not until February 1945 that II Gruppe was formed under Grunherztrager Maj Erich Rudorffer at Briest. Neither II or I Gruppen of JG 7 were in fact fully established, but both flew the Me 262 operationally.

Adolf Hitler, increasingly unable to accept the impending end of the Thousand Year Reich, began, via Goering, in whom he was rapidly losing all faith, to berate the fighter arm's 'failure' to achieve the impossible. On 7 November the Reichmarschall had made a pathetic effort to rally the Jagdflieger to even greater sacrifice, following an examination by Hitler himself, of the disastrous losses they had suffered on 2 November.

In a post-mortem bordering on farce, Hitler made a simplistic deduction. He tried to show that the number of fighters that made contact with the American bombers that day (305) should have related more directly to enemy losses (50). Totally overlooking the fact that the Luftwaffe lost ninety-eight fighters, the conditions under which it now fought and numerous other factors that blunted the German attack, the Fuhrer exploded that it was pointless providing the Luftwaffe with more fighters so it could simply 'play a numbers game'.

Me 262A-2a devoid of markings apart from the Werke Nummer 111603 across the fin, awaits another sortie against a typical backdrop of fir trees during the winter of 1944-45.

Weary Jagdwaffe commanders could only shake their heads in disbelief; given Germany's military situation, a score of fifty US bombers was outstandingly good, even though the cost was getting to be a soberingly normal percentage of the numbers deployed on interception. Had the whole thing not been so serious, such comments would have been appreciated as black humour of the kind German aviators used and understood. In the circumstances, the Commander-in-Chief's constant cajoling and bombast was even more surreal — clearly no one at the top had any idea of how the Luftwaffe fighter force was being bled to death. Worse, few seemed to care.

In those grim days, only the weather offered some respite from the constant courting of death and injury at the hands of the enemy formations. The hard-fighting Jagdgeschwa-deren continued to take punishing blows. On 21 November two more JG 54 pilots were killed in action when IV Gruppe took off from Hopsten to intercept the bombers on the homeward leg. Sighting their quarry in company with the Bf 109Gs and Ks of II./JG 27, the Gruppe's Fw 190A-8s fell foul of P-47s of the 266th Fighter Group, 9th Air Force.

Although JG 27 suffered higher casualties in the resulting combat, JG 54's total loss for the day was five aircraft; three pilots were injured in addition to the two fatalities from 15./JG 54, Fw Hemut Stix and Gefr Hans-Herbert Strakhof. Both the latter are believed to have been the result of a collision over the Munster-Handorf area.

The air battle with Thunderbolts was yet another illustration of the Jagdwaffe's present predicament — it failed to knock down any enemy bombers because it had its hands full with fighters. Once combat had to be joined with American or British fighters, which were invariably superior on most counts, and especially in numbers, the German fighters were almost bound to have to abandon the primary purpose of their sorties.

And yet few Allied airmen, fighter pilots or bomber crews, could afford to relax their vigilance. Despite their numerical inferiority, the Luftwaffe fighter pilots could still exact a toll. On 26 November a large scale air battle developed when the 8th Air Force bomb divisions despatched 1,137 B-17s and B-24s to attack a variety of industrial installations, primarily marshalling yards, in the Bielefeld, Osnabruck and Hamm areas.

The bomber force was the focus of attack by six Gruppen of Fw 190s and six of Bf 109s. JG 54's Focke-Wulf pilots were among more than 500 German fighters that strove to intercept, but it was clear that any man, be he Experte or novice, had to have a lot of luck on his side if he was to avoid the escort, penetrate the web of fire put out by the bomber gunners, and complete a successful firing pass. That day the escort was 669 P-51s and P-47s, enough to knock down 114 Messerschmitts and Focke-Wulfs, resulting in eighty-seven pilot casualties, fifty-seven of them fatal.

One of the Grünherz men shot down and killed was Ritterkreuztrager Ltn Heinrich Bazi Sterr, who either failed to see or could do nothing about the P-51 that nailed his aircraft as he came into land at Vorden. Sterr, with 130 kills, had joined 16./JG 54 less than two months earlier after transfer from II Gruppe in the East, and had been nominated for the Oak Leaves. Also lost that day was Uffz Wilhelm Seueche, from 13.Staffel.

The American force lost thirty-four bombers, twenty of them to fighter attack. Hardest hit was the 2nd Division's Liberator groups, the 491st BG losing fifteen aircraft, all to fighter attacks in the vicinity of Hanover.

On 27 November twelve Grünherz aircraft had been scrambled from Vorden; the Focke-Wulfs were still in sight of their airfield when one fighter suddenly dropped out of formation and dived straight into the ground. The cause was apparently catastrophic engine failure. It was the start of another grim day. Shielding a relatively small force of 530 US bombers briefed to attack marshalling yards, 770 Mustangs and Thunderbolts were more than able to blunt the Luftwaffe's challenge. American pilots claimed ninety-eight. No bombers were lost and only fifteen US fighters failed to return home.

Among the German casualties were two pilots killed and one wounded from JG 54 in addition to the early post-take-off loss. The month rounded off badly with an American mission on 29 November that the Jagdflieger totally failed to intercept, and one on the 30th, when four German fighters were lost for three of the AAF.

It did not take much calculation to reckon the odds the Luftwaffe fighter force now faced — twenty to thirty or more to one was getting to be the norm when the enemy laid on a 'maximum effort' mission. During November 1944, forty-five fighters had been destroyed for 115 aerial combat claims. By far the worst aspect of the figures for the Germans was that although both sides were capable of making good the materiel losses quickly, replacing the dead pilots with highly capable men was a luxury long since denied to the Luftwaffe. More and more responsibility was heaped on the shoulders of the surviving Experten.

The Luftwaffe fighter units in the West now faced the strength of three Allied strategic bomber forces (the US 8th and 15th, plus RAF Bomber Command), each with huge fighter elements tasked primarily with escort but with an important secondary ground attack capability, and two tactical air forces (the US 9th and the 2nd Allied Tactical) composed of light and attack bombers. Again, the latter forces could field vast numbers of fighters. In addition, the Allies mounted pure fighter and 'armed reconnaissance' sweeps designed first and foremost to blast the Luftwaffe out of the sky.

For the defenders, the distinctions were academic — projected forward and assuming a loss rate similar to that presently being inflicted by the combined efforts of this mighty force, the figures added up to nothing less than utter defeat. But the German emphasis would continue to be the destruction of heavy bombers; apart from the devastation caused to cities, primarily by RAF night raids about which the day fighters could do little, the Americans had, since May 1944, begun a systematic campaign against a particular type of vital industrial target that many, even in the German high command, thought would have been bombed much earlier. These production centres were at the very heart of the Luftwaffe's ability to fly and fight, and their destruction hit at its very lifeblood — oil.

The Bulge

Seasonal bad weather in December did not prevent the Allied air forces continuing their pounding of German strategic and tactical targets, but the blanket of snow, fog and low temperatures kept the Allied tactical air forces away from the battlefield long enough for Hitler to launch his last great gamble in the West. But even the initial success of this eleventh hour feat of German arms was a nail in the Jagdwaffe's coffin; instead of Galland's 'Big blow' against the enemy in the air, Hitler ordered the bulk of the fighter force westwards to support von Runstedt's optimistic drive aimed ultimately at securing the port of Antwerp. Having at first thought that only JG 300 and 301 would be sufficient to guard Reich airspace, Luftflotte Headquarters Germany had to throw in the shattered JG 27 and IV./JG 54 — the homeland still had to be defended.

For many months the Americans had been perfecting the technique of bombing blind, and the RAF had little difficulty in adapting its terrifyingly efficient destructive power by night to bombing in daylight. Bomber Command made a total of eleven day raids in December 1944 and if Lancasters and Halifaxes were airborne as well as Fortresses and Liberators, the Jagdwaffe had even greater difficulty than usual, for the two forces only rarely struck the same targets and this fact spread *Reichsverteidigung* fighter effort even more thinly. A sudden need to provide support to ground forces was all but beyond its capability. It was small compensation that the British heavy bombers were marginally less well-protected than their US opposite numbers against fighter attack, for they too did not venture far without a huge escort.

Any division of its forces caused the Jagd-waffe chronic problems, as the events of 5 December showed. While the fighter force waited until the Jagddivision operations centre at Doberitz vectored it onto a worthwhile target, the US bombers made their way unhindered to Berlin.

Making contact with the fighters covering a Bomber Command force targeting the railway yards at Soest, the German fighters took casualties even before the main air battle of the day took place, as the 8th Air Force was withdrawing. Once again the escort was all but impenetrable. Having wasted precious time awaiting their ground control's intructions, the Fw 190 and Bf 109 pilots lost the initiative. The result was another fifty-three pilots killed when the American escort pounced.

Again JG 54 managed to avoid the worst of the enemy's attention — the grim reaper's scythe fell more heavily that day on JG 1 which lost fifteen pilots — only one Grünherztrager, Fw Heinz Marz of 16.Staffel being killed. But even this nibbling away at available pilot numbers was deeply felt, as nobody knew which individual Gruppen would get the worst of it on the next scramble.

One of the grimmer side effects of the air fighting from the German point of view was the fact that a crippled fighter could fall in dense woodland or the waters of a lake and not be discovered for months, if at all. Much of the fighting on 5 December took place over the Lake Muritz area in southern Germany: an attempted ditching in a lake could spell disaster, even to a pilot who had not been wounded in aerial combat.

At this time, III./JG 54 continued under the command of JG 26 while IV.Gruppe flew as part of JG 27, in effect giving the respective Jagdgeschwaderen four and five Gruppen respectively. Hannes Trautloft, as Inspekteur der Jagdflieger, visited Fürstenau, home of JG 26 on the 5th. Awaiting the twenty-nine Focke-Wulfs as they landed after combat with P-47s, Trautloft awarded the RK to Maj Karl Borris. Borris had answered an *alarmstart* at 13.15 by leading four Fw 190s off almost immediately afterwards. As if to enforce his suitability to wear the decoration, he shot down a B-17.

I Gruppe JG 26 returned at 13.45 only to be ordered up again at 14.32. Nine Fw 190s were away by 14.35. Thunderbolts were intercepted at 15.05 and for some ten minutes the German fighters tangled with fifty of the enemy. They landed again at 16.01 with no losses to report.

As the Ardennes offensive gathered momentum, the bulk of the Jagdwaffe was placed under the command of Luftflotte West. Dietrich Peltz, not Adolf Galland, now directed the fighters, there being forty Gruppen available for what were essentially ground support operations. Not all the Gruppen had aircraft suitable for this task, as a large percentage were equipped with Bf 109 G and K models, configured primarily as interceptors. Such was the urgency attached to the ground offensive that these fine distinctions were ignored.

As far as operational casualties went JG 54 gained a respite of two weeks or so after Uffz Gerhard Mutke of 14.Staffel was killed on 6 December. The lull was due to the weather, which approached the worst conditions the German fighter force had long experienced in Russia, but on 17 December, rain and heavy overcast did not prevent a large force of enemy fighters penetrating west of the Rhine. Among the US units involved that day was the 404th FG with P-47s and the P-38-equipped 474th Group. Scrambled to find the Thunderbolts, JG 26 had no success in the low morning overcast, but JG 27 certainly did. While claiming some kills themselves, the Jagdflieger nevertheless lost six pilots killed and four wounded. The 404th had a busy day, as the group was back in the afternoon to again be met by a spirited defence.

JG 27 also had to contend with RAF Tempests, I.Gruppe losing four pilots in combat with the aircraft of No. 56 Squadron. A second encounter with the 474th saw another four Fw 190s shot down. IV./JG 54's losses for the day were three pilots killed in combat when the two sides met high above the towns of Bonn and Duren. Two 14.Staffel pilots, Oberfh Werner Timpke and Uffz Heinz Winkler, flying an Fw 190A-9 and an A-8 respectively, went down, as did Fh Fw Otto Schelnest of 13.Staffel, at the controls of an Fw 190A-8. In total, over a wide-ranging aerial battlefront, the Germans lost fifty-five fighter pilots killed and twenty-four wounded. JG 27's tally of sixteen kills matched exactly those admitted as lost by the AAF.

The Germans' last major ground offensive in the West, the so-called Battle of the Bulge, gradually ran out of steam — or to be more precise, fuel. Reacting as quickly as the weather allowed to the crisis, the Allies stepped up the bombing of synthetic oil plants and fuel centres, with the 15th Air Force increasingly making its presence felt over the furthest such targets in the Reich. The predominantly Liberator-equipped force appeared over Poland on 17 December, the intercepting Jagdwaffe being able to do little to prevent it.

To help strangle von Runstedt's offensive, the bombers also initiated a wide-ranging campaign against German lines of communication to prevent supplies getting through. Much of this effort was handled by the medium bombers and fighter-bombers of the 9th Air Force. On 18 December IV./JG 54 was in the thick of the fighting that developed over the city of Cologne. The weather was about as bad as it could be for air operations — freezing rain and mist reducing visibility to dangerous parameters, increasing the horrifying prospect of mid-air collisions. As they strove once more to find the American bombers, 9th AF B-26 Marauders and A-26 Invaders, the Jagdflieger instead became the target of the escort. Part of this was made up of the Thunderbolts of the 365th and 368th Fighter Groups. Three JG 54 aircraft were lost, Fh Fw Otto Schelnest and Fw Erich Fike being killed and Uffz Dieter Schmidt wounded.

Although the overall German losses for the day were relatively light, at twenty-one pilots killed in action plus twelve wounded from the fourteen Gruppen that took off to intercept, even this level of casualties cut swaths through the Jagdwaffe's strength, particularly as events showed every sign of getting far worse. Frequently, the Jagdflieger found fighter versus fighter combat awaiting them to send their casualty rate soaring.

Gradually the level of Allied air activity increased in proportion to the better weather conditions. A week after the German ground offensive started, the carnage inflicted on the Luftwaffe rose to its old, pre-winter level. On 23 December large scale air battles developed as the 8th and 9th Air Forces again went out after communications targets.

Once again the Jagdwaffe fielded almost its entire available strength and by noon around ninety Fw 190s and Bf 109s had passed over Cologne en route to intercept the bombers. But the Americans had sent 400-plus fighters to protect their four-engined charges — even before they had made contact with the enemy bombers, the Germans were bounced by P-47s of the crack 56th Fighter Group over the Eifel mountains. Among the resulting victims of the dogfights that ensued was Uffz Willi Bach of 16./JG 54. Taking hits, his Fw 190A-8 went down near Rottingen. Eye-witnesses stated that Bach had probably been killed or wounded, as he made no attempt to bail out.

A second Focke-Wulf from JG 54 fell near the hamlet of Villip. This one did not have the pilot in the cockpit, Uffz Klaus Gehring having bailed out. Unfortunately his parachute wrapped around the tail unit, the stricken machine dragging Gehring down to his death. To these two downed pilots, JG 54 had to add a third, who was wounded, to its casualty list.

A series of separate air battles had developed, ranging over many square miles of German territory; it was at this time that the Ardennes offensive reached a critical point, with St Vith in German hands and Bastogne surrounded. But as the enemy air forces could virtually plan missions with little or no regard to significant Luftwaffe interference the German ground situation would soon become desperate. The white-starred bombers came on in continuous streams, to shatter their targets, turn and fly home, ready to return later the same day or the next, always with their fighters providing any protection that was necessary.

With von Runstedt's tanks having driven a wedge into the Allied lines in Belgium, the Jagdwaffe faced an additional hazard — any pilot who was shot down now had an even chance of being captured. Also, with strong Allied tactical air forces operating from continental bases, P-47s, P-38s, Spitfires and Tempests had the range to give chase over substantial distances. As a result, Luftwaffe fighter pilots could find themselves miles from their home bases after their sorties. Out of ammunition and low on fuel, they were often forced to put down at the nearest available airfield.

Although they were then invariably able to refuel and rearm, they faced an additional hazard in reaching home base — flying of any kind was fraught with danger and the ever-present risk of interception.

Unhappy Christmas

Following the loss of more pilots from IV./JG 54 in the combats of 23 December, on Christmas Eve both 9. and 12.Staffeln of JG 54 returned to Varrelbusch to once more link up with the rest of III Gruppe. A further improvement in the weather, although it remained bitterly cold, saw continual air activity, and JG 54 experienced both successes and losses during the day. IV Gruppe, busy attacking Typhoons at about midday, were themselves bounced by No. 274 Sqn Tempests, which claimed one Fw 190 shot down, probably that flown by Ltn Paul Brandt, who was killed. Two Typhoons which were lost are believed to have been destroyed by the Grünherz' fighters in this engagement. Two other pilots were missing when the Fw 190s returned home.

It was a period when the fighter leaders often had to make rapid changes of plan; they had to countermand orders to attack bomber formations in order to preserve some of their forces when fighters came on the scene. This happened on 24 December, when the appearance of RAF fighters in considerable force took JG 54 and other units by surprise. To the Germans' slight advantage, the British pilots were surprised too!

There was hardly time for any kind of break for either side to celebrate Christmas for the Allied fighters were out in some force, air combat resulting in eight casualties from JG 54. Another pilot went down on the 26th, and on the 27th, III Gruppe was placed under the command of JG 26. The Gruppe now divided its time between jet protection and sporadic Jabo sorties as well as bomber interceptions, all of which were exhausting in the extreme. In an effort to imbue confidence, Kommodore Robert Weiss addressed the Gruppe pilots, emphasising that everyone who now flew operational sorties, irrespective of rank, needed mutual support from his fellows.

He said, 'We have little to lose but our lives.

We will continue to fly in the sure knowledge that our NCO pilots are backing us up.'

To their credit, all pilots indeed continued to fly against the enemy however hopeless the cause seemed. The Luftwaffe rank structure had always placed a heavy responsibility on the shoulders of non-commissioned officer pilots, much more so than did the Western Allies, and these men continued to represent the backbone of the fighter force. All ranks, from the commander to the newest recruit, knew that many of those remaining in front line units would be unlikely to live to see the final defeat of Germany. . . .

Weiss was an inspiration to all, especially the younger men. And there were numerous individuals of the Jagdwaffe who needed all the help they could get to fight down the mind-numbing fatigue of operational flying — not to mention naked fear, born largely of inexperience. To a man they wondered if they could beat the odds and just stay alive; every sortie brought the brutal realisation that their proud and once-mighty force was being hunted down like a pack of wild dogs.

Each passing day brought its share of grim tidings: the fighting on Christmas Day removed another sixty fighters from the Jagdwaffe's collective strength. The Grünherz' casualties were the worst suffered by the Luftwaffe in the day's engagements, which saw JG 1, 3, 6, 11, 26, 27, 53 and 77 committed. IV./JG 3 lost seven pilots out of the total of forty-nine killed in action that day.

By 27 December, the Ardennes offensive was halted. Bastogne was destined to be the limit of the German advance and the route of the last great offensive in the West was marked out by the blazing hulks of tanks and vehicles, held and then annihilated by Allied power on the ground and in the air.

Another seven aircraft of JG 54 became coffins for their pilots on the 27th. This time the casualties were shared by III and IV Gruppen, which lost five Fw 190D-9s and four A-8s respectively. III Gruppe's antagonists were Thunderbolts and Tempests.

Crump's 10.Staffel and Dortenmann's 11.Staffel fought a running battle which began at 13.00. Although the Dora-9s managed to destroy one Tempest, four of them were shot down by a quartet of RAF pilots. The day also recorded an instance of the occasional 'help' the Jagdwaffe received from the presence of Tempests — American fighter pilots tended to confuse both this and the Typhoon with German types and often mistakenly engaged in combat. There were casualties from such incidents but usually the mistake was quickly rectified. No force was immune from recognition mistakes in the heat of battle and the Germans themselves had to contend with similar occurrences.

While III Gruppe was battling with Tempests over Munster and Telgte, IV./JG 54 was, with elements of JG 26 and JG 77, flying tactical support sorties, trying to relieve the pressure on German ground forces in the St Vith area. Their armoured Fw 190A-8s tangled with US fighter bombers, probably P-47s, and four of their number were shot down, their pilots, Ltn Alfred Budde, Uffz Herbert Muller-Welt, Ltn Hans-Georg Baur-Berger and Obltn Ludwig Dresler, all being posted as missing, presumed killed.

Then, on 29 December, Jagdgeschwader 54 suffered another disaster, perhaps its greatest of this phase of the war. III Gruppe's black men had somehow marshalled seventy Fw 190D-9s to provide take off and landing cover to the Me 262s of KG (J) 51 based at Rheine. Their task was to take on any Allied aircraft that appeared to threaten the security of the jet base, similar duty being assigned to elements of JG 6 and JG 27.

Responding to such an alert, the Dora-9s took off under VHF R/T ground control of the Jagddivision 3 station at Wiedenbruck, part of the *Reichsjagerwelle* or air defence fighter network. This system determined the location of friendly aircraft by slant range measurement of FuG 16 ZY radio transmissions from each aircraft. The height and location of enemy formations could also be determined so that German fighters could be vectored onto them. It was a reliable enough system — but it failed on this day.

In response to an alert, the ground station directed JG 54 to commit itself in Staffel, rather than Gruppe strength. The orders were nothing short of a death sentence for the Grünherz fighters.

Leading 10.Staffel off at 19.00, Ltn Crump's

aircraft were followed by 11. and 12.Staffeln at hourly intervals. Control reported strong enemy fighter formations in the vicinity of Tecklenburg and across Munsterland in general. And there they were, a dozen Fw 190s, heading into an unknown size of enemy formation: it was extremely unlikely that the Jagdflieger would meet inferior numbers.

It was 9.Staffel that was taken by surprise. Just as it reached the area Lingen-Rheine, Ltn Willi Heilmann was vectored by ground control right into the flightpath of a vastly superior force of Spitfire IXs of No. 411 Sqn RCAF. Apparently, the German controllers either did not detect the large enemy force or failed to pass on the fact to friendly fighter units operating in the area Munster-Osnabruck-Rheine, although they could hardly fail to have known they were airborne. The designated ceiling was 6,500 feet and Heilmann clawed desperately for altitude as the Spitfires opened fire. It was a one-sided massacre. The Canadians had a field day, shooting down at least six aircraft which carried pilots to their deaths.

Robert Weiss watched in horror as the remnants of 9.Staffel drifted back to Varrel-busch. His own aircraft was quickly made ready and he took off, leading his Stab back to the area where the battle had taken place. Following close behind was 11./JG 54 led by Ltn Prager.

Closing the right area, map reference 'Foxtrot-Quebec', Weiss spotted a large formation of Spitfires of Nos 331 and 501 Squadrons. The Dora 9s immediately dived on them and a number of dogfights ensued. At that moment more British fighters arrived on the scene, identified as Typhoons belonging to Nos 168 and 438 Squadrons. Now heavily outnumbered, the Germans battled it out above Lengerich, near Lingen.

The odds were simply too great. After Fw Gerhard Neerson and Obltn Eugen Schreiner had gone down, Weiss himself succumbed, in a combat involving several Spitfires. By this time 11.Staffel had waded into the melee and individual Focke-Wulf 190 pilots were fighting for their lives, pursued and pursuers scattering over a wide area.

In the meantime, Ltn Dortenmann's 12.Staffel scrambled and immediately climbed at full throttle to 20,000 feet. Dortenmann was determined not to be caught by the Allied fighters at low altitude. It was nearly noon as the twelve grey-painted Dora-9s set course for Munster. Combat was joined with British fighters between Dummer Lake and the River Ems. Against the Tempests, 12.Staffel lost two aircraft. Uffz Adam Siebert was shot down and Uffz Gunther Zessin was forced to bail out of his aircraft 'Red 42' when he was wounded by cannon fire. The opposition was believed to have been from Nos 3 and 56 Squadrons. The RAF lost four Tempests.

At least sixteen Fw 190s, including that flown by Robert Weiss, whose score then stood at 121 victories, were shot down. RAF figures stated that 2nd TAF scored thirty-one kills for the loss of eleven fighters. The Germans admitted to the loss of twenty from JG 54 and

Hptm Robert Weiss, who scored 121 victories before his death at the hands of Spitfire pilots in December 1944. 'Bazi' Weiss tended to look younger than his twenty-four years, despite the pressures of flying. *(B. Robertson)*.

three other Staffeln, of JG 6 and JG 27, which were involved in this wild, confusing air battle. The British figure was for aircraft seen going down, and as the Germans did not count pilots who had bailed out of crippled machines the above figure of twenty almost certainly referred only to pilots killed, as was standard in reports at the time. The actual figures for JG 54 were thirteen killed, one missing and two injured.

Losses of leaders such as Robert Weiss elevated more junior officers to positions of command very quickly; pending the appointment of a new Kommandeur, Obltn Dortenmann took over III Gruppe, followed by Obltn Heilmann. To these men fell the now-Herculean task of holding their Gruppen and Staffeln together. There was no thought but to carry on flying and fighting for as long as Germany survived.

As the final full year of World War II drew to a close, the Luftwaffe fighter force was in desperate straits. Replacement pilots were still arriving on operational stations, but the old hands were aghast at how young they were and worst of all, at their lack of flying hours, not only on high performance fighters, but any aircraft at all. A few hours at the controls of a trainer or a converted bomber was often all they could claim. And these boys, for they were little more than that, were still expected to give their all and somehow turn the tide in Germany's favour. Little wonder that the survivors confided their sheer horror at the tide of events to diaries and notebooks.

Fighter pilots the world over are by nature somewhat irreverent and devil-may-care in their attitude to authority; even fewer then had any interest in or knowledge of politics and the German Jagdflieger were no exception. There had previously been little need to question the wisdom of the decisions taken higher up. Now, in the sanctity of the mess, they began openly to challenge what Goering and others had been doing to get them into this impossible situation.

Walter Nowotny with a member of his groundcrew on top of one of his Bf 109Gs. *(Petrick).*

But they had to be guarded with whom they discussed such matters. In its death throes, Nazi Germany began turning on itself. News of the short shrift handed out to 'traitors' and those who did not show the right spirit, even in the face of almost inevitable defeat, permeated even the inner sanctums of fighter airfields.

At command level, the fighter leaders were brought to such a pitch of frustration over the wastage of the Jagdwaffe that they knew that nothing short of a direct confrontation with Hitler or Goering would relieve the martyrdom of their pilots. Men like Trautloft, Steinhoff, Lutzow and Galland were forced to walk a delicate tightrope between the conflicting edicts from above. Hitler, raging at the impotency of the Luftwaffe one minute and then suddenly, seeming to regain his composure — and indeed, considerable grasp of the technicalities of aviation — issued orders that countermanded orders with bewildering rapidity, most of them overlaid with extreme optimism and many of them far removed from reality.

Galland's position was growing increasingly precarious, and by the end of 1944 he attended conferences concerning the operation of the fighter arm more or less as a matter of routine; he became almost a bystander, neither expecting to offer or to receive any practical solutions to Germany's defence in the air. Any meeting with Goering, now increasingly a rare occurrence, served little more purpose than to confuse the issue even further. The constant theme seemed to be that the Jagdwaffe had failed to save Germany from Allied bombing as a result of its own incompetence, rather than that of the High Command. Out of favour with Hitler himself, Goering lashed out at anyone on to whom he could attach blame for his own failings.

The upshot was that the post of General der Flieger was all but eliminated. Galland was not informed officially until mid-January 1945, but Dietrich Peltz was by then handling his responsibilities. Yet irrespective of who was supposed to be in command of the fighter arm, its losses continued.

As the last days of December 1944 ebbed away, the Luftwaffe fighter force took more savage blows. For JG 54, the loss of Robert Weiss had been bad enough, and other Jagdgeschwaderen had suffered far higher casualties, but December's balance sheet was appalling. Apart from losses directly associated with supporting the Ardennes offensive, the fighter arm had to contend with eighty bombing raids on its airfields. In defending these targets 128 fighters had been lost in aerial combat, with a further 129 aircraft destroyed on the ground. In addition, 140 machines had been damaged by the rain of bombs.

To add insult to injury and to strengthen doubts as to the 'effectiveness' of the fighters against bombers, the flak arm claimed three times the total of sixty bombers (and twenty-three escort fighters) shot down by I Jagdkorps. Figures such as these made Hitler waver even more in his belief in the worth of the fighter arm. In his increasing paranoia he more than once threatened to completely disband the Luftwaffe or place the remnants under the control of the SS. The Fuhrer's final hold on reality was rapidly ebbing away. . . .

For the front line Jagdgruppen personnel, such political pontification would have been of little interest even if they had been party to it. there was no time for ruminating on what the future might hold nor, sadly, to mourn the loss of good comrades. The Fatherland was bleeding to death and they, and they alone, held the slim hope of stopping the haemorrhage.

Less than forty-eight hours after the last debacle, JG 54 was in action again. The focus this time was the Bremen-Hamburg area, the 8th Air Force sending 1,327 B-17s and B-24s, escorted by 785 P-51s and P-47s, to attack oil installations, communications centres and targets of opportunity in the vicinity of the two cities. To exact a toll of twenty-seven American bombers and ten fighters, the Luftwaffe was obliged to sacrifice thirty-seven pilots. The USAAF claimed more than sixty-one aircraft shot down and in total the Germans lost forty-nine pilots when the wounded were tallied up.

JG 54's two Gruppen made contact with the escort at Limburg and Osnabruck. III Gruppe came off lightly, with a single Dora-9 from 10.Staffel shot down, Fw Reinhold von der Starten surviving, while IV Gruppe had the only fatal loss recorded by the Geschwader, a single Fw 190A-8 flown by Fh Gunther Voight.

From the beginning of the month, on all sorties up to the launch of von Runstedt's offensive on 16 December, 136 fighter pilots had gone down. To this figure were added eighty-three in the period 19-22 December, and in the week of the 23rd to the 31st, 316 had been killed or were missing — a grand total of 535 men killed, missing or taken prisoner. The portents for 1945 were as bad as they could possibly be.

On the evening of 31 December most Jagdflieger were informed that all leave passes were cancelled. New Year celebrations were also not advised, for tomorrow every available pilot would be required to fly an important operation. Just how important they would know soon enough.

'White 4', an Me262A day fighter of JG7, the unit that grew out of Kommando Nowotny's hurried but vital operational evaluation of the world's first combat-worthy jet interceptor.

Chapter 8

BODENPLATTE

Whether or not the Jagdwaffe's 'Big blow', the mass storming of a single USAAF heavy bomber formation by wave after wave of German fighters in such strength that upwards of 300 B-17s or B-24s would have been destroyed, would have done any more than bring even greater Allied retribution down on the remaining German fighter forces, is academic, for it never took place. But there is little doubt that such an aerial armageddon — the Germans were prepared to accept the loss of 400 fighters — would have been more of a morale booster than the 'last ditch' effort that was actually planned and executed on New Year's Day 1945.

The task of planning a mass fighter strike on Allied airfields in Belgium and Holland fell to Generalmajor Dietrich Peltz, commander of II Jagdkorps and responsible for air operations over the Ardennes region. Peltz was an able commander with wide experience, albeit of bomber rather than fighter forces, and on the face of it, the operation had a more definite tactical purpose when it was originally thought of than the mass bomber attack previously proposed.

Launched to coincide, as was the intention, with von Runstedt's Ardennes offensive, it might have had a more disruptive effect on the Allies and in particular would have reduced the inventory of fighter bombers immediately available to wreck offensive operations on the ground. It therefore made some sense to attack the opposition based in Germany's own backyard, so to speak — but the bulk of the Luftwaffe fighter losses continued to be from the long-range fighters based in England. Some 8th AF units had by that time also moved to the continent, which undoubtedly gave some impetus to 'Operation Bodenplatte'.

Quickly, Galland's plan to unleash 2,000 fighters to bring about a crushing Allied defeat in the biggest air battle of the war, had been shelved. Instead, in December, Goering had

ordered that the General der Flieger instigate plans to carry out a large scale ground attack. But neither Galland nor anyone else could stop the daily attrition of the Jagdwaffe — by the time Peltz had briefed his field commanders for *Bodenplatte*, the number of available German fighters was very much less than had been anticipated for the big aerial attack.

Peltz had held a secret conference to outline the attack plan as early as 15 December; he wanted the strike to go ahead at the earliest possible opportunity (in a matter of days from that date), provided the weather brought clear conditions. There was no reason other than that to postpone it until 1 January — certainly the fact that the enemy pilots on the bases to be hit might be suffering from New Year hangovers did not enter the pictures, and it would hardly have been tactically sound to rely on such a slim chance.

Good visibility was though, very necessary, as the bulk of the inexperienced young pilots who would fly the operation would probably have been hard put to find their allotted targets in low cloud or mist. They would rely heavily on their comrades, and to do so they had to see their commanders flying steadfastly at the head of their formations. The weather proved so unreliable in the intervening days that it was late December before the forecasters could confidently predict clear skies. Finally, on the last day of 1944 they indicated that the following day would be clear.

As finally outlined, the plan called for elements of eleven Jagdgeschwaderen — a total of between 650 and 800 aircraft — to attack sixteen airfields in Belgium and Holland, plus one in France. A total of thirty-four available Gruppen, boosted by the strength of Stab flights, one Staffel of JG 104 and some Me 262As of KG(J)51 would mount the operation. Due to the attrition of the last months of 1944 and the fact that it had only its III and IV Gruppen stationed in the West, JG 54's contribution was smaller than that of some of the other Jagdgeschwaderen. Nevertheless, the ubiquitous black men were able to muster seventeen Fw 190D-9s from III Gruppe and twenty-five Fw 190 A-8/A-9s from IV Gruppe. Even that was a very creditable achievement in the circumstances.

On the afternoon of 31 December, all bases received the codeword *Varus 1.1.45*, confirmation that Bodenplatte would go ahead the following day. The second codeword, *Teutonicus* indicated that all Geschwaderkommodoren, Geschwaderkommandeurer and Staffelkapitanen should now be briefed. Apparently, the details were not passed onto every participating pilot: some were merely told that a big operation was underway and that they should follow their leaders. Receipt of *Hermann*, the third codeword, ordered the attack to take place at 09.20. To achieve maximum surprise, it was intended that all the leading aircraft would be over their allocated targets simultaneously.

Briefings were held at various times through the night and into the early hours, depending on the decision of the various commanders. At Varrelbusch, III./JG 54's Fw 190D-9s had been airborne early on 31 December, briefed to fly a patrol in the vicinity of Bastogne. Instead the pilots found the inevitable American bomber formation and had actually jettisoned their external fuel tanks prior to plunging into a 370-plus Liberator formation when the recall order came.

Bad visibility forced most of the airborne formation to land at Achmer rather than their home base. From there JG 54 headed for Handrup, an airstrip near Furstenau from which it would fly the Bodenplatte operation the following morning in company with I./JG 26. When the Grünherz pilots had landed, they were briefed by Major Karl Borris, Kommandeur of I./JG 26. It was around 18.00 when the pilots who would lead the formations filed into the briefing room.

Borris stressed the need for total radio silence en route to the various targets, and revealed why a Ju 88 night fighter was standing out on the airfield. This machine would carry out the navigation for the fighters, flying as near to the targets as necessary before turning away.

Among the comprehensive list of orders issued to each pilot were maps and printed cards, listing the primary objectives of the operation. These latter appear to have reflected the tender age and lack of combat experience of some of the participating pilots, for they included reminders to switch on the radio at the jumping-off point, to illuminate formation-keeping lights and to arm the guns. Testing of armament was advised before starting the strafing run, as was the need to note the number of enemy aircraft that appeared destroyed or damaged on the airfield under attack. To find the way home, pilots were advised to look out for en route airfields and other landmarks and to note their location.

Most of the Grünherz pilots opted for a good night's sleep on New Year's Eve, although other Gruppen decided that they would celebrate the occasion, come what may. Some pilots who tried to sleep found it hard; the air strike planned for the morning seemed as though it would be some revival of Luftwaffe fortunes, the first time in months that the fighter force might achieve a decisive victory over the enemy. That at least was something to look forward to.

At the main briefing, Maj Borris rose to address a room full of pilots. Conversation died on anxious faces as the Bodenplatte plan unfolded. Brussels/Grimbergen was to be the target for III./JG 54. Take off at 08.30; fly below 600 feet to keep below the enemy radar and maintain radio silence whatever happened. Before they left, each man had the chance of a magnificent breakfast — it was obvious, on the face of it, that a good deal of planning had gone into this operation. . . .

All III Gruppe's Dora-9s took off without incident, the plan being for them to join up with the aircraft of JG 26 from Furstenau. These latter consisted of the GeschwaderStab led by the Kommodore, 'Pips' Priller. Three instructors from JG 104, his own I Gruppe and III./JG 54, a total of sixty-seven Focke-Wulf Fw 190Ds.

But almost immediately, the blanket security screen thrown around Bodenplatte began to reap a bitter harvest. Although 16 Flak Division had been informed that strong formations of friendly fighters would pass over German gun

Among the characters who flew with JG 54, few were as colourful as Josef 'Pips' Priller, a fine pilot and enthusiastic leader of II Gruppe. He was eventually to preside over the final demise of the Grünherz as an autonomous unit when it was absorbed by JG 26 which he commanded in 1945. 'Pips' is seen here shoehorning his ample frame into the narrow cockpit of a Bf 109F, probably at Siwerskaja. *(Petrick)*.

positions that morning, the message did not apparently reach all the batteries.

Keeping very low in clear visibility, the JG 26/JG 54 force roared over the southern shore of the Zuider Zee west of Rotterdam and fanned out into the briefed target areas, Priller now heading an armada of fifty aircraft. At least a dozen pilots had already aborted due to a variety of causes. The Jagdflieger were disconcerted to see how ready their comrades in the flak arm were to shoot at approaching aircraft — and how well they did their job. Three machines were brought down by batteries south of Rotterdam before the force had flown out of range. Naval flak at the mouth of the Schelde Estuary was responsible for another two casualties in Priller's force. Five down.

Priller's force appeared over Grimbergen precisely at the briefed time of 09.20, the Kommodore dividing his force into three attack waves — but there was next to nothing to attack. Grimbergen was all but deserted, save for four B-17s, a P-51 and a twin-engined communications aircraft — nothing that resembled a worthwhile target for a substantial force such as this. As numerous pilots briefed to strafe other airfields found to their chagrin, faulty intelligence had either confused primary and secondary targets, or the information used for briefing had been out of date.

Priller, furious at the stupid reconnaissance failure, nevertheless led his men into their strafing runs and the US aircraft were duly set on fire, as were a number of petrol bowsers and trucks. Frustrated that they had no better targets, some pilots sprayed cannon shells over the buildings adjacent to the runway, doing their best to shield their eyes against the blinding rays of the sun.

Not that Grimbergen airfield was bereft of any defence; the RAF Regiment had ample Bren guns and small arms with which to make low level attacks hazardous. As the Focke-Wulfs made a second pass, they were greeted by a hail of machine gun fire. It was enough to force three fighters down, the third being that flown by Ltn Theo Nibel of 10./JG 54.

Screaming around a church near the airfield, Nibel's machine was hit by rifle fire; he continued his run on the communications aircraft and was turning his attention to a gun position when his engine cut. With no power, Nibel glided down to make a controlled forced landing near Wemmel, the windmilling propeller shattering its laminated wood blades as it slid along the ground. When it came to a stop, the hot engine pinking ominously, Nibel quickly divested himself of his harness. There was no fire and Nibel was able to get clear and surrender to a group of Belgian policemen who were then approaching the aircraft.

One of the first units to be issued with the superlative Fw 190D-9, JG 54 was to lose at least sixty-two of them on operations before the end of the war. An unidentified pilot poses in the cockpit of a 'Langnase-Dora' coded 'Yellow 4' with a personal nickname and lucky four-leaf clover painted under the cockpit. *(Crow)*.

Nibel's Dora-9, 'Black 12' had been brought down by the proverbial lucky hit in a vital spot (in this case a single round through the radiator). It was one of the first intact examples of the D-9 to fall into Allied hands and was consequently very closely examined to yield much useful data on the performance of the latest Focke-Wulf. Considering similar incidents that had taken place with the Bf 109E in 1939 when that too was new to the Allies, it seemed that JG 54 was still making an unwitting habit of this sort of thing!

In the meantime, IV./JG 54 operating from Vorden, was opening its Bodenplatte attack on Melsbroek, its Fw 190A-8s and -9s flying in company with the eighty-five Bf 109G-10s, -14s and K-4s belonging to JG 27, to which it was attached for the operation. En route, this force had also suffered from the attentions of German flak. Two aircraft were shot down, including the Staffelkapitan of 2./JG 27.

Following JG 27 in low from the west, the Grünherz pilots had in their sights one of the fattest targets of the day — fighters, bombers and transports which had not even been dispersed, as few Allied commanders dreamed that the Luftwaffe would or could mount such an attack as that now taking place.

Making straight strafing passes along the airfield's north-south runway, the German fightes had far more targets than had their comrades at Grimbergen. These Spitfires, Mitchells, Mosquitos, Wellingtons and ancient Handley Page Harrows, they systematically destroyed or damaged, at a cost of four pilots, one of whom was taken prisoner. These casualties fell to the airfield defences, an early morning Mitchell operation having departed before the Luftwaffe arrived. The combined racket of two dozen-plus Wright Cyclone engines was more than sufficient to wake up the base and see most personnel, including the airfield defence gun crews, at their posts by the time the German attack began.

With the attack over, the visitation of the German fighter force was marked by the funeral pyres of dozens of Allied fighters, bombers and transports on the majority of the airfields attacked. But the quality of some of the individual strafing runs was so poor that Allied airmen felt safe enough to yell encouragement to these obviously green Jagdflieger as they swept over too high, wasting their ammunition — and getting hit from the ground defences which had acted with commendable speed. The rising columns of smoke were not all from Allied aircraft. . . .

As the German pilots streaked for home, their carefully planned attack formations had become ragged due both to losses and the attentions of enemy and friendly flak. The flight leaders tried their best to call all their flock in, but without success in every case. Some of the youngsters simply got lost and a few disappeared without trace.

Ground strafing, always an exacting business, needed a good deal of practice; although the burning and exploding targets looked impressive to inexperienced eyes, the old heads must have known very soon that overall, Bodenplatte was a dismal failure for the Luftwaffe, an all but final nail in the coffin. Rapid Allied reaction, both in ground defence and air combat, exacted a toll of 151 pilots killed or missing and sixty-three made prisoner from those members of the day fighter force that actually carried out the airfield attacks.

Supplementary casualties — those aircraft and pilots lost in action in other areas later in the day — brought Luftwaffe losses up to 170 pilots killed. Including wounded pilots, the total day fighter force casualties for 1 January reached 232, although some of those wounded were subsequently able to return to duty.

JG 54 had lost twelve aircraft from its two Gruppen, and a dozen fatalities were reported by JG 26, which also had eight pilots captured. The breakdown of losses for the Grünherz Staffeln was:

Unit	Pilot	Fate	Aircraft
9./JG 54	Deutschmann, Fw Paul	PoW	Fw 190D-9 210102/Wht 3
9./JG 54	Kroll, Uffz Gerhard	Inj	Fw 190D-9 210960/Wht 19
10./JG 54	Nibel, Ltn Theo	PoW	Fw 190D-9 210079/Blk 12
11./JG 54	Egli, Fw Gunther	PoW	Fw 190D-9 210084/Yel 14
11./JG 54	Thoss, Uffz Gerhard	MIA	Fw 190D-9 210120/Yel 15
11./JG 54	Eckert, Ofw Walter	KIA	Fw 190D-9 210071/Yel 7
11./JG 54	Bottlander, Hptm Willi	MIA	Fw 190D-9 210045/Yel 2
12./JG 54	Steinkamp, Fhr Hans-Joachim	PoW	Fw 190D-9 210028/Red 2
12./JG 54	Hooven, Uffz Aloysius von	KIA	Fw 190D-9 210957/Blu 18
12./JG 54	Ratzlaff, Ltn Jurgen	MIA	Fw 190D-9 600346/Yel 6
13./JG 54	Kopp, Uffz Werner	KIA	Fw 190A-8 734038
15./JG 54	Ohlenschlager, Uffz Gerhard	MIA	Fw 190A-8 732088
15./JG 54	Bachhuber, Fw Frindolin	MIA	Fw 190A-8 750093

If the actual attack had proved hazardous for the Jagdflieger, the dash back to base was only marginally less so. III./JG 54 had the not uncommon experience of running into alerted Allied fighters en route home after the attack, and lost two Fw 190s. Willi Heilmann, leading 9.Staffel, had split his formation. Keeping low with the bulk of the Gruppe, he had sent Ltn Hans Dortenmann's 12.Staffel up to 5,000 feet as high cover and was over Hasselt when the Fw 190s were attacked by Spitfires.

Heilmann quickly responded to his comrade's call for assistance, taking his entire force up. The Spitfire pilots, initially surprised at seeing so many German fighters in the air at once, engaged in a running battle, losing three of their number for one Focke-Wulf shot down.

One of the reasons for the high number of German losses to friendly flak was due to some units taking off up to twenty minutes late, thereby putting them in the defended areas much later than they should have been. Some anonymous administrator also planned one of the return routes straight across a V-2 launching zone — where the gunners might have been expected to be more trigger-happy than virtually anywhere else in Germany. . .

Other Gruppen suffered a worse loss rate than the Grünherz and coming at a time when just one more casualty was one too many, the loss of so many pilots on a single operation lasting four hours showed Bodenplatte up for the worthless gesture it was. Despite a widely-held belief that the big early morning attack would have kept the enemy — at least that part of it based in Holland and Belgium — grounded, the Germans apparently failed to appreciate just how rapidly the Allies could replace materiel losses.

Had a high number of pilots been killed in the attack, the setback would have been marginally worse — but by that stage of the war, the RAF and USAAF were hardly lacking in trained aircrew, either. There was ample evidence of both these factors and it remains one of the unanswered questions of World War Two as to why Bodenplatte was ever thought to be a viable proposition almost any time after the summer of 1944 — apart that is, as a direct support for the offensive into Belgium, for which it turned out to be too late.

While a German communiqué of 27 January put the number of Allied aircraft destroyed in the Bodenplatte operation at 479 ground and air victories, the total was actually slightly higher, at 500. Had this number represented heavy bombers shot down in aerial combat, the day would surely have been remembered as the worst Allied loss of the war, for a substantial number of aircrew would inevitably have been killed and wounded. As it was, the number of trained pilots and aircrews killed or injured on the bases was minimal, compounding the Luftwaffe's failure. The pilots were back in action as soon as new aircraft arrived.

In the long term, Bodenplatte only hardened Allied resolve to finish the war as quickly as possible, thus denying the Germans the slightest chance of mounting any similar surprise attack. No respite would be offered from relentless attack in the air and on the ground.

A traumatic indicator of the quality of the opposition was provided even on 1 January. Not all the Allied airfields were taken by surprise and there were a few commanders who made an educated guess that the 'hangover factor' might just tempt the Luftwaffe to try something of the sort. One man who had such foresight was John C. Mayer, CO of the 352nd Fighter Group, then based temporarily at Asche, Belgium. Advising his pilots that a very early take off would be posted on the operations board for New Year's day, Mayer snatched a few hours sleep. His prediction came true shortly after 08.00.

Taking off in the middle of the Luftwaffe attack, Meyer's Mustangs, aided by P-47s of the 366th Group, fought magnificently. As the Bf 109s and Fw 190s swept in the P-51s were at a decided disadvantage, still clawing for altitude and with pilots hardly settled down for combat. Gun switches were temporarily forgotten as they sought multiple targets. Nevertheless they recovered their composure to hack down twenty-three of the attackers, bringing the immediate award of a Distinguished Unit Citation.

Lull before the storm

January's weather nevertheless brought the Jagdwaffe a temporary lull in combat; the Grünherz had a relatively quiet period for two weeks as the worst European winter for years kept Luftwaffe air activities to a minimum. Most of the continent was blanketed by heavy snowfalls and freezing temperatures and for more than a week those US bomber missions that were sent out ranged over Germany with little interference from the Jagdflieger. On 14 January the 8th Air Force despatched 911 bombers to a variety of targets, the majority of them being oil refineries and storage depots in central Germany. This time the Luftwaffe rose to do battle.

Twenty-four Gruppen of piston-engined fighters and one of Me 262s found the majority of the 860 P-51s and P-47s that had taken off from England waiting for them. Black Sunday was about to unfold its catalogue of death and destruction. Trying to break this screen of fighters was tantamount to trying to penetrate a brick wall. From 10.45, when Mustangs of the 357th Fighter Group chanced on a hapless Arado 96 trainer and shot it down in flames, the hunt was on.

By far the largest number of Jagdwaffe casualties were suffered by JG 300 and JG 301. At the end of the day their respective losses were thirty-nine and thirty pilots respectively killed or wounded. IV Gruppe of JG 54 suffered a similar fate, although the number of casualties was less. Over Munsterland the Fw 190A-8s and -9s came off worst in combat with enemy fighters. The Gruppe lost ten pilots killed and two wounded, all four Staffeln suffering casualties. Coming so soon after the debacle of 1 January, this was the last straw for IV./JG 54, which had in fact, flown its final operation of the war.

Ordered up to challenge an enemy combat mission which included virtually the entire 8th AF fighter force, it was small wonder that the Luftwaffe was decimated. Highest scoring US-AAF group was the 357th from Leiston, which notched up 56½ kills, the best record of air-to-air kills by one AAF group on a single mission during the war. In total the Jagdflieger lost 107 aircraft, the casualties including five Staffelkapitanen killed and three wounded.

Continuing bad weather and the empty dispersals at the Luftwaffe fighter bases brought air combat to a low ebb over Europe for the rest of January, although pilots were still

One of the pilots who flew the Fw 190D operationally with JG 54 was Fritz Ungar. (*via R. Kuhnert*).

killed, injured or posted as missing in the skirmishes that did take place. The Grünherz lost six aircraft on the 23rd. Even the mighty American and British bomber fleets remained grounded during the last week of the month and they did not return in force until the 28th, when the weather showed some improvement. No JG 54 losses were reported until the 29th, this and the 31st being regarded as good days, with only one aircraft failing to return on both dates.

But the disaster of 14 January was to have even wider repercussions for the Jagdwaffe. The long-brewing, desperate confrontation with Hermann Goering by a dedicated group of the surviving Experten, to make the Luftwaffe Commander-in-Chief understand the extreme plight of the fighter force, took place at the *Haus der Flieger*, the Luftwaffe club in Berlin, on the 22nd. Among those present were Hannes Trautloft, Gunther Lutzow, Hermann Graf and Johannes Steinhoff. Lutzow was the spokesman for the pilots.

It turned out to be futile; any attempt to get one of the highest authorities in Nazi Germany to accept the stark truth that defeat stared him in the face would almost certainly have failed — as most of the assembled fighter pilots probably knew in their hearts. But they had to try to rescue something from the chaos that the air defence of the Third Reich had plummeted into.

But even if the Luftwaffe Commander-in-Chief had lent a sympathetic ear to their suggestions, it was really far too late — as must also have been crystal clear to everyone in the room, including Goering. What this group of the most successful and highly decorated fighter pilots received, rather than commiseration, was threats, abuse and flights of fancy. Goering's ramblings harked back to the old days of World War One. He likened war over the Reich to combat over the trenches in 1917. His accusation that fighter attacks on bombers were not being pressed closely enough showed that he totally failed to appreciate what was going on in the skies above Germany on an almost daily basis.

Franzl Lutzow could hardly believe his ears. He tried without success to bring his chief back to reality but the Reichmarschall, with a final threat to have Lutzow shot, swept out. The last chance to salvage something from the wreckage of one the finest fighter forces in the world was gone forever.

Of Lutzow's death sentence, nothing more was heard. That perhaps said a good deal. Goering, for all his pontification and bombast, was far from stupid. The fact that his best pilots had summoned up the courage — and it took a great deal of courage to do what they did in the general atmosphere of terror generated inside the Third Reich, at a time when almost anyone could be executed for 'treason' — probably had more effect on him than was realised at the time.

Unfortunately, in keeping with a style so typical of the man in later years, Goering did absolutely nothing to revive his old favour with Hitler, which was then at its lowest ebb, and perhaps try to check the inevitable slide into utter oblivion. Instead he appeared to take the challenge as a personal insult, which could not have been further from the intention of the assembled company of some of the most highly-decorated men in the German armed forces.

There were however, some changes in the Jagdwaffe command structure after the pilots' confrontation with Goering. On 26 January Walter Dahl was appointed Inspektor General der Jagdflieger in place of Peltz. Adolf Galland was all but cast into limbo, along with others without a posting, including Macky Steinhoff, by Goering's extraordinary order that they be placed under *Reichsacht* or 'ban of the Reich'. I Jagdkorps was redesignated IX Fliegerkorps that same day. Gordon Gollob was also promoted, to become Inspektor der Flieger, based at Kladow. Lutzow, as a direct result of his contretemps with Goering, found himself with little choice but to accept the all-but-meaningless post of *Kommandeur der Flieger* in Italy. He was never to take up this command posting, simply because the fighter force in the Mediterranean had ceased to exist.

Jet Experten

While the Luftwaffe's piston-engined forces were being destroyed en masse, the Me 262 continued to stab at the enemy in small numbers, invariably giving its antagonists an almighty scare whenever it appeared. It was equally true that the aircraft often gave its pilots a few anxious moments, primarily due to the unpredictability of its turbojets.

As early as July 1944, Karl Schnorrer, the Grunherztrager who had had such a frustrating debut to combat flying on the Eastern Front, was involved in testing the new jet aircraft. It was Schnorrer who, by surviving what could have been a catastrophic airframe failure, brought back from a test flight mute evidence of an airframe stressed almost to its limits. Important data on the behaviour of high speed aircraft was thus available to Messerschmitt technicians, despite the fact that the early production machine that Schnorrer had managed to land was pronounced a write off. His flight followed a number of fatal crashes, which were probably the results of the effects of compressibility when the aircraft went out of

control in a high speed dive.

Schnorrer was one of the Jagdflieger who mastered the temperamental jet fighter and used it to good effect. He was eventually to become one of the leading jet Experten, along with at least three other ex-JG 54 pilots — Erich Rudorffer, Rudolf Rademacher and Wolfgang Spate. The latter had courted death at the controls of the notorious Me 163 rocket fighter, and had seen his friend Joschi Pohs, also a Grunherztrager, killed in a landing accident on 30 December 1943.

Schnorrer and Rademacher both flew with III./JG 7. The latter claimed his first kill, a Spitfire, on 1 February 1945, but there is evidence to suggest that this aircraft was actually a Tempest. Two days later Schnorrer opened his score with a B-17 when the 8th AF sent over 1,000 Fortresses to Berlin and 434 Liberators to Magdeburg. It was more than a week before both pilots scored again (although Rademacher had claimed two Fortresses on 3 February).

On 1 February the bombers were intercepted over Berlin and Rademacher accounted for two B-17s, Schnorrer's kill being a P-51. Rademacher claimed one more P-51 on 16 February. The balance of Schnorrer's seven kills were all B-17s and all of them were shot down in March.

During February, Rademacher shot down two B-17s, a P-51 and a B-24, the last of these being one of six Liberators lost by the 8th AF that day. These Me 262 attacks rarely involved high numbers of aircraft; since the advent of the 'jet menace' Allied pilots were warned to keep an extra sharp look out for them. The 8th and 15th Air Forces had to position strong Mustang formations at extreme altitude if their pilots were to have any chance at all of catching the sleek, shark-like enemy jets. In a power dive from altitude, the P-51 pilots had an even chance of keeping the Me 262 in their gunsights just long enough to open fire. The trick was to make the bounce count — the minute the German pilot was able to open his throttles, the piston-engined fighters would be left standing.

In combatting the Me 262, American pilots were immeasurably aided by the excellent K-4 lead-computing sight, whereas the Germans were marginally hampered by sighting through a device that was hardly more effective than an old fixed-graticule reflector sight. Some Me 262s were fitted with a gryroscopic gunsight, the EZ 42, but this suffered from faulty installation which rendered it all but useless and it was invariably locked and used as a 'fixed' sight.

The Jagdflieger also found the Mustang flights so positioned that from virtually every approach angle they had to go around or through them to get at the bombers, tucked safely inside the escort screen. Only by dividing their available force into small numbers did the Germans have any chance; the escort could not usually be drawn away by an attack from just one direction — the Americans knew that this was just what the jet pilots wanted.

But, being forced to seek their targets alone or accompanied by their Rottenflieger was highly dangerous. Even with its healthy speed margin, the Me 262 might have to run the entire length of the bomber formation, with fighters poised to dive from the rear, sides and front. It was extremely difficult for any wingman to keep station with his leader in such circumstances and the Kette of three aircraft was found to be more practical than the normal Schwarm of four.

In the maelstrom of air combat when the skies were so full of enemy aircraft, the Me 262 Jagdflieger did remarkably well. Although their victories now came in single numbers and therefore could hardly affect the outcome of the war, they kept the enemy guessing. AAF and RAF air commanders were never quite sure just how many Messerschmitt jets were in service — there was always the possibility that the next heavy bomber mission would meet larger numbers than before.

The upshot of the Ritterkreuztragers' confrontation with Goering was that a new unit, Jagdverbande 44, was established at Brandenburg, cheek by jowl with JG 7. It was one of the strangest fighter formations the Luftwaffe or any other air force had ever supported. Even in the chaos of the Third Reich it was unique. Steinhoff, Lutzow and other surviving Experten volunteered their services for the unit when Adolf Galland had been told that he had the pick of the best pilots in the Luftwaffe

if he could use the Me 262 to good effect. The fact that these men regarded themselves as outcast and condemned — and despite their experience and decorations for valour in combat were very much 'on probation' to prove themselves — was indeed a strange situation.

Most of the men who had invited Goering's displeasure during the so-called 'pilots' plot' against him were highly enthusiastic about joining JV 44, set up expressly at Hitler's suggestion and the subject of an official order on 24 February. But even though JV 44's commanders were all at least holders of the Knight's Cross, the Ritterkreuz becoming almost a badge of acceptance, pilots later seconded to the unit as its strength was built up were, with some exceptions, relatively inexperienced.

JV 44 was directed to draw its personnel from 16./JG 54, Erg 2 and Factory Protection Unit 1; it was the job of the Experten to mould these men into a fighting unit and although this was done with all speed, it took time to instil a basic measure of confidence in men who had never flown an aircraft anything like the Me 262.

It was consequently not until 8 April that a JV 44 Me 262 made its first kill. The unit was subordinated to Luftflotte Reich and took its operational orders from Luftgaukommando III (Berlin) and had, to quote the original directive, '16 operational Me 262s and 15 pilots.' By 8 April out of 200 serviceable Me 262s remaining in front line units, JV 44 had an inventory of around fifty.

In the meantime JG 7 and the retrained Kampfgeschwaderen pilots continued to fly their respective fighter and ground attack sorties. Individual pilots managed to overcome operational difficulties facing the Me 262 force and to steadily build up their victory tally. By late March, Karl Schnorrer had accounted for a total of nine enemy aircraft, his last B-17s falling on the 30th when he got two. Rudorffer also had a successful sortie that day, he too denying the 8th Air Force two more B-17s.

Most of Rademacher's jet victories were also bombers, his last one being shot down on 10 April. Spate, transferred from JG 400, claimed the first of his five jet kills on 17 April and his last on the 25th. All of these were B-17s.

It was on 10 April that the Luftwaffe put up the highest number of Me 262 sorties — fifty-five. Contact with US bombers was reported by forty-eight pilots, who managed to shoot down ten. But the swiftly-reacting escort deprived the intercepting force of twenty-seven jets. Five pilots were killed and fourteen reported missing.

Such losses in jet pilots could no longer be made good and the ever-worsening ground situation forced a slimming down of the Me 262 force. On 11 April, in a move designed to concentrate the jet fighter force so that available resources would not be stretched further, I./JG 7 and three Gruppen composed mainly of ex-bomber pilots flying jet Jabo sorties were disbanded. The Me 262 fighter units were dispersed to areas not immediately threatened by the advance of the Russians and the Western Allies, III./JG 7 abandoning its bases near Berlin and flying to Prague/Ruzyne.

Chapter 9

RED TIDE

The steady westward push of the Soviet Army continued into the spring of 1944, the main weight of the assault falling on the territory occupied by Army Groups Centre and South. Slower progress was made by the enemy forces facing Army Group North, although here too the Germans were forced to give ground, with little chance that modest counter-attacks or the holding of fortified 'hedgehog' positions would hamper the Russians for long.

The Luftwaffe, relatively free of the almost microscopic examination of its performance by Hitler in the battles in the West, did what it could to reduce the weight of Russian airpower now being thrown at the Wehrmacht on all fronts; Soviet production of armaments of all kinds was now burgeoning onto the battlefields in the East and nowhere was the renewal more marked than in the air.

While the war would be decided by troops, tanks and artillery, Red Air Force ground attack units, equipped with the elegant Pe-2, deadly Il-2 and Lend-Lease types such as the Bell P-39 Airacobra — which the Russians arguably used to far better effect than anyone else, anywhere else during the war — became a constant hazard to German units.

It had been stated that the Luftwaffe's losses on the Eastern Front could have been higher had the enemy fighter regiments flown more independent sorties similar to the Frei Jagd sweeps regularly mounted by the German fighter force. Fortunately for the Jagdwaffe the Soviets never planned or executed an all-out annihilation campaign for the fighter force similar to that which took place in the West. That is not to say that huge formations of enemy fighters were anything ususual over the

Fw 190A Jabo 'White 10' with a 500kg bomb under the fuselage, taxying out for yet another crack at the advancing enemy long after the issue of Germany's survival had been decided. Along with bomber interceptions, fighter bomber sorties were flown right until the end of hostilities. (Petrick).

Eastern Front, or that air combat was a rare occurrence!

But as an integral part of the 'combined arms' doctrine prevailing throughout the Soviet armed forces, the air force was inevitably bound to the fortunes of the armies, and while no air arm can be entirely subordinated to what happens on the ground, the Russians showed a marked propensity to operate in the vicinity of their ground forces. Like the Germans, the Soviets did not possess a large long range bomber force; the only four-engined type to see service was the Petylakov Pe-8. Relatively few in number, these could not be used on anything like the scale of the air armadas of the Western Allies.

Instead, the Soviets tended to deploy large numbers of tactical aircraft in a medium altitude, semi-strategic role. Targets were generally small in area and more often than not mobile rather than static. Such tactics often resulted in heavy casualties, as the bombers, primarily twin-engined types, would often fly in long columns to drop their bombs, pounding the target until it was destroyed. While these 'steamroller' assaults were often successful, they denied the crews much flexibility and if the column was attacked by the Jagdflieger, casualties were all but inevitable.

Soviet strength was biased heavily towards strongly built, highly manoeuvrable fighters and ground attack types. These could be produced in vast quantities and flown with relative ease by the thousands of young pilots and crews upon which the Red Air Force was obliged to rely after the disasters of 1941-42. The successful deployment of these enthusiastic amateurs, led and encouraged by comparatively few men of long experience in air combat and tactics, steadily whittled down the Luftwaffe's strength in the East to the point where it became critical. The Wehrmacht could no longer expect air support to make the difference between success and failure, as had happened in the past.

By mid-1944 the Luftwaffe fighter force could only hope to maintain local air superiority over the numerous fortified positions the German army defended, often at Hitler's behest, as it retreated. With about half its strength compared with 1941 gone the Luftwaffe never-

theless fought tenaciously and maintained an aerial presence until the end. The very scale of the Russian land-mass often allowed air operations to go ahead unhindered by the Red Air Force, which did not place much store on attacking rear areas — everything was geared to the main thrust of the offensive to clear the Germans from Soviet territory.

German fighter strength on the entire Eastern Front at the end of 1943 had dwindled to 385 aircraft, 305 of which were operational. While this number constantly fluctuated as new fronts demanded a continuation of fire brigade deployments, it said much for the fighting spirit of the German airmen that the sheer weight of numbers opposing them rarely inhibited operations. It was a David and Goliath struggle in which the giant stumbled but never fell. . .

For JG 54 and other fighter units defending the territory captured by Army Group North, the scale of the assault against their occupied territory was not initially as heavy as on that held by the two other original German army groups. The Grünherz Geschwader was therefore able to loan its strength to bolster sectors more immediately threatened by the Russian advance. This saw the Grünherz fighters temporarily spread across the USSR, as far south as Iwanoka, and Winniza and Poltava in the Ukraine.

During the spring of 1944 JG 54 continued to fall back in orderly retreat along the line of airfields it had used during the Barbarossa drive into Russia and in May Wolfgang Späte, ex-Staffelkapitan of 5./JG 54 returned from testing duties at Rechlin to lead IV Gruppe. Späte would return home later in the year to organise JG 400 and fly the Me 163 in action, prior to becoming the *Gefechtsverbandsfuhrer* (Operational Unit Commander) of JG 7.

The June 1944 offensive saw the Soviet juggernaut becoming all but unstoppable as it thrust through the centre of the Russian front aimed at engulfing Poland and splitting the German army front. A huge bulge thus developed in the line, which was inexorably dragging westwards as the southern areas were evacuated by German troops.

On 19 June JG 54 mourned the loss of another Experten when the seventy-five-victory pilot Helmut Grollmus was killed in action north of Viipuri, the Finnish town that had been renamed Vyborg after 1940. Also lost that day was Ofhr Hans-Viet von Obernitz of 5.Staffel.

Summer offensive

The ebb and flow of the air fighting saw the Luftwaffe's daily fighter patrols constantly in action with Red Air Force units, and steady attrition in pilots and aircraft. Throughout the spring and summer months, JG 54 experienced the loss of one or two aircraft per day. Sometimes the figure rose to four or five pilots killed, posted as missing or injured during combat operations, and while these losses could still be replaced, the invaluable experience which was lost with the men who became casualties was difficult to duplicate if the replacements were novices. Fortunately for the Luftwaffe, the policy of switching experienced leaders from unit to unit around the war fronts maintained a cohesion that was little short of incredible.

An example of how the attrition rate sapped the Luftwaffe fighter force can be illustrated by the record of JG 54 for the month of August 1944. While the component Gruppen flew on every day of the month, weather permitting, action — in which casualties were sustained — took place on fifteen days, less than half the period. Total pilot casualties were twenty-nine. Of these, eleven were killed, five were missing and thirteen sustained injuries of varying degrees.

All aircraft involved in the August combats were Fw 190A-5s, -6s and -8s, with a solitary Fw 190A-2 being lost on the 18th. It was being flown by Uffz Karl Klar of 6.Staffel, who was killed. All but one of the Fw 190s were as far as is known, configured as fighters, although an A-8/R2 of 8.Staffel was the mount of Uffz Fritz Haunsch when he was injured on 2 August.

By mid-September, JG 54 had pulled its Focke-Wulfs back to Libau-Grossin, where the GeschwaderStab and II Gruppe remained for a short period. By month's end, I Gruppe was at Cirava.

September also saw a valuable ally of the Germans suddenly discontinue hostilities against the Russians. Bowing to Soviet pressure,

Finland entered into peace negotiations. Fighting broke out between Finnish and German troops and the Finns compounded Hitler's problems in the East by closing some Baltic ports to German shipping. This led to extreme difficulties when the coastal ports of Latvia and Estonia had to be evacuated in the face of the Red Army advance.

On 3 October, the Finnish Air Force destroyed an Il-2, claiming the last aerial victory scored in the Continuation War. While the Finns only reluctantly ceded territory to the USSR under the terms of the armistice and the Finnish Army had never fought alongside the Germans, it had been useful to have the greater part of Finland as a buffer zone, preventing any Soviet thrust to cut off German forces in the Far North. With the end of the Finnish involvement, the Germans were obliged to stretch their military resources even further.

Victories continued to accrue to the Jagdflieger, despite the ever-lengthening odds on almost every sortie now flown over the front lines. More than ever before, the Russian Front became the arena of the Experten, the master of the quick stab-in-the-back-kill, the pounce on an enemy formation, to shoot and zoom away before the opposition could react.

September saw more command changes for JG 54; Oblt Mader, who had been Kommodore since Nowotny's return to Germany, was also posted. Into his shoes stepped none other than Dieter Hrabak, now with the rank of Oberst. The ex-leader of II Gruppe became the last Kommodore of JG 54 in the East.

By 13 October, the town of Riga was back in Russian hands and the German Eighteenth Army was consolidating in the Courland pocket. Subjected to a strong Soviet blockade, it fell back behind well fortified positions.

Oblt Otto Kittel, Staffelkapitan of 2./JG 54, who scored his 250th victory during this period, became the third Grünherztrager to be awarded the coveted Swords to the Ritterkreuz, on 25 November. That the Geschwader was still very much in action was demonstrated on 15 October when Oblt Helmut Wettstein, Staffelkapitan of 6./JG 54, scored the 8,000th kill of the war. Soon afterwards came confirmation that another Grünherz pilot had been honoured with the Swords when Maj Erich Rudorffer got his

210th victory. Few could say that in the Major's case the decoration had been won easily — having been shot down on no less that sixteen occasions, Rudorffer had taken to his parachute nine times. The Swords were duly presented to him on 25 January 1945.

Throughout its time on the Eastern Front, JG 54 had flown a high number of ground attack sorties with both the Bf 109 and Fw 190 and a number of pilots had become adept at disabling and destroying Soviet tanks. One man who made something of a name for himself for his prowess in this far from easy task was Paul Brandt. Operational with the Grünherz in the East until March 1944, he was posted to the Western Front, only to be killed in action on 24 December. Having flown well over 400 sorties on the Eastern Front, Brandt was then Staffelkapitan of 16./JG 54.

Making an average rate of progress of fifteen miles a day, the Red Army had crossed the Polish frontier on 18 July. Sweeping through Moldavia and into Rumania in August, Russian tanks were in Bucharest by the end of the month. The link-up of Rumanian and Russian divisions effectively cut off sixteen German divisions in the East. The reversal, started at Stalingrad, had turned into a disaster for the Germans.

In the North, Latvia and Estonia were all but cleared of German troops by mid-September and when the Finns sued for peace with Russia, the Germans were barely holding on in the East. But the sound principal of leaving pockets of resistance to be mopped up later and not to hinder the main assault by diverting strength meant that the Russians all but bypassed territory on the Baltic coast, including a number of vital seaports.

The remnants of Army Group North were squeezed into Courland, there to be well protected by the fighters of JG 54. Occupying the airfields at Windau and Libau-Grobin on the coast and inland airfields at Zabeln, Skundra, Tukum and Grava, the Grünherz had little choice but to make any operation to capture the well-fortified 'last ditch' defensive pocket as costly as possible for the enemy.

Apart from two Gruppen of JG 5 in Norway, JG 54 was the only Jagdgeschwader to be deployed by the Luftwaffe left in the Northern

The Courland area saw the last wartime sorties for JG 54 in the East, flying various models of the Fw 190, including the A-9. Hptm Hellmut Wettstein, Staffelkapitan of 6./JG 54, climbs out after a successful sortie early in 1945. *(Petrick).*

sector of the Eastern Front by December 1944. At that time its inventory of Fw 190s was one aircraft in the GeschwaderStab; thirty-four in I Gruppe and forty-four in II Gruppe. Luftlotte 4, in the Southern sector had II./JG 51, II./JG 52 and I./JG 53 and Luftlotte 6, in the Central sector, deployed the remaining Gruppen of JG 51 and JG 52. In addition, there were over 500 Fw 190s dispersed among ground attack units.

Low priority

On 13 February 1945 the Luftwaffe divisional headquarters at Arnhem, Doberitz, Metz, Schleissheim and Stade issued a Top Priority directive to clarify the position vis-a-vis the use of precious aviation fuel. In effect, it grounded all but the most competent pilots throughout the Luftwaffe. Yet still, incredibly, it allowed the 'operation of fast bomber formations in the front-line area by day'. It went on to stress that night fighter units should deploy only their top 'A' crews against the bombers, while it saved the worst aspect until last. The directive finished with the words, 'On account of the loss of the production of the synthetic oil refineries, the operation of fighter defence is minimum priority.'

Subsequent events point to the fairly rapid modification of this edict, and its almost complete disregard on the part of those fighter unit commanders who had fuel, serviceable aircraft and pilots available to fly them. This had to be the case if any form of aerial defence of the Reich, by day or night, was to continue. The devastating raids of the RAF's Operation Thunderclap, directed at Dresden and Chemnitz in February and March saw a relatively poor rate of fighter interception, a fact that more or less forced a change of mind.

But the readiness state of some of the day fighter formations was by then appallingly low. On 15 February Hptm Klemm, on promotion to Major, assumed command of III./JG 54 which then comprised 9., 10., 11. and 12.Staffeln, plus a number of smaller formations.

For the Grünherz, only a handful more independent sorties were possible. On the 14th a number of Fw 190s had taken off to protect Me 262 bases, the German jets operating against Allied targets in the Kleve area. The Doras ran into seven Spitfire XIIs of No. 41 Squadron RAF and two NCO pilots, Uffz Oskar Seidenfuss and Ogefr Rudolf Zogbaum, both members of 9.Staffel, were shot down and killed. With the Focke-Wulfs engaging them, the Spitfire pilots were at least prevented from attacking any of KG (J) 51's Me 262s stationed at Rheine, the primary purpose of their 'Rat catching' patrol.

III Gruppe fought on; a 22 February dogfight with Mustangs in the Cloppenburg area chopped down two more aircraft, those flown by Fw Robert Grasser and Fw Gustav Westedt. A further Grünherz Dora 9 was damaged in this action, which for the Allies was the first day of Operation Clarion, a final assault on remaining German rail and road communications. Again,

all available 8th AF fighters participated and overall they shot down six German fighters. As was usual at this time, fighter strafing of airfields further decimated the Luftwaffe, with twenty-four aircraft destroyed on the ground. By the standards of the time, this figure was modest.

Now there simply were not enough pilots for III Gruppe to continue operating as an independent unit and on 25 February, it was retitled IV./JG 26. So all but ended the existence of the Grunherz Geschwader in the West, at least as a separate entity. The change was really only cosmetic and many individuals' loyalties remained firmly rooted in the unit that had once been; the original identification still appeared in Luftwaffe records, as far as these were still being maintained. The former JG 54 Staffelkapitans, Ltn Crump (now in command of 10./JG 26), Oblt Dortenmann/ Ltn Prager (11./JG 26) and Oblt Heilmann (9./ JG 26) continued to lead their men into action as the death throes of the Third Reich were played out.

There were further losses in air combat as the German fighters flung themselves on the American bomber formations now ranging over the Fatherland with impunity, trying to avoid the hordes of Mustangs that were there for the primary purpose of destroying the attackers — which they did with terrifying efficiency and regularity. Alternatively, the Jagdflieger could try their luck with the RAF Spitfires or Tempests, neither of which were easy opponents — their only merit in German eyes was that they tended to be slightly fewer in number than American fighters.

It was a period when marauding Allied fighters expended vast amounts of ammunition on airfields packed with piston-engined bombers, trainers and other second-line types, most of which had long ceased to have any operational value to the Germans. On some sorties, the Allied pilots reported no contact or even any sighting of enemy fighters — there was little point in the Jagdwaffe braving such massive opposition.

Attempting to rationalise what remained of the Jagdwaffe, Oberst Gollob drew up a plan for the re-equipment of the day fighter force then based on the Western and Eastern Fronts,

A Bf 109G-6 retro-fitted with the taller wooden tail unit to give greater stability, displays the full late war markings of III Gruppe. *(Ungar)*.

although the distinction between the two formerly separate theatres of war was now all but superfluous. In essence, it envisaged that all units then flying the Fw 190A-8/9 (as were the majority, a total of sixteen Gruppen) would receive the Fw 190D-9, D-12 or the Me 262. II./JG 1 would receive the He 162 (I./JG 1 was already equipping with the aircraft) and I./JG 301, then flying the Fw 190A-9/R-11, was to re-equip with the Ta 152H-1 as indeed did III./JG 301 in time to fly some operational sorties.

The directive additionally confirmed that the Bf 109K-4 would be the last production version of the Messerschmitt fighter and all units flying any Bf 109 version would be re-equipped with jets. An irony here was that far from this desirable option, a number of Kampfgeschwaderen which were resurrected to fly the Me 262 in the bomber role, actually converted to Bf 109s due primarily to a need to conserve the jet fighter (as against fighter bomber) force. Any dissolution of strength into new units which by that time would have been hard put to make any useful contribution to the war effort, was seen to be pointless.

Taking note of the fact that there were still three Gruppen of JG 54 in existence, the directive also listed IV./JG 26, and there may well have been plans to resurrect III Gruppe at

some future date. All Gruppen of JG 54 were slated to receive the Dora 9, with IV./JG 26 converting to the improved Fw 190D-12.

These seemingly futile attempts at regrouping Luftwaffe fighter units had to be done, if only to find a home for numerous pilots who had previously been on the strength of bomber and other units who either had no aircraft to fly or had no required offensive role other than at the controls of a fighter, and to utilise the fighters that were still steadily pouring from the production lines. Whether the available pool of pilots were skilled enough to fly them was quite another, far more difficult question.

An equally large question mark hung over the supply of aviation spirit and lubricating oils. Few people really knew how much longer the war would last, and in any event this particular reorganisation list only projected forward to May. But some units did partially convert to new aircraft before the cessation of hostilities.

At operational unit level, it was only an extreme optimist who looked very far ahead, even in an atmosphere of great confusion and uncertainty with rumours of an 'eleventh hour' revival of German fortunes, possibly linked with a Western Allied confrontation with the Russians, seeming to have some credence. In the meantime, officers and men alike could only measure their lives in days. Some saw little point in continuing to fly when even to take off meant almost certain death. Such sacrifice could hardly affect the issue now.

On 24 March, Varrelbusch itself was heavily bombed by the US heavies. Once more JG 54's veteran pilots and groundcrews had to absorb casualties and the destruction of installations and equipment. On the following day, the overwhelming pressure on all remaining Jagdgeschwaderen led to the disbanding of III./JG 26.

IV Gruppe soldiered on, inevitably becoming less and less effective as a fighting force. On 25 March Fw Gerhard Kroll, wounded during the Bodenplatte attack and now back in action, made what was to be his last operational sortie. Flying as part of 16./JG 26, his Staffel was being led by Willi Heilmann. All day long IV Gruppe had been on alert. Orders were received, cancelled and changed, without a take-off being made. Finally, the Dora 9s were ordered up when Tempests were reported. Kroll and his unit made contact near the Dutch border and Heilmann dived away as a trio of Tempests overhauled the Focke-Wulfs.

Kroll knew the British fighters more than had the measure of the D-9 and suddenly one of them was opening fire at his aircraft. He was then at 23,000 feet.

Cannon fire ripped into the Focke-Wulf and Kroll shoved back the canopy to bail out. It opened about a foot, then stuck momentarily before the slipstream whipped it away. At around 13,000 feet, Kroll jumped.

Terrified that his parachute had been burned when his instrument panel had exploded under the impact of the Tempest's shells, the German pilot waited for the right moment to pull the ripcord. He saw trees below and estimated that he might just survive dropping into their branches, even if the 'chute had been damaged. He pulled. The chute snapped open, swung once and Kroll was down, having deployed his canopy at 500 feet. He had suffered burns during the combat, with the result that he saw no further action.

It could not last much longer for the decimated piston-engined fighter units and on 11 April the final dissolution of the former III./JG 54 took place at Klein-Kummersfelde, when all remaining pilots and some ground personnel were formally transferred to JG 26. This was little more than another 'paper' transfer, as the end of the war was only weeks away.

For some personnel the ultimate ignominy was at hand; without adequate fuel it was pointless servicing aircraft that were unlikely to fly again and some of the ground crewmen reluctantly donned army uniforms to fight (often for the first time) as Wehrmacht infantry.

Bitter end

The turn of the year 1945 saw the remnants of the Luftwaffe fighter force in the East somehow being held together. Although all units had suffered grievous losses and in some cases, experienced almost total renewal of personnel during the period on the Eastern Front, the majority of the single-engined Gruppen were still in existence. The belated realisation that the fate of Germany turned on how many fighters could be put into the air meant that the Jagdgeschwaderen never faced the wholesale disbandment that befell other branches of the Luftwaffe, particularly the piston-engined bomber formations. In those cases where fighter Gruppen were disbanded, it was usually because they had been all but wiped out.

With the Russian advance having swept the Wehrmacht from its primary areas of occupation, isolated pockets, all but cut off from the main areas of fighting, held on — if the main weight of the Soviet offensive had left them in something of a backwater, there were still plenty of enemy troops left for mopping up operations. The remains of the Wehrmacht and the Luftwaffe fought on in the East.

It was on the Courland peninsula that JG 54 was to fly its final sorties as an independent Jagdgeschwader. With their backs to the sea, the Grunherz continually flew in support of the German defenders, who resisted six separate attempts to dislodge them from Courland. It was a front about 155 miles (250 km) deep and 93 miles (150 km) wide, a pocket of land into which the Russians poured a massive weight of firepower to annihilate the last remnants of the Germany army in the East.

That these desperate rearguard actions were not carried out without cost to the Jagdflieger goes almost without saying; JG 54 was now squaring up to the elements of three Russian Air Armies, the 3rd, 4th and 15th, the aircraft of which mounted thousands of sorties against the Germans.

To retreat from Russia the German armies used sea as well as land routes. Baltic ports were heavily utilised and although the number of Kriegsmarine units available to protect transports was hardly numerous, the danger to be faced from the Russians at sea was marginally less than that prevailing on land.

Regular calls were made on JG 54's fighters to fly protective patrols over the transports plying the dangerous waters of the Baltic, as well as to keep up the pressure with Jabo strikes on Russian tank columns. In this latter role, the effectiveness of such strikes could only be limited — but there were no longer any German bomber formations operating in the area of Courland that was under siege.

Evacuating German troops and civilians from the Baltic ports turned into the largest exodus of its kind ever. Ably supported by the ships of the oft-maligned Kriegsmarine, the slow and vulnerable liners and freighters faced a terrible voyage to get their human cargoes to

the dubious safety of German territory. The Navy performed magnificently and was instrumental in saving thousands of lives. JG 54 put up as many sorties as possible to ward off marauding Russian aircraft flying anti-shipping strikes. When ships were hit by Soviet submarines the hapless passengers faced a grim ordeal in the freezing waters of the Baltic, and many thousands perished.

The 'Grünherz' problems were compounded by dwindling fuel supplies, which inevitably led to a decrease in the number of sorties that could be flown. Despite this, JG 54's pilots were to score more than 400 victories in the period 1 January to 8 May 1945.

One pilot whose run of victories had appeared to reflect little of Germany's current predicament was Ltn Otto Kittel. He finally succumbed to the odds on 16 February with a personal score of 269, battling with Il-2s while trying to protect sorely-pressed ground forces. It was during the early part of 1945 that JG 54 also received a memorable 'testimonial' as to its prowess in combat. A Russian pilot who had been shot down stated, while he was being interrogated:

Scoreboard. The 7.Staffel trailer showing the unit badge and tally of kills to date during the fighting on the Eastern Front. *(Petrick)*.

'The fighters of the green heart are generally in the minority — but when they are around, things heat up!'

A part of the general retreat from Soviet territory had included most of JG 54's ground crews. Anyone not needed to service the Geschwader's remaining fighters had been ordered to leave the Courland area. Many individual black men went to Heiligenbeil to join II Gruppe, while others were welcomed by I Gruppe at Neuhausen. These airfields had been designated as repair and overhaul centres to prepare replacement aircraft for the Staffeln still in the front line, Maj Rugenstein being placed in command of the 'support force'.

On 7 April, *Luftwaffenkommando Courland*, the old Luftflotte 1, now virtually isolated in Latvia, noted its fighter strength as:

Unit	Aircraft	Strength	Serviceable
StabsSchwarm JG 54	Fw 190	5	5
I Gruppe JG 54	Fw 190	38	33
II Gruppe JG 54	Fw 190	41	38
III Gruppe JG 54	Fw 190	43	41
NAGr 5	Bf 109/Fw 189	25	18
NSGr 3	Go 145	18	16

Other Luftwaffe men were not so lucky; the defensive chaos that was now the Eastern front found high numbers of Luftwaffe ground personnel with a rifle or machine pistol in their hands instead of their more familiar tools. Drafted into the Luftwaffe field divisions or the Wehrmacht, the casualties in the final battles around Pillau included a number of Grünherz men, whose poor skills as marksmen can hardly have effected the outcome. The majority had received basic military training many years previously and their knowledge of modern combat techniques was at best sketchy. Germany had reached the position that any man, however limited his fighting ability, was deemed to have a place in the front line. To argue the point was not only futile, it risked the dreaded label of traitor, with fearful consequences.

On 29 April Adolf Hitler committed suicide in the ruins of Berlin's Reich Chancellery and Admiral Donitz became the nominal head of the remains of Nazi Germany. One of his first acts was to despatch emissaries to the Allies agreeing to the terms of unconditional surrender. Three days later, Berlin fell to the Red Army and on 3 May, as British troops entered the rubble of Hamburg, Montgomery prepared to accept the final surrender of all German forces in western Europe at midnight on 8 May 1945.

On 7 May General-Oberst Hilpert, Commander-in-Chief of the only German army group still holding a front line, surrendered his Courland Army to the Russians. The troops laid down their arms the following day. That night Dieter Hrabak received a telephone call from the commander of Luftwaffenkommando Courland, who stated:

'The German Army has capitulated. The flying sections of JG 54 are ordered to fly out to Flensburg at daybreak under the command of its Kommodore (Hrabak). Transport aircraft from Norway will fetch as many of the ground personnel as possible out at first light. Equipment is to be destroyed.

'Evacuation of ground personnel unable to be lifted out by air will, as far as possible, be affected by sea. The Commander-in-Chief will remain behind and will go into Russian captivity'.

This last sobering order reflected the inevitability of the German position and was terrible in its stark simplicity. It was a fate that befell numerous Luftwaffe pilots including those handed over by the Western Allies, even after a great many Germans had risked life and limb to get themselves into areas occupied by what was widely regarded as the lesser of two evils. Even in what had become the Western zone of occupation German prisoners found considerable hardship in the weeks and months following the end of hostilities.

In compliance with these final orders, Hrabak quickly informed the personnel of both Gruppen, many of whom could hardly have been surprised at the news. The Kommodore also contacted the Kriegsmarine units which still had ships available to take his men to Germany, and ground columns were organised for transfer to the port of Libau.

To all intents and purposes, the war in Europe was over and in the succeeding days of May the remnants of Jagdgeschwader 54 departed from Courland, the majority ending up at Flensburg. Most of the ground personnel arrived via surface transport or air — and more than a few volunteered to take the fastest method of all. Rather than a marginally more comfortable seat in a Ju 52 troop-carrier, they chose the very cramped, dark and cold interior of an Fw 190.

Lightened by the removal of all surplus operational equipment, a single-seat Focke-Wulf could carry up to three passengers on a one-way ferry flight across the Baltic, destination Flensburg. It may have been just as well that these men could not see the icy grey wastes of the waters below them.

No sooner had a sizeable proportion of JG 54 gathered at Libau when the airfield and harbour were bombed by the Red Air Force on 8 May. Heavy casualties were caused by this seemingly pointless raid.

At Flensburg, the heavily-laden Gunherz Fw 190s touched down to disgorge their cramped and cold occupants who were nevertheless pleased to be back on German soil. By 8 May some 200 men had arrived there.

That World War Two had not entirely run its course was evidenced by the fact that at 07.45 on 8 May Oblt Thyben, Staffelkapitan of 4./JG 54, found a Pe 2 flying a maritime reconnaissance sortie west of Libau and out over the Baltic. Thyben promptly shot it down, the victory being witnessed not by his wingman Fritz Hangebrauck, but by the latter's chief mechanic Albert Mayers, who was squatting behind the seat in Thyben's aircraft.

On a day that recorded a good deal of air activity on the now-merged Eastern and Western fronts, 8 May was also to be remembered as the date of the last Allied victory when at 20.00 an F-6 reconnaissance Mustang of the 10th TacRecon Group shot down an Fw 190. There was otherwise little combat, as most of the aircraft in the air were German machines moving to designated 'surrender airfields' and being escorted by their erstwhile antagonists.

As the war on the Eastern front petered out, the last of the Grünherz aircraft left in orderly fashion. The final flight of four pilots to leave Libau were Heino Cordes, Staffelkapitan of 2./JG 54, accompanied by Arthur Lotz, Hans Gott and Oskar Renner.

Not all the departing Focke-Wulfs reached Denmark. Uffz Ludwig Nitsch of 1.Staffel, having listened to the Geschwaderkommodore's message on 8 May, took off from the base at Windau. He was one of the last to leave as the starter battery in his aircraft refused to function. With the help of men from a flak unit, Nitsch hand-cranked the 190's engine into life.

After take off, Nitsch dropped the external fuel tank attached to the aircraft and pointed its nose towards Denmark. Due probably to a navigational error, Nitsch made landfall at Fosie, south of Malmo in Sweden. Electing to make a belly landing, Nitsch put his fighter down on open ground with only superficial damage. It is assumed that like numerous other Germans who found themselves in Sweden at the end of the war, he was interned and later handed over to the Russians.

Four other JG 54 men who landed in Sweden on 8 May became unwilling guests of the Russians. Their arrival caused a few raised eyebrows, for they had flown in an Fw 190. Having left Zirava in Latvia that morning, Fw 190A-8 'Blue 11' of 5.Staffel put down at Valby. The crash landing must have shaken up the three passengers, although they apparently emerged unscathed. They were: Unteroffiziers Walter Staender and Rudolf Vogel, and Gefreiters Heinz Tatenhorst and Gunther Herchet. Later in 1945 these and other German internees were shipped to the Soviet Union.

The Luftwaffe men who arrived at Flensburg were interned by troops of the British Army and although the reception of Germans was a large-scale undertaking, there was little attempt to disarm each individual. The British, acting under orders to the effect that all German military personnel in Schleswig-Holstein and the zone lying between the Eider and North-Baltic Canal were to be interned, were quickly faced with a mass of some 13,000 prisoners. This large group was moved from Flensburg into the allocated zone and more or less broken down by branch of service and unit.

Odderate was chosen as the last location of the wartime Jagdgeschwader 54; personnel of

Austrian nationality, which included the bulk of II Gruppe, were placed in a separate camp, with the surviviors of III Gruppe being located at neighbouring Suderhastedt under the command of Major Klemm.

The Geschwader continued to welcome late-comers from the East, as transports brought in the last of the men who had been stationed in Courland, shipping them to Flensburg via Kiel. All personnel led a peaceful, if boring existence through the summer of 1945 and it was not until September that the Grünherz finally stood down.

It had been decided by the Western Allies that the bulk of German troops would be allowed to return to their homes and following processing, personnel were informed that they would be released. Oberst Hrabak presided over a final roll call in September 1945 and made a short address to the assembled men to officially dissolve the Luftwaffe unit in which they had served — for one of the most illustrious fighter units of either side, the war was over.

But for some men, the conflict would not finally be put behind them for years. Those who had been captured by or were turned over to the Russians were forced to endure an even greater fight for survival than they had in their front line unit. For a few, World War II's hardships and deprivations were to last until well into the 1950s.

This incarceration was an unfortunate and, in many eyes, grossly unfair victimisation of a vanquished foe; by making no distinction between the German services and the rank and responsibilities of the individual, airmen were, by implication, charged with 'war crimes'. The Russians were the only ones to officially make such an example of the ordinary fighting man.

As far as aerial victories went, the figures returned by German pilots stationed in the East hardly reflected the scale of the defeat — they read like the scores achieved by whole Allied units or groups of units, rather than individuals. The Gemans were able to achieve such impressive victory tallies by dint of the fact that so many pilots were flying combat for years on end. Consequently, no Allied fighter unit came anywhere near the Germans in terms of victories scored.

The Eastern Front was the arena for fighters,

the Germans claiming about 45,000 Russian aircraft shot down. The Russians themselves put the figure of operational losses higher, at 70,000 and some sources state that this might even have reached the staggering total of 90,000. And the vast majority of these were destroyed in air-to-air combat, ground victories not being counted by the Luftwaffe. It may well be that the larger figure quoted above is boosted by the aircraft lost on the ground.

It was only the German lack of planning for a protracted war that obliged these highly experienced and decorated men to carry on flying and fighting. Ultimately, it led many of them to make the supreme sacrifice, as the odds became too great.

The contribution to the German war effort made by such men was out of all proportion to their numbers and the quality of their equipment, particularly on the Eastern Front. Good as their aircraft had been when Operation Barbarossa was launched in 1941, both the Fw 190 and Bf 109 were being significantly outclassed by 1945, particularly when they were flown by pilots not trained well enough to use them effectively.

But when an Experten was at the controls, both the piston-engined fighters were nothing short of lethal — the figures spoke for themselves. With 352 kills, Maj Erich Hartmann emerged from the war as the most successful fighter pilot in history; the list of Luftwaffe fighter pilots who scored over 100 victories ran to 107, and there were thirty-five with 150-200 or more. Taking the US yardstick of an ace as a pilot with five or more aerial victories (a somewhat arbitrary figure as the Germans did not use it) there were over 5,000 pilots with this baseline score.

In the table of those with the highest scores, Oblt Otto Kittel's 267 and Maj Walter Nowotny's 255 made them the fourth and fifth highest respectively, only Hartmann, Gerhard Barkhorn (301) and Gunther Rall (271) of JG 52 overtaking the top-scoring Grunherztrager. All these individuals scored the vast majority of their kills on the Eastern Front. In terms of total victories, JG 54 took third place with JG 52 first and JG 51 second. By any yardstick, the German Jagdfliegers' achievement was remarkable.

Appendix 1

THE DAILY ROUND

A major part of the day-to-day life of a military pilot is spent in simply waiting. In World War II fighter pilots, who did not usually have to attend the kind of detailed briefing necessary for bomber crews, probably had more time on their hands between operations than any other branch of the service. The duration of their combat sorties was invariably shorter and as in other air forces, the Jadgflieger partook of a long list of recreational activities to relieve the boredom. Apart from sleep, which was probably the universally favourite pastime, pilots enjoyed chess and card games, particularly Skat.

As the elite of the air arm, fighter pilots were certainly not averse to civilised surroundings, even when their unit operated from a forward base. As soon as the unit moved in, requisitioning parties were sent out to find the best possible living quarters. A castle, a French chateau or other fine house, provided that it was within a reasonable distance from the airfield, would do fine. And when JG 54 was based at Sivertskja, its pilots' quarters were among the most magnificent in the Luftwaffe – nothing less than the summer palace at Gatschina. Once occupied by the Tsars, this huge, imposing complex also housed Stuka and Kampfgeschwader personnel – indeed it was large enough to accommodate the greater part of the Luftwaffe on the Eastern Front!

To overcome the tension of day-to-day combat flying, calming recreational activities were encouraged. Numerous individuals would renew their acquaintance with favourite half-forgotten hobbies where these were possible and it goes without saying that music was very popular. The harmonica, trumpet and violin probably led the field in the Luftwaffe. Anyone with musical talent was drafted into the numerous orchestras or bands that served to entertain not only the resident personnel, but visitors. One of the more sombre duties was the provision of suitable music for the funerals of fallen comrades.

Lengthy stand-down periods allowed for organised sports of all kinds and time for long-term projects such as drawing or painting. The art of wood-carving was widely practised to decorate the popular *Abschuss-stocke* or victory stick to record individual prowess in combat. With their heads occasionally carved into a variety of striking animal or bird-head shapes, these sticks recorded victories in the form of bars or miniature reproductions of the national insignia of the fallen enemy which were carefully painted.

Most units requisitioned vehicles or trailers (Wohnwagon) as temporary flight-line pilots' quarters. These would invariably be decorated, outside as well as in, with Gruppe or Staffel badges. When a move of airfield became necessary, such vehicles usually went along. Vehicles would also be adapted as mobile cinemas or saunas. At one stage of the war, JG 54 is reported to have shown a different feature film every evening to help relieve fatigue.

Pets were very popular with flying personnel and they too would accompany their owners from place to place. Dogs — dachshunds, terriers, schnauzers and so on — were the most popular and the most practical animals, as they needed little maintenance. Many a 'Staffelhund' also accumulated flying hours — and not always in transport aircraft. Numerous fighter pilots found room for their dogs in an Fw 190 or Bf 109, the hapless animal sometimes suffering the indignity of unexpected air combat if the enemy happened to put in an appearance during a routine or enforced base move. Dogs invariably became airfield personalities in their own right and one Kommodore of JG 54 had a 'Grünherz-Dackel' complete with a tiny green heart collar tag.

Other animals would invariably be kept on any airfield the unit occupied for any length of time. These included dairy animals and other livestock which were primarily a source of

Fritz Ungar with the terrier 'Struppi', perched on top of an FW 190D-9 under camouflage netting, probably at Varrelbusch. *(via R. Kuhnert).*

food, a fact that did not stop geese, pigs, hens and even cows being given pet names, even though their fate was invariably the cooking pot!

Having been trained to use small arms, pilots were often able to supplement basic rations with the results of forays into the local hinterland, although professional hunters might have looked askance at the range of weapons used — Lugers, Mausers and machine pistols were not exactly recommended for such sport. Handguns also featured in organised and impromptu shooting competitions, which were encouraged to maintain marksmanship in the air. It was invariably the case that a man who was a good shot with a rifle or pistol on the ground was able to adapt his skill to accurate shooting in the air, particularly in judging the degree of deflection required.

Any unit with a strong tradition and *esprit de corps* would make its presence felt in a given locality in a variety of ways. The easiest way to do this was in paint. Most Luftwaffe units travelled with an ample supply of stencils and the Geschwader, Gruppen and Staffel badges would turn up on a variety of fixed and

mobile installations. In JG 54's case, the Grünherz personnel even decorated railway carriages with Gruppe insignia.

'Liberated' items left by a retreating enemy indulged the pilots' sense of humour, examples being the Union Jack proudly waving from the top of a Grünherz Staffelwagen used on the Channel coast in June 1940, and the widespread commandeering of foreign cars and other vehicles liberally decorated with badges.

Every unit travelled with its official regalia in the form of standards, flags and banners for ceremonial occasions. Smaller sized Gruppe or Staffel emblems were also applied onto fabric flags and pennants, the latter occasionally being stamped out in metal and designed to be attached to the radio mast of the Bf 109 to indicate command aircraft. On airfields, large-size unit emblems were used to indicate dispersal points or marshalling areas.

Crew rooms the world over have some kind of visual indication of what branch of service is located at a given airfield and the Luftwaffe was no exception. JG 54 sported an Abschuss board to provide an at-a-glance accumulative record of victories by each Gruppe in various campaigns. Throughout the Luftwaffe (more so than any other combatant air arm of World War Two) there was a strong tradition of providing visual evidence of achievement. All units indulged in the display of carefully decorated placards, boards, garlands and banners which proclaimed a milestone in operations, these being displayed alongside — or festooned about — the successful pilot immediately after he returned from the relevant sortie.

In the case of fighter units the garland or wreath invariably announced the latest Staffel, Gruppe or individual score in aerial combat — in multiple hundreds and thousands! The German propaganda machine took full advantage of such milestones and the pilots who accomplished each feat of arms were duly photographed for editorials and biographies in service and domestic publications.

Rarely exhibited outside the environs of the airfield were huge cardboard iron crosses or other artistic creations that implied a degree of levity. Duly paraded for the unit's own cameras, such embellishments reflected a widespread and very necessary ability to relieve the tension of operational flying through humour.

German air force humour manifested itself in different ways, from ribald graffiti chalked on aircraft — easily washed off by hand or the next rain shower if the 'old man' did not heartily approve — to a whole compendium of slang expressions and terms. These latter were part and parcel of any operational unit in most of the world's air arms. As practical as it was succinct, such terminology speeded up communications in the air, and became an integral part of speech on the ground. Accompanied by expansive hand gestures to show the relative positions of hunter and hunted during air combat, fighter pilots spoke a language all their own.

The majority of pilots also picked up nicknames or first name shortforms during the course of their military service, these coming to be in common usage throughout the Staffel or Gruppe. Slang was widely applied to everyday items of equipment, uniform and decorations. It was hardly surprising that the enemy came in for his share of slang, too.

Examples of slang have been quoted throughout this text, but some others were: Air Cabbies/Cab Drivers — bomber pilots; Bulge (Buhl) — derived from the Bf 109G's engine cowling contours; Cementer — the Il-2 Schturmovik; Cauliflower — the Oak Leaves; crate — aircraft; Crows/Cyclists — own fighters; Experten — fighter ace; Fat Dog/Furniture Van (Viermot) — enemy bomber, invariably an Allied heavy; Garden Fence — own airfield; heavy buses — Allied bombers; Hitler saws — German machine guns; Horrido — victory cry (from St Horridus, the saviour saint of the Luftwaffe fighter pilot); Indians (Indianer) — enemy fighters; Ivans — Russian aircraft; Old Heads/Old Hares — long-serving, highly experienced fighter leaders; Wooden Eye (Holzauge) — Rottenflieger/Katchmarek or wingman.

The Luftwaffe's top Experten were literally front page news for much of the war and such popularising of the nation's warriors helped to keep the German people informed of what was happening on the fighting fronts, and did its bit to maintain morale. The propagandists delighted in emphasising the courage and prowess of pilots and if the man of the hour could be

persuaded to pose with an exotic pet such as a lion cub, so much the better.

As well as its regular aircraft, a fighter unit maintained a number of second-line machines for communications and liaison flights. In JG 54's case the inventory extended to the Fiesler Fi 156 Storch, the Arado Ar 68 and the Klemm Kl 35. Normally fitted with wheeled landing gear, such aircraft could be adapted to take skids or skis — a useful asset in the Russian winters. In the Grünherz and other Jagdgeschwaderen, second-line aircraft would often be as well decorated as the fighters.

Ground crews

All Luftwaffe flying formations, irrespective of size, would hardly have been able to function without the dedicated support of the ground crew. Their duties were manifold and the various specialist trades available to a first-line Jagdgeschwader included all skills, ranging from that of driver and teleprinter operator to airframe fitters and weapons and radio specialists. In addition, there was a headquarters staff consisting of operations room clerks, accountants, cooks, clothing and quartermaster personnel, and so forth.

The men who undertook ground duties came, like the pilots, from all walks of life. although the geographical associations reflected by the operational Gruppen tended to extend to non-flying personnel. The pre-war core strength of regular airmen was supplemented significantly by a large number of reservists who were drafted at the start of World War II. In their case, the age range was from eighteen to fifty.

Within each component Staffel was a cadre of specialists who looked after the aircraft; a first and second mechanic was assigned to each machine, the whole group being under the command of an Oberwerkmeister. A senior NCO armourer, along with his armament team, was responsible for all the weaponry carried by each of the fighters in a Jagdgeschwader, while an equivalent-rank NCO, who in turn had his own team of specialists, looked after radio and other communications equipment.

On an operational airfield, large-scale maintenance such as engine changes, repairs as a result of battle damage, maintaining stocks of radios and keeping airfield vehicles in good working order, was the responsibility of second-echelon working parties. They lived and worked in and around the hangars and repair shops and were under HQ control.

Day to day duties did not enable the 'black men' to easily maintain the smartness of dress so evident in the uniforms of the pilots, but few people would hand out reprimands for any laxity in this area. Most of the time, ground crews wore their ubiquitous black (or dark blue-grey to denote a specialist trade) overalls with regulation leather belt and other ranks' sidecap or 'Schiff'.

The average Luftwaffe working day lasted the full twenty-four hours and it was small wonder that at any given time, individuals could be seen sleeping, dead to the world, slumped in chairs, in the shade of the aircraft if it happened to be hot or huddled around a stove in barely adequate huts in the middle of a frigid wasteland — until a call or whistle from the senior NCO sent them obediently scurrying to their allocated task. Sleep was often the only available diversion from the rigours of duty.

In a crack fighter unit, anyone on the ground crew who could wield a paintbrush with a fair

Fighter pilots were often photographed with members of their unit's groundcrews as an acknowledgement of the part the latter played in every victory. Sharing the laurels in this snapshot taken for one of JG 54's multiple kill milestones are pilots and ground personnel — whose dress was as individualistic as the aircraft they serviced! *(Petrick)*.

degree of skill was kept busy updating each pilot's victory tally. These most commonly took the form of coloured bars applied to the rudder of the fighters, often with miniature reproductions of the national insignia of the enemy aircraft shot down. So many pilots in the Luftwaffe ran up high scores that the room to place all these markings soon ran out. Then the painters would be called upon to make tiny reproductions of wreaths, medal ribbons and the medals themselves as a suitable frame to a 'rounded up' score.

In a different category, but still concerned with paint, was the continual need to mark aircraft with badges, numbers, rank symbols and tactical camouflage. In the course of the average Luftwaffe Jagdgeschwader's operational career, the amount of paint required was substantial: not only did replacement aircraft have to be given the appropriate local camouflage, but a whole range of identifying markings as well. And it was a notable fact that the Luftwaffe, almost without exception from the first day of the war to the last, never went into action with unpainted aircraft. Neither were warplanes allowed to get too scruffy and oil-stained. Not only did this reduce operational efficiency, it was seen to reflect adversely on the pride — and by implication — the fighting spirit of the unit. Bf 109s and FW 190s were therefore kept as clean as possible. How much this could be done naturally depended on the location of the unit and the amount of equipment, particularly spray guns and power units, that were available.

There were few pilots who were not amazed at what the Luftwaffe ground crews managed to achieve even under the most arduous conditions. When JG 54 and other units were based in Russia, the winters were among the worst that any air force unit has had to endure. Even so, the black men managed to coax life out of frozen engines and have aircraft on the line for the next sortie. Minor miracles were performed by the black men almost as a matter of routine and Luftwaffe literature is liberally punctuated with praise from pilots for the men who 'kept them flying'.

Appendix 2

LUFTWAFFE RANK EQUIVALENTS

German Officers:	British	American
Generalfeldmarschall	Marshal of the RAF	General (5-Star)
Generaloberst (Gen Obst)	Air Chief Marshal	General (4-Star)
General der Flieger (Gen d Fl)	Air Marshal	Lieutenant General
Generalleutnant (Gen Ltn)	Air Vice-Marshal	Major General
Generalmajor (Gen Maj)	Air Commodore	Brigadier General
Oberst (Obst)	Group Captain	Colonel
Oberstleutnant (Obstltn)	Wing Commander	Lieutenant Colonel
Major (Maj)	Squadron Leader	Major
Hauptmann (Hptmn)	Flight Lieutenant	Captain
Oberleutnant (Obltn)	Flying Officer	First Lieutenant
Leutnant (Ltn)	Pilot Officer	Lieutenant

Non-Commisioned Officers (NCOs):

German	British	American
Stabsfeldwebel (St Fw)	Warrant Officer	Warrant Officer
Oberfeldwebel (Ofw)	Flight Sergeant	Master Sergeant
Feldwebel (Fw)	Sergeant	Technical Sergeant
Unterfeldwebel (UFw)	–	–
Unteroffizier (Uffz)	Corporal	Staff Sergeant
Hauptgefreiter (HGfr)	–	Sergeant

Other ranks:

German	British	American
Obergefreiter (Ogefr)	Leading Aircraftsman (AC)	Corporal
Gefreiter (Gefr)	Aircraftsman First Class (AC1)	Private First Class
Flieger (Fl)	Aircraftsman Second Class (AC2)	Private
Oberfahnrich (Oberfh)*	–	–
Fahnrich (Fh)**	–	–

*Senior Officer Candidate
**Officer Candidate

NB: Neither of these junior flying grades had any equivalent in the RAF or the USAAF. It should also be stressed that many of the above do not directly equate with Allied ranks but are the nearest equivalent. The listing shows how much lower down the scale of rank the Luftwaffe allowed pilot training to be undertaken, a fact which partly reflects Germany's military situation, particularly in 1944-45. In the RAF or USAAF, the lowest flying rank was that of Sergeant and Second Lieutenant respectively.

Appendix 3

TABLE OF JG 54 PILOT CASUALTIES DURING THE BATTLE OF BRITAIN

Date	Pilot	Fate	Aircraft	Unit	Location
12 Aug	Dress, Oblt Albrecht	PoW	Bf 109E-4	III Gr	Hengrove, Kent
12 Aug	Stabner, Gefr	MIA	Bf 109E-4	III Gr	Channel
15 Aug	Schnaar, Fw	KIA	Bf 109E-4	2./	Courtrai, France
15 Aug	Gerlach, Ltn	MIA	Bf 109E-4	2./	Channel
15 Aug	Hautkappe, Uffz	MIA	Bf 109E-?	5./	Channel
15 Aug	Niedermaier, Uffz	KIA	Bf 109E-4	9./	Cranbrook, Kent
16 Aug	Knedler, Fw	MIA	Bf 109E-4	3./	Channel
25 Aug	Hild, Oblt	MIA	Bf 109E-4	I Gr	St Nicholas, Kent
28 Aug	Schottle, Fw Otto	PoW	Bf 109E-1	I Gr	Hythe, Kent
28 Aug	Kleeman, Uffz	MIA	Bf 109E-4	II Gr	Channel
30 Aug	Ziegler, Ltn R	PoW	Bf 109E-4	II Gr	Oxted, Surrey
30 Aug	Roth, Oblt Hans	PoW	Bf 109E-4	II Gr	Chelsham, Surrey
1 Sept	Stangl, Oblt Anton	PoW	Bf 109E-4	II Gr	Ashford, Kent
2 Sept	Elsing, Oblt	KIA	Bf 109E-4	II Gr	Calais, France
2 Sept	Schelcher, Oblt Ekkehard	KIA	Bf 109E-4	III Gr	Chilham, Kent
2 Sept	Frauendorf, Uffz	KIA	Bf 109E-1	II Gr	Calais, France
2 Sept	Elbers, Uffz Heinrich	PoW	Bf 109E-1	8./	Ashford, Kent
4 Sept	Witt, Oblt	MIA	Bf 109E-4	3./	Channel
5 Sept	Hotzelmann, Uffz Fritz	PoW	Bf 109E-4	I Gr	Maidstone, Kent
5 Sept	Behze, Uffz	KIA	Bf 109E-4	5./	Channel
5 Sept	Ultsch, Hptm Fritz	KIA	Bf 109E-4	III Gr*	Pitsea, Essex
5 Sept	Dettler, Fw	KIA	Bf 109E-4	9./	Benfleet, Essex
8 Sept	Biber, Fw	KIA	Bf 109E-1	I Gr	Channel
23 Sept	Knippscheer, Obfw	KIA	Bf 109E-4	3./	Barham, Kent
27 Sept	Schon, Oblt Anton	KIA	Bf 109E-?	8./	Faversham, Kent
30 Sept	Marke, Uffz Fritz	PoW	Bf 109E-4	9./	Bexhill, Kent
30 Sept	Braatz, Uffz Wilhelm	KIA	Bf 109E-4	9./	Tonbridge, Kent
9 Oct	Schweser, Fw Fritz	PoW	Bf 109E-4	7./	Hawkinge, Kent
9 Oct	Eberle, Ltn Josef	KIA	Bf 109E-4	9./	Channel
12 Oct	Malischewski, Ltn Bernard	KIA	Bf 109E-4	II Gr*	Tenterden, Kent
12 Oct	Behrens, Ltn	MIA	Bf 109E-4	7./	Channel
20 Oct	Iburg, Fw	PoW	Bf 109E-4	9./	New Romney, Kent
25 Oct	Schypek, Oblt Joachim	PoW	Bf 109E-4	5./	Lydd, Kent
25 Oct	Wagner, Ltn	PoW	Bf 109E-4	5./	Dungeness, Kent
27 Oct	Zimmermann, Uffz Arno	PoW	Bf 109E-4	7./	Lydd, Kent

*Stab

NB: The above listing is for the period to 31 October 1940, the date set by the RAF as the end of the main daylight phases. As emphasised in the text, the Luftwaffe did not recognise this date as having any significance.

Appendix 4

JG 54 PILOTS

Name & final rank (where known)	Unit(s)	Final score	Fate
Adameit, Maj Horst (RK, El)	I Gruppe	166	MIA 7/8/44
Addicke, Uffz Herbert	III		KIA 28/7/44
Alber, Uffz Erwin	I		
Aloe, Hptm Herbert	II	31	MIA 21/6/44
Altendorf, Uffz Erich	IV		KIA 27/11/44
Altendorf, Uffz Fritz	IV		KIA 26/9/44
Aman, Uffz Hermann	II		MIA 17/9/43
Angeli, Ltn?	I		
Arnecke, Ltn Dieter	II		KIA 1/8/44
Asche, Uffz Heinrich	II		
Assmann, Uffz Jakob	II		KIA 2/7/44
Artzfeld, Ofhr Jean Gustav	III		KIA 12/7/44
Augskelis, Ofhr Reinhard	I		KIA 29/7/44
Ausmann, Uffz Jabo	II		KIA 26/8/44
Backhaus, Ltn Otto-August	10(J)		KIA 9/4/43
Bachhuber, Fw Frindolin	IV	11*	MIA 1/1/45
Bachleitner, Uffz Karl	II		KIA 8/7/43
Banse, Uffz Gunther	Umrust Kdo, JG 5		KIA 9/4/43
Bartak, Ltn Fritz	III		KIA 29/12/44
Barth, Ofw Gustav	IV		
Bartling, Uffz Gunther	II	11	KIA 2/42
Bauer, Fw Gerhard	IV		KIA 21/9/44
Baur-Berger, Ofhr Hans-Georg	IV		MIA 27/12/44
Bach, Uffz Willi	IV		MIA 23/12/44
Becker, Fw Gerhard	IV		KIA 25/9/43
Becker, Uffz Heinrich	II		KIA 4/1/44
Belcire, Oblt Ernst	III		KIA 29/12/44
Behrens, Ltn ?	III		MIA 12/10/40
Behze, Uffz ?	II		KIA 5/9/40
Beims, Ltn Walter	I		KIA 28/12/42
Beinhorn, Uffz Hans Werner	I		KIA 21/4/43
Besisswenger, Oblt Hans (RK, El)	II	152	KIA 3/43
Bell, Ltn Kurt	IV	7	KIA 24/12/44
Bergau, Ltn Julius	10		KIA 9/7/44
Berndt, Fw Paul	? & JG 11	10	
Bester, Uffz Wilhelm	II		KIA 28/8/43
Beutin, Ofw Gerhard	?	60	KIA 2/43
Biber, Fw ?	I		KIA 8/9/40
Biedenweffer, Uffz Helmut	IV		KIA 12/8/44
Biederbick, Ltn Helmut	III	14	

Bienecke, Fw Paul	II		KIA 21/2/45
Bienricher, Gefr Rolf	III		KIA 8/9/44
Bietfeld, Ltn Werner	IV		
Bisngort, Fw Erich	IV		
Bleck, Uffz	III	5	
Bleich, Ltn Hans	II		
Bloens, Uffz Hans-Joachim	I		KIA 8/6/44
Bob, Maj Hans-Ekkehard (RK)	III & JG 3, JG 51, JG2, JV44	60	
Boes, Oberfh Ludwig	I		KIA 2/1/45
Boesch, Fw Emil	10(J)		KIA 12/3/43
Bogdahn, Uffz Horst	I		KIA 8/9/43
Bonin, Maj Hubertus von	I & JG 52	?	
Born, Uffz Gerhard	I		MIA 25/3/44
Bos, Uffz ?	I	10	
Boschl, Uffz Ludwig	II		KIA 21/12/44
Bottge, Uffz Erich	IV		
Bottlander, Hptm Willi	IV		MIA 1/1/45
Braatz, Uffz Wilhelm	III		KIA 30/9/40
Brandt, Uffz Helmut	I		PoW 16/1/43
Brandt, Ltn Paul (RK)	IV	34	KIA 24/12/44
Braunshirn, Ofw ?	III	13	KIA 8/41
Brechtl, Fw Josef	?	27	KIA 1/43
Breger, Oblt Paul	IV		KIA 27/12/44
Bremer, Ofw Peter	?	40	PoW 13/7/43
Breitfeld, Oblt Werner	IV		KIA 14/1/45
Brill, Ltn Karl	IV & JG 7	35	
Brinkmann, Ltn Heinz	III		MIA 10/6/44
Broch, Ltn Hugo (RK)	II, III	81	
Brock, Oblt Fritz	III	8	
Brodt, Ofw Heinrich	III		KIA 15/10/44
Broennle, Ltn Herbert	II & JG 53	58	KIA 7/43
Bruggenmeier, Gefr Franz	II		
Bruggmann, Ofw Heinz	III		KIA 1/3/45
Bruhn, Ofw Heinrich	I	9	
Bruns, Gefr Johann	III		
Bruck, Ofw Heinz	IV		KIA 14/1/45
Buch, Uffz Heinz	III		KIA 29/12/44
Buckeberg, Uffz Heinz	10(J)		MIA 14/3/43
Budde, Ltn Alfred	IV	21	MIA 27/12/44
von Bulow, Oblt Hakon	III	6	KIA 5/42
Bulling, Uffz Rolf	III		KIA 8/8/44
Bundschub, Oberfh Frindolin	IV		MIA 26/8/44
Bune, Fh Alfred	IV		KIA 25/12/44
Bungert, Fw Erich	II		KIA 7/4/44
Burger, Uffz Horst	I		KIA 1/8/43
Buschan, Uffz Heinz	II		KIA 14/5/44
Buschmann, Uffz Ludwig	I		MIA 12/7/43
Carstens, Fh Werner	II		KIA 24/10/44
Celtjen, Ofw Fritz	I		KIA 25/8/43

Chalupka, Ogefr, Stephan	III		KIA 9/5/44
Clare, Ltn Paul	III		KIA 13/7/44
Clerico, ? Max	III	7	
Cordes, Ltn Heinz		62	
Crump, Ltn Peter	III & JG 26	31	
Dahn, Fw Karl	IV		KIA 27/12/44
Deutschmann, Fw Paul	III		PoW 1/1/45
Deterra, Oblt Paul-Rudolf	IV		MIA 16/7/44
Dettke, Fw Alfred	?	33	KIA 1/43
Dettler, Fw ?	III		KIA 5/9/40
Dobele, Ltn Anton (RK)	I	94	KIA 11/11/43
Doering, Gefr Heinz	IV		MIA 24/12/44
Dorr, Uffz Hans	I		KIA 7/8/44
Dorner, Oberfh Helmut	II		KIA 16/8/44
Dortenmann, Oblt Hans	III & JG 26	38	
Drecker, Ltn Heinz	II		KIA 12/2/44
Dresler, Oblt Ludwig	IV		MIA 27/12/44
Dress, Oblt Albrecht	III		PoW 12/8/40
Dressler, Uffz Fritz	II		KIA 15/7/43
Dudnitzek, Uffz Paul	II		KIA 24/8/43
Dutel, Oblt Edwin	I		KIA 10/4/43
Easer, Uffz Walter	III		
Eberle, Ltn Josef	III		KIA 9/10/40
Ebert, Uffz Fritz	10(J)		KIA 3/4/43
Eberwein, Oblt Manfred	? & JG 52	56	
Eckerle, Hptm Franz (RK, El)	I	62	KIA 2/42
Eckert, Ofw Walter	IV		KIA 1/1/45
Eckl, Fj Fw Johann	IV		KIA 25/12/44
Egener, Uffz Ernst	IV		MIA 29/9/44
Eggers, Ltn ?	III		
Egli, Uffz Gunther	I		Pow 1/1/45
Eisenach, Maj Franz (RK)	I & JG 1, ZG 76	129	
Eisenach, Oblt Karl	I		
Elbers, Uffz Heinrich	III		PoW 2/9/40
Elsing, Oblt ?	II		KIA 2/9/40
Etzler, Ltn Gerwin	10(J)		
Ewart, Ltn Walter	I		
Fadrich, Uffz Gerhard	II		MIA 26/7/43
Fernau, Uffz Joachim	III		KIA 29/12/44
Feuser, Gefr Hans	I		KIA 7/4/44
Fike, Fw Erich	IV		KIA 18/12/44
Findeisen, Hptm Herbert (RK)	II	67	
Fink, Hptm Gunther (RK)	III	56	KIA 5/43
Finkler, Ofw Paul	IV		KIA 13/10/43
Fischer, Uffz Karl	I		KIA 26/7/44
Fischer, Oblt Karl-Reinhardt	I	33	KIA 11/43
Fischer, Oblt Kurt	I		KIA 8/12/43
Fischer, Uffz Rudolf	II		KIA 1/7/44
Francke, Ltn Gunther	IV		KIA 25/12/44

Frauendorf, Uffz ?	II		KIA 2/9/40
Florsch, Uffz Rudolf	Stab		KIA 8/12/43
Forbig, Ltn Horst	?	58	MIA 12/6/44
Foss, Uffz Albin	III		KIA 15/10/44
Friebel, Oberfh Heinz	I		KIA 5/8/44
Frohling, Uffz Dietrich	II		KIA 16/6/44
Fuchs, Uffz Erich	I		
Fuchs, Ltn Karl	I	67	KIA 10/10/43
Fuchs, Ofw Robert	?	39	
Fureder, Ltn, Georg	?	26	
Gartner, Uffz Arthur	?	22	
Gasser, Fw Robert	IV		KIA 22/2/45
Gehrke, Uffz Bruno	I		KIA 18/9/44
Gehring, Uffz Klaus	IV		KIA 23/12/44
Gerecke, Fw Rudolf	IV	27	KIA 22/7/43
Gerlach, Ltn	I		MIA 15/8/40
Glaser, Uffz Erhard	I		
Golingen, Uffz Bernhard	IV		
Goos, Ofw Ludwig	IV		MIA 23/1/45
Gottslein, Fw Eugen	IV		KIA 20/9/44
Gotz, Oblt Gunther	I		KIA 1/2/43
Gotz, Oblt Hans (RK)	I	82	KIA 4/8/43
Gotzelt, Uffz Hans	IV		
Grabe, Uffz Karl-Heinz	I		
Grasser, Uffz Robert	III		
Griessel, Oberfh Julius	II		KIA 24/10/44
Grollmus, Ltn Helmut	II	75	MIA 19/6/44
Gross, Ltn Alfred (RK)	III & JG 26	52	
Grube, Uffz Helmut	IV		
Grubert, Uffz Hans	I		KIA 15/9/43
Grubert, Uffz Joachim	I		KIA 15/9/43
Guse, Uffz Richard	IV		MIA 21/9/44
Haala, Oblt Sigurd	?	40	
Haase, Ltn Gunther	I		KIA 30/1/44
Haase, Oberfh Heinz	II		KIA 27/7/44
Hagel, Uffz Karl	I		MIA 9/12/44
Hahn, Maj Hans	II & JG 2	108	
Hahnlein, Ltn Georg	I	40	KIA 25/8/44
Halfmann, Fw Hans	III	11	
Haller, Ltn Gunther	Stab	30	KIA 9/44
Hammerschmidt, Uffz Georg	III		
Handel, Uffz Julius	IV		KIA 23/9/44
Handtke, Ogefr Erich	II		KIA 17/2/45
Hangebrauk, Fw Friedrich	II		
Hank, Uffz Josef	IV		KIA 15/8/44
Hankammer, Fh Darl-Heinz	IV		
Hannig, Ltn Horst (RK, El)	II	98	KIA 5/43
Hannig, Ltn Norbert	II	34	
Happatsch, Uffz Hans-Joachim	I	20	KIA 9/7/43
Hartmann, Uffz Johann	I		

Haufe, Gefr Wolfgang	II		
Haunsch, Uffz Fritz	III		
Hautkappe, Uffz ?	II		MIA 15/8/40
Heck, Uffz Karl	10(J)		MIA 9/4/43
Heck, Fw Walter	II	32	KIA 22/5/43
Hegels, Uffz Karl	III		MIA 29/12/44
Hegener, Ofw Hans	IV		KIA 13/2/45
Heilmann, Hptm Wilhelm	III	34	
Heinzeller, Oblt Josef	I	35	
Held, Uffz Anton	I		KIA 23/7/43
Henrich, Uffz Hans	I		
Herquerdt, Ofw Erich	III		
Herrmann, Ofw Helmut	III		KIA 12/7/44
Herschel, Oberfh Andreas	III		
Herstreapf, Oblt Horst	IV		
Herzog, Fw Emmerich	IV		KIA 27/11/44
Hesse, Ofw	?	29	
Heyer, Ltn Hans-Joachim (RK)	III	53	KIA 11/42
Heyn, Gefr Max	I		KIA 14/10/43
Hild, Oblt ?	I		MIA 25/8/40
Hils, Uffz Markus	II		KIA 6/6/44
Hirschfeld, Oblt Ernst-Erich (RK)	II & JG 300	24	KIA 7/44
Hofer, Uffz Hans	IV		KIA 22/3/45
Hofmann, Oblt Rudolf	II		KIA 9/8/44
Hoffmann, Oberfh Ernst	IV		KIA 25/12/44
Hoffmann, Gefr Heinrich	IV		
Hoffmann, Ltn Reinhold (RK)	III	66	KIA 19/5/44
Holy, Fw Otto	II		KIA 21/7/44
Holtkamp, Oberfh	IV		KIA 26/8/44
Holzinger, Fw Franz	? & JG 7	10	
Homuth, Maj Gerhard (RK)	I & JG 27	63	MIA 23/8/43
Hooven, Uffz Aloysius von	IV		KIA 1/1/45
Hopp, Gefr Helmut	I		KIA 5/3/45
Hotzelmann, Uffz Fritz	I		PoW 5/9/40
Hrabak, Maj Dietrich (RK, El)	II & JG 52	125	
Hunerfeld, Ltn Udo	?	28	
Hunger, Gefr Klaus	III		MIA 18/7/44
Husing, Ltn Walter	I		
Huth, Fw Walfried	IV		MIA 27/12/44
Huss, Fw Werner	II		
Iburg, Fw ?	III		PoW 20/10/40
Ihlenfeld, Fw Kurt	I		KIA 4/1/44
Jager, Uffz Anton	IV		
Jasper, Gefr Theodor	IV		KIA 7/10/44
Jess, Fw Gerhard	III, II		KIA 8/2/45
Jost, Ltn Detlef	IV		
Jung, Ltn Detlef	IV		MIA 21/9/44
Jung, Hptm Heinrich (RK)	Stab, III, II	68	KIA 30/7/43
Jungbluth, Stfw Max	I		MIA 12/7/43

Kaltenbach, Uffz Heinrich	IV		MIA	24/7/44
Kalwatz, Uffz Karl-Heinz	I		KIA	26/2/45
Kammerl, Uffz Josef	I		KIA	27/10/43
Kampf, Fh Herbert	III			
Keller, Ltn Friedel	I			
Keller, Oblt Paul	10(J)		KIA	24/3/43
Kemethmuller, Ltn Heinz	III, II & JG 26, JG 3	89		
Kempf, Ltn Karl-Heinz (RK)	III & JG 26	65	KIA	9/44
Kinzinger, Oblt ?	I			
Kirchmeier, Ofw Oskar	IV			
Kittel, Oblt Otto (RK, El, S)	I	267	KIA	16/2/45
Klar, Uffz Karl	II		KIA	18/8/44
Klatt, Ofw Leo	IV			
Kleemann, Uffz ?	II		MIA	28/8/40
Klemm, Maj Rudolf (RK)	III, IV & JG 26	42		
Klesse, Uffz Arnold	III, II		MIA	7/2/45
Knedler, Fw ?	I		MIA	16/8/40
Knippscheer, Obfw ?	I		KIA	23/9/40
Knobel, Uffz Erich	II		MIA	21/6/44
Koall, Hptm Gerhard (RK)	I, IV & JG 3, EJG 1	37	KIA	4/45
Kobeck, Uffz Karl Kurt	III		KIA	27/5/44
Koch, Oberfh Georg Heinrich	II		KIA	16/10/44
Koch, Uffz Gunter	III		KIA	13/2/45
Koch, Uffz Joachim	10(J)		KIA	24/3/43
Koch, Uffz J	10(J)		KIA	29/3/43
Kohler, Fw Ainfried	10			
Kohlert, Uffz Josef	I		KIA	1/5/44
Kohloff, Ltn Dietrich	III		MIA	2/2/45
Koller, Ofw Herbert	II	49		
Kolodzie, Ltn Erich	III		KIA	13/10/44
Konig, Uffz Karl	III		KIA	15/10/44
Kopp, Uffz Werner	IV		KIA	1/1/45
Korfges, Ofw Werner	I		PoW	15/10/43
Korn, Uffz Hans	I			
Korthen, Uffz Rudolf	III		KIA	24/6/44
Kossmann, Uffz Friedrich	IV		KIA	14/1/45
Kranz, Uffz ?	I			
Krarsch, Oberfh Franz	I			
Kraut, Maj ?	Stab, II			
Krawack, Uffz Hans	IV		KIA	14/1/45
Kreisel, Fw Karl	IV		KIA	29/12/44
Kremers, Uffz Willi	I		MIA	6/12/44
Kriegel, Ltn Gerhard	III	28	MIA	19/5/44
Knedler, Fw ?	I			
Kroll, Uffz Gerhard	III			
Kroschinski, Ltn Hans-Joachim (RK)	I, III	76		
Kuhn, Uffz Gerhard	III		KIA	12/6/44
Kulke, Uffz Karl	I		KIA	1/2/43
Kurz, Uffz Gunther	IV		KIA	6/11/44
Kuzay, Uffz Konrad	10		MIA	9/7/44

Lampert, Uffz ?	10(J)		
Lang, Hptm Emil (RK El)	III & JG 26	173	KIA 9/44
Lange, Fw Erich	IV		KIA 24/2/45
Lange, Ofw Erwin	III		
Lange, Maj Heinz (RK)	III & JG 51	70	
Lange, Uffz Kurt	IV		MIA 27/3/45
Langer, Uffz Gunther	III		KIA 23/1/45
Lautenschlager, Fw Gerhard		31	KIA 5/42
Lechmann, Fw Heinz	IV		KIA 14/1/45
Lehert, Uffz Horst	II		KIA 10/8/43
Leiste, Ltn Hermann	?	29	KIA
Leiter, Uffz Karl-Heinz	IV		KIA 3/9/43
Leopold, Oblt Fritz	IV		KIA 1/12/44
Lepszy, Uffz Heinz	III		KIA 8/8/44
Lewe, Uffz Walter	II		KIA 15/12/44
Leykauf, Oblt Erwin	III & JG 26	33	
Licha, Ltn Ludwig	II		KIA 8/6/44
Licht, Uffz Albrecht	II		
Licht, Gefr Alfred	II		
Liebezeit, Uffz Gerhard	IV		KIA 23/9/44
Lignitz, Hptm Arnold	III & JG 51	25	KIA 9/41
Linke, Fw Hebertus	I		
Lober, Uffz Fritz	10(J)		MIA 3/4/43
Lohmann, Ltn Werner	II		MIA 26/5/43
Loos, Oblt Gerhard (RK)	I, III	92	KIA 6/3/44
Luchau, Ltn Karl-Heinz	II		
Lucke, Fw Gebhard	IV		KIA 6/9/43
Luckscheiter, Ltn Gunter	IV		
Lude, Ofw Eugen	IV		KIA 25/12/44
Luer, Uffz Friedrich	IV		
Luer, Fw Fritz	II	19	
Luneberg, Fw Artur	II		KIA 14/7/44
Lutz, Uffz Karl	I		MIA 29/3/44
Mack, Uffz Wolf	II		KIA 21/7/44
Mader, Obstlt Anton (RK)	? & JG 76, JG 2, JG 11, JG 77	86	
Mai, Uffz Hans	IV		MIA 25/12/44
Mai, Ltn Wilhelm	IV		KIA 14/9/43
Malischweski, Ltn Bernard	Stab		KIA 12/10/40
Mahlau, Ofw Erich	II		KIA 23/12/44
Mangel, Fw Hugo	III		
Mannlein, Uffz Hans	III		
Manstein, Ltn Erich	IV		KIA 22/3/45
Marke, Uffz Fritz	III		PoW 30/9/40
Marquadt, Ofw Erich	III		
Marx, Uffz Friedel	I		
Marz, Fw Heinz	IV		KIA 5/12/44
Matrtens, Ltn Rudolf	I		MIA 13/7/43
Mattmuller, Gefr Erich	IV		KIA 23/10/44
Graf Matuschka, Oblt Siegfried	I, II	29	KIA 4/43

Maul, Gefr Karl	I		KIA 9/12/43
Maul, Oblt Werner	III		MIA 2/2/45
Meiniecke, Uffz Gerhard	I		KIA 10/10/44
Meis, Fw Helmut	I		KIA 4/8/43
Meisener, Ofw Klaus	IV, III		KIA 11/2/45
Meissing, Uffz Otto	III		KIA 18/1/45
Meitzke, Ltn Ulrich	III		MIA 3/2/45
Mertgen, Uffz Karl	III		KIA 7/7/44
Mettig, Maj Martin	Stab		
Meyer, Oblt Walter	? & JG 26	18	KIA 1/43
Michalek, Maj Georg (RK)	I	59	
Miezala, Fw Walter	II, IV		MIA 21/9/44
Migge, Uffz Werner	III		KIA 27/7/44
Mischke, Uffz Reinhard	III		MIA 25/7/44
Missner, Ofw Helmut (RK)	I	82	KIA 9/44
Muders, Fw ?	IV		
Muhleisen, Fh Otto	II		
Muller, Ogefr Arthur	III		KIA 4/2/45
Muller, Ofw Siegfried	III	33	
Muller, Fw Wilhelm	III		
Muller, Ofw Xavier	II	47	KIA 27/8/43
Muller-Riensburg, Hptm ? von	?		
Muller-Welt, Uffz Herbert	IV		MIA 27/12/44
Munderloh, Ofw Georg	II	20	
Munster, Ogefr Siegfried	IV		KIA 21/2/45
Mutherich, Oblt Hubert	II & JG 77, JG 51	43	KIA 9/41
Mutke, Uffz Gerhard	IV		KIA 6/12/44
Neerson, Fw Gerhard	IV		KIA 29/12/44
Niedermaier, Uffz ?	III		KIA 15/8/40
Nibel, Ltn Theo	IV		PoW 1/1/45
Nikoleit, Uffz Heinz	I		KIA 16/3/43
Nitsch, Uffz Erwin	I		KIA 18/10/43
Noak, Uffz Bruno	IV		KIA 29/9/44
Nowotny, Maj Walter (RK, El, S, Br)	I, III, I & KdoNty	258	KIA 8/11/44
Obernitz, Ofhr Hans-Viet von	II		
Ohl, Uffz Hans Joachim	II		MIA 11/8/44
Ohlenschlager, Uffz Gerhard	IV		MIA 1/1/45
Ohler, Ltn Karl von	IV		MIA 14/7/44
Olsen, Ltn Kurt	IV		
Ohlsten, Ltn Kurt		54	
Ostermann, Oblt Max Hellmuth (RK, El, S, Br)	II, III, I & ZG 1	102	KIA 8/42
Pabler, Uffz Kurt	I		KIA 10/10/43
Patzak, Oblt Rudolf	III	15	KIA 2/44
Paul, Gefr Walter	II		
Pausinger, Ofw Paul	IV	26	KIA 4/8/43
Peele, Uffz Friedel	IV		KIA 22/3/45
Peschke, Ogefr Manfred	III		

Peters, Ofw Willi	III		
Pfeiffer, Uffz Norbert	IV		KIA 3/11/43
Philipp, Obsltn Hans (RK, El, S)	II, I & JG 76, JG 1	206	KIA 10/43
Philipp, Ofw Wilhelm (RK)	I, IV & JG 26	81	
Pichon-Kalau, Hptm Werner	? & JG 51	21	
Plaffe, Fw Walter	I		MIA 17/6/44
Pohs, Oblt Josef (RK)	II & JG 76	43	KIA 12/43
Posemann, Uffz Willi	IV		KIA 26/12/44
Postgers, Ltn Hans	I		KIA 26/8/43
Pott, Uffz Franz	I		KIA 24/9/44
Prager, Ltn Hans	III & JG 26	32	
Prause, Oberfh Alfons	II		KIA 3/9/44
Preschnitz, Uffz Stefan	II		KIA 27/10/44
Preupger, Fw Helmut	IV		MIA 6/8/44
Proske, Fw Gerhard	I	27	PoW 30/1/44
Pruess, Fh Dietrich	III		
Quarda, Fh Sepp	?	52	
Queck, Uffz Herbert	IV		KIA 27/2/43
Rademacher, Ltn Rudolf (RK)	I & JG 1, JG 7	126	
Radtke, Oblt Helmut	IV		KIA 14/1/45
Rapke, Uffz Hermann	IV		
Raschke, Oberfh Gunther	I		KIA 18/11/44
Ratz, Fw Paul	II		MIA 19/7/43
Ratzlaff, Ltn Jurgen	III, IV		MIA 1/1/45
Raupach, Ofw Richard	? & JG 7	23	
Rausmayer, Ltn Hans	IV		MIA 20/9/44
Rausch, Uffz Gunther	I		KIA 25/8/44
Reichardt, Uffz Emil	III		KIA 29/12/44
Reinhardt, Fw Hans-Gunther	?	44	KIA 10/43
Reiter, Oberfh Erich	III		MIA 7/6/44
Resch, Ltn Karl	IV		KIA 14/1/45
Richter, Ofw Ernst	III?	20	
Richter, Uffz Karl	II		KIA 22/8/43
Ritter, Uffz Rudi	IV		MIA 3/8/43
Ritzel, Oblt ?	I		MIA 8/10/44
Rochan, Uffz Gunther	4.(J)		MIA 3/12/43
Rosenthal, Uffz Friedrich	II		KIA 22/9/43
Rossmann, Uffz Friedrich	IV		
Roth, Oblt Hans	II		PoW 30/8/40
Ruben, Ofw Karl	II		KIA 17/11/43
Rudorffer, Maj Erich (RK, El, S)	II & JG 2, JG 7	222	
Rupp, Ltn Freidrich (RK)	III	52	KIA 5/43
Rupp, Uffz Werner	IV		KIA 29/12/44
Sablatnig, Gefr Karl	IV		
Sanzenbacher, Uffz Rudolf	I		
Sattig, Hptm Karl (RK)	II	53	KIA 8/42
Schalkelberg, Ogefr Alfred	III		
Schelcher, Oblt Ekkehard	III		KIA 2/9/40
Scheel, Ltn Gunther (RK)	I	71	KIA 16/7/43

Schelnest, Fj Fw Otto	IV		KIA 17/12/44
Schiebeler, Uffz Kurt	? & JG 400, JG 7	6	
Schilling, Oblt Wilhelm (RK)	III & JG 1	50	
Schlaef, Fw Erich	III		KIA 23/7/44
Schlecht, Ofw Willi	10(J)		
Schleinhege, Ltn Hermann (RK)	II, III & JG 3	96	
Schlipke, Uffz Karl	III		
Schlohmann, Uffz ?	II		MIA 1/8/44
Schluter, Uffz Werner	I		KIA 3/8/44
Schmuser, Fh Hans-Joachim	III		KIA 29/12/44
Schmeilder, Uffz Willi	II		MIA 21/9/44
Schmidt, Fw Bruno	IV		
Schmidt, Uffz Dieter	IV		
Schnidt, Uffz Toni	?		
Schmitt, Ltn Jan	I		KIA 29/1/44
Schmidt, ? Heinz	10(J)		
Schmoller-Haldy, Hptm Hans	I	14	
Schmude, Ltn Karl-Heinz	? & JG 7	31	
Schnaar, Fw ?	I		KIA 15/8/40
Schneiker, Uffz Fred	IV		
Schnell, Hptm Siegfried (RK, El)	III, IV & JG 2	93	KIA 2/44
Schnorrer, Ltn Karl Rk	I & JG 7	46	
Scholz, Maj Gunther	? & JG 5	34	
Schon, Oblt Anton	III		KIA 27/9/40
Schonert, Fh Erwin	IV		MIA 25/12/44
Schonwald, Uffz Gunter	III		
Schonwaldt, Uffz Gerhard	III		
Schottle, Fw Otto	I		PoW 28/8/40
Schrape, Fw Siegfried	IV		
Schreiner, Oblt Eugen	IV		KIA 29/12/44
Schroer, Maj Reinhard (RK, El)	III & JG 27, JG 3	114	
Schroder, Uffz Alxander	III		MIA 6/7/43
Schroder, Uffz Otto	I		KIA 16/9/44
Schroter, Uffz Martin	IV		KIA 14/1/45
Schulten, Oblt Bernhard	?		KIA 25/9/42
Schulz, Oberfh Egon	IV		KIA 25/12/44
Schulz, Ltn Karl	I		
Schuster, Uffz Gottfried	IV		KIA 3/9/43
Schuster, Uffz Martin	IV		
Schuts, Uffz Karl	III		
Schwarz, Uffz Eduard	IV		KIA 14/1/45
Schwarz, Gefr Hans-Herbert	III		
Schwarz, Uffz Helmut	III		
Schwarz, Uffz Konrad	III		KIA 27/7/44
Schweser, Fw Fritz	III		PoW 9/10/40
Schwital, Oberfh Gerhard	IV		MIA 24/12/44
Schypek, Oblt Joachim	II		PoW 25/10/40
Seevers, Ltn Albert	II		KIA 22/11/44
Seibert, Uffz Adam	IV		KIA 29/12/44
Seidenfuss, Uffz Oskar	III		KIA 14/2/45
Seifer, Oblt Heinz	IV		KIA 23/1/45

Seifert, Ofw Heinz	IV		KIA 14/1/45
Seiffert, Oblt Heinz	IV		KIA 13/1/45
Seifried, Uffz Willibald	III		
Seiler, Maj Reinhard (RK, El)	I, III & JG 104	109	
Senner, Uffz Wilhelm	III		KIA 20/6/44
Seueche, Uffz Wilhelm	IV		KIA 26/11/44
Sichert, Ltn Herbert	IV		KIA 18/12/44
Siebe, Ltn Kurt	III		
Siegler, Fw Peter (RK)	I	49	KIA 9/42
Sinz, Fw Hermann	III		
Slabon, Fl Roman	II		KIA 10/12/43
Spate, Maj Wolfgang (RK, El)	II, IV & JG 400, JG 7, JV 44	99	
Spickers, Ofw Joachim	IV		KIA 23/1/45
Sprenger, Uffz Otto	I		KIA 17/11/43
Sosner, Oblt Heinz	IV		KIA 23/6/44
Stabner, Gefr ?	III		MIA 12/8/40
Stadelmann, Uffz Eugen	III		
Stahlberg, Fw Georg	IV		MIA 9/3/45
Stangl, Oblt Anton	II		PoW 1/9/40
Stanglmayr, Uffz Heinz	II		
Steinkamp, Fh Hans-Joachim	IV		PoW 1/1/45
Sterr, Oblt Heinrich (RK)	II, IV	130	KIA 11/44
Sterr, Oblt Heinz	IV		KIA 26/11/44
Steuerkamp, Uffz Hans-Joachim	I		
Stirringhaus, Uffz Rudolf	I		
Stix, Fw Helmut	IV		KIA 21/11/44
Stober, Fw Kurt		36	
Stoeber, Uffz Herbert	II		KIA 28/4/44
Stotz, Oblt Max (RK, El)	II	189	MIA 19/8/43
Strakhof, Gefr Hans-Herbert	IV		KIA 21/11/44
Straten, Fw Reinhold von der	IV		
Strehlow, Fw Friedrich	I		KIA 5/9/43
Streichan, Ofw		25	
Swenteberg, Ofw Alfred	III		MIA 17/7/44
Syroth, Uffz Seigfried	II		
Tauchen, Ltn Alfred	III		KIA 8/6/44
Tegtmeier, Ltn Fritz (RK)	I & JG 7	146	
Teumer, Hptm Alfred (RK)	I, III, IV	76	KIA 10/44
Tezzele, Uffz Bruno	I		KIA 15/9/44
Tangermann, Ltn Kurt	? & JG 52, JG 7	46	
Thielen, Ltn Werner	III		KIA 12/6/44
Thies, Ltn Otto	4(J)		MIA 3/12/43
Thoss, Uffz Gerhard	IV		MIA 1/1/45
Thyben, Obltn Gerhard (RK, El)	III & JG 3	157	
Tichel, Fw Hans	III		
Timpe, Oberfh Werner	IV		MIA 17/12/44
Tittel, Fw Hans	III		KIA 23/2/45
Trautloft, Oberst Hannes (RK)	Stab & JG 77, JG 51	57	
Tschaffon, Uffz August	II		

Ucker, Uffz Walter Hermann	III		KIA 19/5/44
Ulbrecht, Uffz Gunther	III		KIA 13/3/45
Ultsch, Hptm Fritz	Stab/III		KIA 5/9/40
Ungar, Fw Fritz	III		
Unger, Fw Martin	III		MIA 22/3/45
Unterlerchner, Ltn Ossi	?	27	
Vaart, Oblt Albert	II		
Venjakob, Uffz Otto	III	16	KIA 23/6/44
Vincent, Oblt Otto	I	45	KIA 4/1/44
Vogelbacher, Fw Peter	IV		KIA 21/9/44
Voight, Uffz Ernst	III		
Voight, Ofw Gunther	IV		KIA 31/12/44
Volkmar, Ltn			
Werner Gustav Edua	III		
Vollath, Hptm ?			
Wagner, Uffz Hans	III		KIA 14/1/45
Wagner, Ltn ?	II		PoW 25/10/40
Walde, Uffz Paul	I		KIA 7/7/44
Walter, Uffz Rudolf	IV		
Wandel, Hptm Joachim (RK)	II	75	KIA 10/42
Wefers, Ofw Heinrich	?	52	KIA ?
Wegner, Uffz Hans	III		
Weidlinger, Uffz Hans	III		KIA 22/3/45
Weinbergmayer, Uffz Hans	II		MIA 1/8/44
Weiss, Hptm Robert (RK, El)	I, III & JG 26	121	KIA 29/12/44
Welsch, Fw Hugo	I		MIA 9/10/44
Welzel, Ltn Hans-Werner	II		
Wermter, Gefr Adolf	I		
Wernicke, Ltn Heinz (RK)	I		KIA 6/3/45
Wernitz, Ulrich (RK)	I	101	
Wernitz, Ulrich Rk	I		
Westedt, Fw Gustav	IV		KIA 22/1/45
Wettstein, Hptm Hellmut	II	34	
Wichmann, Ltn Fritz	I		KIA 25/8/43
Wieden, Uffz Gerhard	III		
Willmann, Ltn Kurt	II		KIA 14/7/43
Windisch, Uffz ?	I		
Winkler, Uffz Heinz	IV		KIA 17/12/44
Winterer, Hptm	?		
Witt, Oblt ?	I		MIA 4/9/40
Witt, Uffz Werner	I		KIA 25/7/44
Wohnert, Ltn Ulrich (RK)	I, II	86	
Wolf, Ltn Albin (RK, El)	II	144	KIA 2/4/44
Wrigge, Uffz Rudolf	I		KIA 6/7/44
Wubbe, Uffz Heinrich	I		KIA 26/10/44
Wubke, Hptm Waldemar	III & JV 44	15	
Zander, Fw Fritz		31	
Zapfl, Ogefr Johann	I		
Zeidler, Uffz Georg	I		KIA 19/9/44

Zemke, Uffz Egon	I		
Zessin, Uffz Gunther	IV		
Ziegler, Ltn R	II		PoW 30/8/40
Zilling, Oberfh Gunther	III		MIA 1/8/44
Zimmermann, Uffz Arno	III		PoW 27/10/40
Zimmermann, Fw Konstantin	IV		
Zoch, Uffz Gunther	I		KIA 23/9/44
Zogbaum, Ogefr Otto	III		MIA 14/2/45
Zurn, Ltn Helmut	I		MIA 5/7/43
Zweigart, Oblt Eugen-Ludwig (RK)	Stab, III	69	KIA 8/6/44

RK – *Ritterkreuz* (Knight's Cross); El – *Eichenlaub* (Oak Leaves); S – *Schwerten* (Swords); Br – *Brillianten* (Diamonds).

NB: It will be noted that many pilots in the foregoing appendix are listed as belonging to IV Gruppe; this is because any Staffel number higher than nine has been noted as belonging to a IV Gruppe inventory. This is more for convenience than anything else, as Staffel numbers are not known in every case and consequently the Gruppe to which the individual pilot belonged has had to be left blank. Any reader who can add to this list, and in particular identify the scores of those pilots who are not shown to have achieved any victories — a relatively unlikely event — are urged to contact the author through the publishers.

Stoically getting down to it on the iron-hard surface of a Russian airfield, armament specialists make sure that all four 50-kg bombs are secured on the belly rack of a Bf 109E-7 of I./JG 54. Note the domestic watering can, which probably held engine coolant. *(Bundesarchiv).*

Index

Messerschmitt Bf 109E–4, II./JG 54

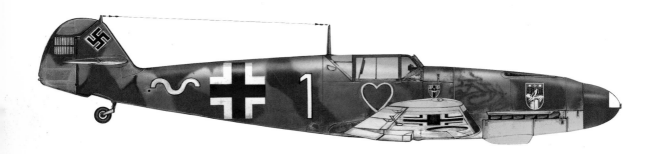